THE NIGHT BEFORE Christmas

VICTORIA ALEXANDER, SANDRA HILL, DARA JOY, NELLE MCFATHER

LOVE SPELL NEW YORK CITY

LOVE SPELL®

November 1996

Published by

Dorchester Publishing Co., Inc.
276 Fifth Avenue
New York, NY 10001

PROMISES TO KEEP

VICTORIA ALEXANDER

This story is dedicated to my Dad,
who taught me to believe.

December 24, 1996

This was absurd. Ridiculous. If anyone spotted her here they'd lock her up and throw away the key. She shifted her weight impatiently from one foot to the other and summoned the composure born of a lifetime of wheeling and dealing in a man's world to keep her face expressionless, cool, and controlled.

The line in front of her proceeded at an agonizingly slow pace, feeding the joyous excitement of the youngsters before her and increasing her own sense of foolishness and embarrassment and, yes, perhaps a touch of fear. She was unaccustomed to lines, to waiting even a minute for what she wanted. And she was not used to fear.

The line moved ahead one space. Tension tightened her stomach. Did all women in their seventies act with this odd disregard for sense and sensibility? Did the

7

realization that one was closer to the end of life than the beginning somehow trigger impetuous fits of irrational behavior? Was she succumbing to some irreversible geriatric disease? Dementia? Or worse? Or was she simply, finally, taking a hard look at a long life and finding the assets far overshadowed by the deficits?

Mothers with bright-eyed, stuffy-nosed charges in tow eyed her with mingled caution and curiosity. She ignored the impulse to return their speculative gazes with the scathing, superior glare that had put many a recalcitrant employee or bull-headed business rival firmly in his place and instead drew a deep, steadying breath.

The line progressed. Her firm step belied the anger spiraling within her. How dare these women stare at her with such impertinence as if she were a doddering old fool? Obviously these housewives and baby factories had no idea of who she was. Or rather, she corrected to herself, who she had once been.

Absently she stepped forward, her thoughts far from the lush department store surroundings. Katherine Bedford had been a name in the world of business long before these women were born. In a day and age when most women in the corporate arena had taken dictation and the word "career" was synonymous with "husband hunting" she had parlayed a tiny, regional company into an international conglomerate. And eventually sold it for millions. Her picture once graced the cover of *Time*.

"Ma'am?"

Her attention snapped to the man seated before her. In spite of his red suit, masses of white, curly hair and snowy beard, the face confronting her was that of a young man in his thirties, no more.

Her heart sank. This was simply another department store Santa. A seasonal worker. A temporary employee. There was no magic here. Still . . .

She squared her shoulders and trapped his gaze with hers. "I'm here to ask for my gift."

"Lady." The Santa's gaze slid to the teenage elf standing off to one side in a silent plea for help. The girl, who obviously would be more at home in a T-shirt and jeans than elf ware, shrugged as if to say he was on his own. "Lady," he said again.

She stepped closer and clenched her teeth. "Please."

Confusion colored the Santa's face. "I . . ." His voice lowered. "I'm just here for the kids."

Katherine bit back an irritated retort, annoyed more at herself than at him. This was a foolish, futile, last-ditch attempt to salvage something she'd lost long ago. To change what couldn't be changed. Perhaps she was in her dotage after all. Even so, she had come this far. Katherine Bedford never gave up on anything without a fight.

She leaned forward until her face was just inches from his and stared into uneasy, pale blue eyes. "Once, you offered me a gift, a Christmas present. And I didn't take it."

"Lady, I . . ." He hesitated and a subtle change washed through his eyes. They deepened, darkened to the hue of blue-black midnight. The shade of a winter evening. The color of Christmas Eve.

"You said you didn't need it." His voice came richer, wise and intense.

Her breath caught in her throat. The world around

her, the line of children, the gaudy retail decorations, the junior elf all faded. She couldn't tear her gaze from his. She didn't want to.

"I was wrong," she said simply.

Compassion gentled his voice. "It's too late now, you know."

"Is it?" She fought back a rising sense of desperation. "Why?"

"You've lived your life. Made your choices." He raised his shoulders slightly in a gesture of inevitability. "You can't go back."

"You promised me a gift," she said, stubbornly refusing to succumb to sheer panic and outright failure. She was so close.

He studied her for a long, silent moment. "What do you want, Katie?"

Katie. No one had called her Katie in longer than she could remember. No one would have dared. Hope surged through her.

"Katie?"

"I want"—the words tumbled out of their own accord—"I want a second chance."

"A second chance?" Amusement danced in his eyes. "And do you deserve a second chance?"

Long years of ruthless deals and hardheaded decisions flashed through her mind. A lifetime of ambition and success. A lifetime alone.

"No," she said simply.

He laughed, a deep, genuine ho-ho-ho that somehow lifted her spirit and renewed her soul. "You never were a liar, Katie, I'll grant you that."

"I just thought . . . I had hoped . . ." She stared, speechless, unable to recall the last time, if ever, she had been at a loss for words. "You did promise."

He lifted a bushy white brow. "Santa always keeps his promises."

"Excuse me, ma'am."

Katherine shot the elf an angry glare.

"The other children are waiting," the teen said in that self-important way of people who abruptly rise to a position of power.

Katherine's gaze snapped back to the Santa. He shook his head as if waking from a dream.

"I am sorry, lady," he said, his eyes again pale, his voice immature and ordinary. "I just work here."

She stared for a moment, then nodded abruptly and turned, her position at once taken by an eager child. She stepped away briskly, slowed, turned, and studied the scene.

Santa sat on his throne, children lined before him, a cheery elf by his side. Swags of red and gold cascaded around him and billowed above the aisles of the posh store. The final frenzied day of Christmas shopping was in high gear with only a few hours left to go. Crowds of last-minute gift seekers scurried past with expressions of panic or tired satisfaction. Had nothing changed at all?

Or had everything?

She walked through the quiet house and paused for a moment to listen to the sound of silence, of emptiness. Where was everyone? Of course, she chided herself, the staff was gone, given the day off. It was, after all, Christmas Eve. Annoyance shot through her at being alone, but she pushed the unworthy thought aside. The small number required to attend to her needs these days were excellent workers, loyal and competent. Good people. They deserved to spend the holidays at home with their families. It wasn't their fault she had no family of her own.

She wandered idly through the spacious house. Anywhere else in the country her home would be considered a mansion. But in this affluent Los Angeles suburb it was simply a big house.

Each and every room was pristine and perfect. Every feature, every aspect from sofas to art remained exactly as the high-priced decorator had arranged it twenty years ago. White on white. Unsullied, unspoiled, untouched. It struck her often lately how there was really nothing personal in her home. No photos of friends and family, no knickknacks picked up on fun-filled vacations, no out-of-place gifts cherished for the memory of the giver alone.

She climbed the stairs to the second floor and wondered why her thoughts turned more and more not to what she had but what she didn't. It must be *this* day, nothing more. Christmas Eve was an anniversary of sorts for her, one she had usually managed to ignore. But this year . . . this year things were different.

Katherine stepped into her bedroom, as impersonal as everything else in this house, and reached to turn on the television. No. She pulled back her hand in irritation. One of the hundred or so versions of that damned *Christmas Carol* might be on. She detested that blasted story. Once, years ago, an acquaintance had suggested that perhaps Scrooge wasn't all bad, just misunderstood. Why, wasn't the maligned creature merely a small businessman struggling to keep his head above water while coping with incompetent employees? She'd laughed at the time but privately thought there was some truth to the theory. Poor Scrooge was no doubt simply the nineteenth-century version of a workaholic.

Just like me.

She shook off the idea and cast a critical glance around the sun-filled room. Sunshine in December. Only in southern California. It was enough to make you laugh out loud. It never truly felt like Christmas here. What were the holidays without snow? Her only acknowledgment, or maybe concession, to the season these days was a wreath on the front door and an extravagant arrangement in the foyer, both from a very chic, very expensive florist.

Why was she so restless today? There were any number of things she could do to keep busy. She still retained her seat on several corporate and charitable boards. There was always correspondence or odds and ends to deal with. Today's issue of the *Wall Street Journal* still sat untouched. The latest nonfiction bestseller rested on the table beside her bed. Nothing appeared the least bit interesting.

It was that ridiculous visit. She shook her head in disgust. How could she have given into such an asinine impulse? It was sheer stupidity.

She grabbed the newspaper with newfound determination and settled into a chair. Past time to put that nonsense behind her. But the headlines made no sense, the words swam, the print blurred. All she could see were his eyes. Dark and deep. The color of Christmas Eve. She'd seen those eyes before.

He called me Katie.

The paper fell from her hands as if in slow motion.

He called me Katie.

The realization filled her with a kind of awe. Was there a chance then, after all? Could a woman who'd spent her entire life with her faith based firmly on reality, on statistics and balance sheets and bottom lines, now believe in miracles?

She rose from her chair and stepped quickly to the walk-in closet, afraid now to waste even a second. She knew where it was, had always known where it was, but never sought it out before today. Imagine—the irony pulled a smile to her lips—two impulses given into in one day. This must be some kind of record.

She pushed aside clear plastic boxes of neatly stacked shoes, seldom-used dress pumps, until she found an old-fashioned hatbox. She pulled the cardboard carton from its forgotten corner, ignoring the fine layer of dust that covered the faded gray and white striped design.

The eagerness of a child presented with a new toy or rediscovering a long-lost favorite filled her and she sank onto the plush carpet on the floor. Her hands trembled as she untied the dingy white cord binding the ancient box together. Her breath seemed to stop and she lifted the lid.

There was so little here. She knew, of course, before she opened the carton; still, the pitiful store of memories brought a lump to her throat. She grasped a handful of letters, tied with a string, all unopened, and relived the long-ago moment when she'd received them and knew exactly what they meant. She pulled out a delicate glass ball, frosted with glitter and the magic of Christmas, the kind of no-longer-seen ornament that could capture the imagination of children who stared into its enchanted depths.

There was only one item left.

With a careful touch, she picked up a small, rectangular box, its cellophane window yellowed and brittle with age. The brown, withered remains of a flower within bore no resemblance to the fragrant, snowy white gardenia it had been, what was it now, fifty plus years ago?

Her excitement crumbled and sorrow washed over her. For what might have been. And what was.

He called me Katie.

The meager bits and pieces of the past were Katie's, not Katherine's. Nobody called her Katie. Not anymore. But once, nobody had called her anything else . . .

". . . Katie."

Snowflakes flurried against the glass, incandescent fireflies flitting through a blue-black night.

"Katie Bedford, would you please stop staring out the window and take this?" Mary Ann Hanson held up a hand-blown glass ball and glared with obvious irritation.

Katie reached down from her perch on the rickety ladder and plucked the ornament from her friend's hand. "I was looking at the snow. It's really coming down now."

Mary Ann's expression softened as if the beauty of Mother Nature's display washed away her annoyance. "It is pretty, isn't it? Just like a greeting card."

Katie wrinkled her nose. "I didn't mean that exactly. Oh, it's nice enough, I suppose, but I'm tired of snow.

Winter's barely started and it feels like it's been snowing forever."

"Katie!" Mary Ann raised a chastising brow. "Don't be such a Scrooge. Why, snow for Christmas is practically perfect."

"I suppose," Katie murmured, her gaze wandering to the window once again. "But don't you ever wonder what Christmas would be like someplace warm? Someplace where you didn't have to fight icy sidewalks and slick roads all the time? Where the grass was green and flowers bloomed even at Christmas?"

"No," Mary Ann said staunchly. "Never. I love snow, especially at Christmas."

"Still . . ." Katie threw a last glance at the winter display outside the window and shrugged to herself. It was lovely, of course, but even inside the cozy community hall-turned-canteen, the cold beat against the glass and shivers skated along her arms.

Mary Ann released an impatient sigh. "Katie, are you going to hang that ball or sit up there on that ladder all night?"

"Sorry." Katie studied the tall, lush fir and quickly picked a spot for the ornament. "These are beautiful. Where on earth did they come from?"

Mary Ann shook her head. "Beats me. One of the chaperons said they must have been donated, anonymously I guess. There was a big box full of them at the door to the hall tonight when Mrs. Gillum and the others arrived to start setting up for the dance. It must have been somebody who took one look at this tree and thought it needed help."

"Mary Ann." Katie laughed. "I can't believe our very

own spirit of Christmas present is saying such sacrilegious things."

Mary Ann stuck her tongue out. "It doesn't have anything to do with Christmas spirit, it's the truth. Our homemade decorations looked pretty darn pathetic." She tossed the tree a satisfied nod. "This is much better. Those balls give it just the right touch of—"

"Gaudy flamboyance?" Katie teased.

"I was going to say magic." Mary Ann glared. "Honestly, Katie, I don't know what's gotten into you this year. I really—"

"Enough, enough." Katie thrust her hands out in front of her in an effort to ward off any more of Mary Ann's comments. "I'm sorry. You're absolutely right. The ornaments do add a bit of magic."

"And there should be magic at Christmas," Mary Ann huffed.

Katie nodded and stifled a grin. "Absolutely. Now, give me a hand and I'll get off this thing."

Mary Ann cast her a mollified look and steadied her descent down the ladder. Katie brushed off the needles clinging to her skirt and glanced around the rapidly filling room. There would be a full crowd here tonight. She and Mary Ann had served as canteen hostesses every evening since their return home from school for the holidays. The place was always busy. But tonight was different. Tonight was Christmas Eve.

Mary Ann studied the room with a critical eye. "I wonder if he'll be here tonight."

Katie pulled her brows together in a puzzled frown. "Who?"

"Prince Charming, of course." Mary Ann's gaze never wavered from the growing assembly of young men.

"What on earth are you ta—" Abruptly the answer hit her. "Mary Ann Hanson, you're not on that husband hunt of yours again?"

"Um-hum," Mary Ann said, obviously more concerned with her search for Mr. Right than with Katie's words.

"I can't believe—"

"I can't believe you're not doing the same thing." Mary Ann turned eyes wide with exasperation toward her friend. "Look at us. We're not getting any younger. If we don't do something soon, all the good men will be gone. We'll be old maids."

Katie laughed. "I'm sure we have a couple of good years left. We're only twenty, not quite ancient yet. I don't think there's any need to worry."

"Sometimes I don't understand you at all." Mary Ann's eyes narrowed suspiciously. "Don't you want to get married?"

"Sure." Even to her own ears, her answer sounded a little strained. "Of course I do."

"Well, what better opportunity will you have to find a man than right here?" Mary Ann's wide gesture encompassed the room. "Just look at the selection: tall, short, dark, fair, soldiers, sailors, marines. You can practically pick and choose to suit your taste."

"A virtual smorgasbord of men," Katie said wryly. "Or maybe a better description would be 'potluck.' "

"Well, I don't care what you think. I think this is the perfect chance to meet someone special. To find that one man who's your destiny, your fate." Mary Ann tossed her head in a flurry of blond hair. "And I, for one, want that fate. I want to get married and have children and fall in love."

Katie raised a curious brow. "Not necessarily in that order, I hope."

"Don't be silly. Love comes first." Mary Ann's eyes widened as if she'd just been hit by a revelation. "What about love, Katie? Don't you want love either?"

"Of course I want love. And marriage," Katie said impatiently. This entire conversation, even with her closest friend, was getting far too near to a truth Katie didn't especially want to face. "But someday, not now. I'm in no hurry to go rushing down the aisle with anyone. And as for love . . ." Her gaze drifted across the room and lingered on a pretty woman barely ten years older than herself.

Pamela Gillum stood beside the refreshment table doling out cookies and punch and good spirits. She lived next door to Katie's family and, right now, lived there alone with her three children. Her husband was a captain in the Air Corps, stationed somewhere in England. Pamela held up well publicly, but Katie noted how the older woman looked when she thought no one watched. Then her composure crumbled. Scared was the best description. Maybe even terrified. Of every letter, every knock on the door, every newspaper headline. Fear etched tiny lines in her forehead and instilled a barely noticeable tremble in her hands and rimmed her eyes with red.

"I don't think this is the time for love," Katie said under her breath.

Mary Ann's gaze followed hers. "The war can't last forever."

Katie shook her head in disdain. "That's what we said last year. Remember? Right after Pearl Harbor? Everyone said this would be a short war. We'd wipe out the Japanese and march right into Germany and deal with Hitler and it would be over."

"But we can still—"

"Mary Ann, grow up," Katie said sharply. "Don't you read the papers at all? It's 1942. If you're hoping for a quick end to this war you can forget it right now and face the facts. This is going to be a long, hard haul. And all these guys you've got your eye on . . ."

She waved at the still swelling throng. "Look at them, Mary Ann. Half of them are younger than we are. They're just kids. We get to go home tonight when this party's over. They're going places they've never been, to do a job nobody should have to do. And a whole lot of them won't be coming home. Ever. Just like Harry."

"I know that," Mary Ann said quietly. "I just don't want to think about it. I'd much rather have a little fun and help them have a good time before they go. Is that so wrong?"

Guilt shot through Katie and immediately she regretted her harsh words. Mary Ann had a good heart, and there was no excuse for taking out her own frustrations about the war on her best friend.

"Of course not." Katie tossed her an apologetic smile. "I'm sorry."

"I'll tell you something else, Katie." The blonde squared her shoulders and met Katie's gaze straight on. "If I find my prince here, I don't care what happens next. If I have to spend however long this war lasts living like Mrs. Gillum, I can bear it. I could even take finding somebody and . . . losing him."

She shook her head. "I know you think it's stupid, and maybe it is, but I truly believe that when you find love you need to grab it right then and there. So what if life doesn't turn out the way you thought, if you don't get to live happily ever after, at least you'd have something. It might only be for a year or a week or just one night. Love is worth the risk." She glared with defiance. "It's got to be."

"I don't think it's stupid," Katie said softly. "I think it's very brave. I don't have that kind of courage."

"No?" Mary Ann stared at her for a moment as if considering her answer. Then an impish light twinkled in her eye. "But you do have long legs and Rita Hayworth hair and dark, mysterious eyes that make men weak. Let's face it, you're a dish. You don't need courage."

Katie laughed with relief at the return of her friend's good humor. "Maybe not, but I'll always need a friend.

"That you've got, pal." Mary Ann grinned, and the girls shook hands in an exaggerated gesture of friendship.

A moment later, an elderly woman bustled up to them with an authoritative manner that would have had even the most decorated generals at the War Department green with envy. With a few brisk, no-nonsense orders she directed the removal of the ladder by high-school-aged volunteers dressed like elves.

"Some of the local florists got together and donated these for the hostesses tonight." The energetic matron thrust two small, cream-colored boxes at them. "Gardenias, I believe. Isn't it wonderful how everyone wants to do their part for the war effort?"

The girls traded swift glances.

"Wonderful," Mary Ann echoed with a remarkably straight face.

Katie bit back a smile. "For the war effort, of course."

"Of course." The chaperon nodded firmly, oblivious to any possibility of amusement. "Now, you two have a lovely time this evening and be sure to follow the rules. They're there for your protection, you know." She cocked a stern brow as if daring them, right then and there, to break the myriad of rules and regulations designed for the express purpose of allowing healthy young men and women to have fun, but not too much fun. The girls stared back innocently. Apparently satisfied, the formidable guardian of virtue marched off to rally the rest of her troops.

Katie pulled the lid off her box and picked up the corsage. "Gardenias in winter. Very nice. Although they don't do well in the cold."

"Who cares?" Mary Ann plucked the fragrant flower from its carton. "I don't know about the war effort in general, but this certainly does do something for my own personal battle plans." She pinned the blossom on her sweater and cast an assessing gaze around the room. At once her eyes lit up.

"Spotted a potential target?" Katie said, smothering her amusement.

"You'd better believe it." Mary Ann tossed her friend a devilish grin. "See you later."

"Happy hunting." Katie grinned back, and her friend sauntered off with a casual manner that belied the determination in her eye.

A burst of music from the far end of the hall caught Katie's attention. A group that could be called a band by only the loosest definition tuned up with all the subtlety of tortured animals. It was an odd mix of callow youth, who stared at the soldiers with naive envy, and older gentlemen, who cast wistful glances at the men in uniform as if remembering the victorious battles of their own wartime coming-of-age.

She scanned the now packed room, curious to see if anyone she knew was here. A silly idea, of course. All the local boys would be home with their families on Christmas Eve. It might very well be their last Christmas Eve together for a long time.

A wave seemed to undulate through the crowd and it parted for a moment, as if someone had drawn an invisible line down the middle of the hall. Her glance idly followed the open pathway, past one uniform after another, until stopped by a figure smack dab in her line of sight. Her gaze wandered up long, powerful legs, strong hands, and broad shoulders to a face fit for the hero of a movie. No, she amended the thought, make that the hero's best friend.

He was handsome in that kind of wonderful all-American-boy sort of way. Just the type of man she always seemed to fall for: tall with dark hair and darker eyes. He grinned a crooked sort of smile that said without words this was a man of confidence, a man who saw the humor in life, a man without fear.

His gaze caught hers, and a shock of recognition shot through her so strong it staggered her senses and knocked her breath away. At this distance she couldn't tell if his eyes were blue or brown, only that

23

they seemed to see into her very soul.

A startled expression crossed his face. Did he somehow share what she had just experienced? His grin widened and he nodded slightly as if in silent acknowledgment. She wanted to turn away from this odd intimacy with a total stranger but somehow couldn't summon the power to so much as move her head. Then abruptly the crowd shifted once again and he was lost to her sight.

Unexpected, unreasonable panic bubbled through her. Who was this man and why did he have such a dramatic effect on her? She'd never seen him before and would probably never see him again. Unlike Mary Ann, she had no intention of either hunting for a husband or snaring one, so this immediate connection with a stranger was shocking and scary and . . .

Fate?

The thought popped to mind with startling abruptness, and she fumbled with the flower in her hand. The delicate corsage tumbled to the floor, and she swooped down to retrieve it before it could be crushed in the crowd. She reached toward it, but just as her fingertips brushed the petals, a large, male hand gently plucked it off the floor. Her heart thudded faster, and she instinctively knew whose hand it was. Her gaze traveled up the length of his arm to finally settle on his face, the cocky grin she'd seen from across the room, the twin dimples in his cheeks, his dark eyes.

They were blue, dark as the night and just as endless.

"Do you believe in love at first sight?" His voice was mellow and rich and seemed to echo deep within her.

She stared, mesmerized, speechless. Every fiber of her being screamed *Yes!*

"No," she said coolly and pulled herself to her feet. "But that's a great line"—her gaze wandered to the bar on his shoulder—"Lieutenant. Almost as good as 'haven't we met somewhere before?' or 'you remind me of someone I know' or—"

"Didn't we go to school together?" he said, his voice solemn, his eyes twinkling. A challenge shone there, and she couldn't resist the urge to laugh out loud.

"That's better." He grinned. "I'd hate for the prettiest girl here to think I was some kind of a jerk."

She shrugged. "Well, with lines like that . . ."

"Funny," he said under his breath, "it didn't feel like a line."

His gaze met hers and they stared for a long, intense moment.

"Katie." She gasped, breaking the taut silence, and thrust her hand out to shake his. "I'm Katie Bedford."

"Michael Patrick O'Connor." He took her hand in his and she struggled not to pull back at the electric feel of her fingers in his. He nodded toward his shoulder. "Lieutenant O'Connor now, I guess."

"Where you from, soldier?" The routine words slipped out before she could stop them.

He cocked a dark brow. "Now, that's a line if ever I heard one."

"Sorry." The heat of embarrassment flushed up her face. "It's a standard-issue comment these days."

"Like everything else." He laughed again, and she marveled at the warmth that flushed through her at the sound. "I'm from Chicago originally. Fresh from college graduation."

"That's what I thought." She nodded.

"Oh?" The brow rose again. "Does it show?"

"No, of course not. I just meant . . ." She scrambled for the right words. What on earth was wrong with her tonight? She sighed. "Well, I'm not sure what I meant exactly. You just look . . . new at all this."

"I am new"—he gestured toward the room—"at this anyway. And by the way, it's not soldier."

"No?" A sinking sensation settled in the pit of her stomach. Obviously he wasn't a soldier. Even she could see that from the insignia on his uniform. He must think she was a total and complete idiot.

"Close, though. Army Air Corps."

"A pilot?" *Please, don't let him be a pilot.*

"You bet." Pride shimmered in his voice.

"How nice," she said weakly.

A frown creased his forehead. "I take it you don't like pilots?"

"They're okay." She shrugged. "My brother was a flyer. In the Navy." Even to her own ears, her voice sounded strained.

His question was casual, but a hint of concern touched his eyes. "Where?"

"Pearl Harbor."

"I see." He studied her for a moment, his gaze assessing and sympathetic. "Sorry."

"It's been a year. I . . ." She drew a deep breath and favored him with a shaky smile. "Life goes on."

"Sure." An awkward silence stretched between them. His gaze wandered to his hands and he looked surprised, as if he had just noticed the gardenia he still held. "Here." He thrust the flower toward her. "I almost forgot."

26

"Thanks." She accepted the corsage and started to pin it on her sweater. Her hands trembled slightly.

"Let me." With a few deft moves, he affixed the bloom to the wool cardigan. His dark head bent close and a subtle wave of scent washed over her. She breathed in the heady aroma of aftershave and spice and heat, and her knees weakened with an odd ache for something as yet unknown.

"There." He tossed her a satisfied nod and straightened up. Goodness, he was close. He was a good six inches taller than she and her eyes were on a level with his lips.

He was very close.

Firm, sensuous lips that seemed made for smiling or . . . kissing.

When did he get this close?

What would those lips be like against hers? Would they demand or coax? Would they be gentle or urgent? Insistent or tender—

"Miss Bedford?"

His voice jerked her attention upward to his eyes. Amusement glittered there as if he was well aware of her perusal. Once again, an annoying heat spread through her cheeks

"Katie," she sighed. "Call me Katie."

"Michael," he said.

His gaze meshed with hers, and she wasn't quite sure what to say next. She wanted to know everything about him. His hopes, dreams, and ambitions. She wanted him to know everything about her. Her secrets, her passions, her joys. Overwhelmed by her own reactions, she feared that every word she spoke would come out wrong. And it seemed terribly important to be clever and charming to this man.

The band burst into a rousing, if distinctly off-key, rendition of "Chattanooga Choo-choo." Michael winced, and she laughed at the chagrined look on his face.

"Sorry." He shrugged sheepishly. "I didn't mean to be rude. They caught me off guard."

"They're definitely not Glenn Miller but they're all we've got." She leaned forward in a confidential manner. "We'll be playing records when they need a break." She tossed him an impish grin. "Or when we need one."

He laughed, and the music abruptly seemed sweeter. "In the meantime"—he nodded at the dance floor—"would you like to dance?"

"Are you any good?" she teased.

"Am I any good?" He cast her a look of mock indignation. "I'll have you know I am one of the best. Why, women have been known to throw themselves at my feet for the opportunity to spin around a dance floor with me."

"Just like Fred Astaire, I bet," she said solemnly.

"Exactly," he said just as seriously.

"In that case"—she offered her hand and a resigned smile—"call me Ginger."

Michael took her hand in his, and his fingers fit around hers like a glove, natural and comforting and right. A grin still danced across his handsome face, but his eyes held a light that belied the casual tone of his words. "Call *me* lucky."

Lucky? He led her to the dance floor, and before the beat of the music swept away any possibility of coherent thinking, she firmly pushed back a nagging thought in the dim recesses of her mind.

These days, just how long would a pilot's luck last?

The evening and the music and the magic of the man beside her seemed to speed up the hours and the evening flew by. Every now and then she'd catch Mary Ann eying her with a knowing look and a smug smile, and Katie did her best to ignore her. It was easy. Michael occupied her attention completely. He was funny and smart and definitely not shy about his abilities.

"You are a good dancer," she said breathlessly as they spun to a stop at the edge of the floor.

"Told you." The twinkle in his eye belied the modesty of his tone. "I do a lot of things well."

"I'll bet." Friendly sarcasm dripped from her words.

"Surely you don't doubt the word of a man in uniform?" He clasped his hand over his heart and heaved an exaggerated sigh. "That's positively—"

"Un-American?" She grinned.

"Un-American, unpatriotic, un-just about everything you can think of." He leaned closer in mock menace. "I feel it's my duty to report this kind of gross violation of the war-effort act."

She stared, startled. "The what?"

"The war-effort act. Surely you've heard of it," he said in a solemn manner.

She pulled her brows together in confusion and shook her head. "No. Are you kidding?"

"Is this the face of a man who's joking?" His expression was stern but a teasing light lurked in his eyes.

"You are kidding," she said with relief. She didn't

mind a good joke, but she didn't like the vaguest suggestion that she was doing anything even remotely disloyal.

"I still have to report this." He nodded at the bar on his shoulder. "I am an officer, after all."

"Well, Lieutenant." Her serious tone matched his own. "If you must, you must." She glanced around the crowded room and crossed her arms over her chest. "But I don't know who you'll report me to. There doesn't seem to be a single, solitary general in sight."

"That is a problem." He frowned thoughtfully; then a slow grin spread across his face. "I've got it. Come with me, Miss Bedford."

He grabbed her hand and dragged her across the room. She struggled amidst her own laughter to keep up with his long strides.

"Where are you taking me?" she gasped.

"Right here." He pulled to an abrupt stop and she stumbled into him. "I believe this is the highest authority here tonight."

She lifted her gaze, and a giggle bubbled through her lips. Before her sat a most authentic-looking Santa. Who had been corralled into donning a Santa suit tonight? Judge Thomas maybe? Or Mr. Brisch? Regardless, he played the part to perfection.

"Santa, I have a serious infraction to report," Michael said in his best commanding-officer voice.

"Katie Bedford." Santa frowned in a chastising way she thought would have been reserved for misbehaving children. "What have you done to upset this fine young man?"

"Why, Santa," she said with innocence, "I haven't done anything. Nothing at all."

"That's not true, Santa." Michael shook his head sadly and leaned toward the oversized elf. "She doubted my sincerity."

"Katie!" Santa's tone was shocked but his eyes twinkled.

"Well," Katie said confidentially, "would you believe him?"

Michael clasped his hands behind his back, raised his eyes heavenward, and whistled a vacuous tune.

"You look like a choirboy," she accused.

"I was," he said virtuously.

"Now, now, children." Santa chuckled. "It's Christmas Eve. What can I do for you? What would you like for Christmas?"

"I can think of one thing." Michael cast her a wicked glance.

"Michael," she said, shaking her head, "you are incorrigible."

"Thank you," he said humbly

"When are you leaving, son?" Santa's tone was casual, but at once the mood of the conversation darkened.

"Tomorrow."

"Tomorrow?" A heavy weight sank in the pit of Katie's stomach. "But it's Christmas."

His somber gaze met hers. His voice was quiet. "It's a war, Katie."

"But—"

"Enough of that, now. There's still tonight to be enjoyed." Santa's voice rumbled through her, and she thought again what a perfect Santa this man made. "Come now, my boy, isn't there anything you'd like for a Christmas present?"

31

Michael smiled down at her. "I think I might already have everything I need."

The intensity of his gaze brought a flush of heat to her face.

"What about you, Katie?" Santa said softly.

She stared at Michael and wondered at the depth of feeling this virtual stranger triggered in her. "I don't think I need anything either."

"Katie." Santa's words were quiet but some vague underlying tone drew her attention to his face. She stared into his eyes and couldn't seem to pull away. She watched and they deepened to the color of a winter midnight. The color of the sky on Christmas Eve. "The offer's good anytime. That's a promise."

At once his eyes lightened and the odd connection was broken. Santa shook his head as if to clear his mind. Then he grinned at the couple standing before him. "You two go and have a good time. And have a Merry Christmas."

"I think they're playing our song," Michael said.

Katie laughed. "We don't have a song."

"We do now." He pulled her into his arms and out onto the dance floor. The strains of "I'll Be Seeing You" floated through the air.

"I love this song," she said and snuggled closer.

"Me, too."

She gazed up at him and quirked a curious brow. "Really?"

He shrugged sheepishly. "Can I help it if I'm a born romantic?"

"A romantic?" Doubt colored her voice.

"Ah, Katie, once again you question my sincerity." He sighed.

She laughed. "Sorry. It's just not often you run into a man who admits to being a romantic."

"I not only admit it but I have a hard time believing this particular song fails to touch a sentimental chord in anyone. Even a man." He pulled her closer and spoke softly into her ear. Her blood pounded through her veins at the intimate contact. "Just listen to it, Katie."

She closed her eyes and lost herself in the spell of the music and the man.

"Listen to what it says." He hummed a bar or two, then softly sang, " 'I'll be seeing you in all the old familiar places, that this heart of mine embraces all day through.' Do you know what he's saying, Katie?"

"Hmm?" She didn't want to answer, didn't want her words or her thoughts to shatter the enchantment that shimmered around them.

"He's saying that everything they've shared will always remind him of her . . ." He paused for a moment and the music drifted by like a gentle wave or a warm breeze. " ' . . . in every lovely summer's day, in everything that's bright and gay . . . ' and more, Katie, everything he sees that's good and warm and joyous will always bring her to mind for him. He's talking about love."

"Love?" She echoed the word as if she'd never heard it before.

"Love, Katie," Michael said soberly. "The kind that lasts forever . . . 'I'll find you in the morning sun and when the night is through, I'll be looking at the moon but I'll be seeing you.' "

She pulled back and stared into the deep, endless blue of his eyes.

"It's a love song." His eyes enticed her down into their smoldering, hypnotic recesses and she couldn't turn away. "And a promise."

For a long moment, they stared and the world faded to a soft blur. She was afraid to move, afraid even to breathe, afraid to break whatever magic held them here, bound together in a fierce, intimate communion.

"Come on." He pulled her into the corridor where the light was much dimmer than in the main room. Some eager serviceman, or perhaps an equally enthusiastic young hostess, had tacked up a bit of greenery in the secluded area.

"Mistletoe?" She widened her eyes in surprise. "The chaperons would have a fit if they saw that."

"Then let's not let them see it." He pinned her with a direct gaze that melted her defenses. His eyes were dark with desire and intense with something she couldn't quite place. Something that took her breath away. "Kiss me, Katie."

He drew her into his arms and it was as if she'd finally come home. As if this was where she belonged, where she'd always belonged. His head dipped toward hers and she tilted her face to meet him. His lips brushed against hers, lightly at first, and the sparks she'd noted when he merely touched her hand flared into a blaze of need and wanting. Her arms snaked around his neck and he pulled her closer. The rough wool of his uniform pressed against her, crushing the gardenia that clung to her sweater.

Was it his heart that throbbed between them or her own?

His lips demanded more, and she met his insistence

with eager abandon. Her fingers caressed the warm flesh at the back of his neck, and she marveled at the feel of hard muscle beneath velvet skin.

He pulled his lips to the line of her jaw and beyond to a point just below her ear. He nibbled and kissed and teased until she thought her knees would buckle and she would dissolve into a small, quivering puddle. Never had a simple kiss affected her like this. Never had she ached for the touch of knowledgeable hands on previously unknown places. Never had a man done this to her.

"Dear Michael," she murmured, "what will I do with you?"

"Marry me."

His words barely penetrated the thick haze of arousal enveloping her, and she uttered a mindless sigh in response.

Michael drew back from her and his gaze searched her face as if he sought answers to questions only he understood. His gaze locked with hers and it seemed as if time itself stopped just for them. As if they and they alone were the only two people in the world, in the universe, in all of creation.

"Marry me, Katie," he said softly.

"Marry you?" She gasped. "Is that what you said?"

"Twice now." A tiny twinkle of wry amusement danced in his eyes. "I love you, Katie."

The fog of desire that blunted her senses abruptly vanished and her mind sharpened with the meaning of his words. "Love? How can you love me? We just met. I don't even know you."

"I don't know you either, but I still want to marry you." The slight smile on his lips didn't touch the smoldering depths of his eyes. "And you're wrong, you know."

"Wrong?" She couldn't seem to catch her breath.

He nodded. "I do know you. I've known you forever."

"Forever? That's ridiculous." He was standing way too close. That's why she couldn't breathe. It had nothing to do with the passion in his eyes. Nothing to do with the fervent tone of his words. Nothing to do with how her body seemed to fit so perfectly with his own. She tried to pull away but he held her tight.

"I knew the moment I saw you across the room, we were meant for each other. It was the strongest sensation I've ever felt. Like being hit by a bolt of lightning. We're soul mates, Katie." His words rang with quiet conviction. "I know it as surely as I've ever known anything in my life; you're my destiny. My fate."

Fate?

She laughed weakly. "Fate? Now that's a good line. You *are* a romantic."

A frown furrowed his forehead and he shook her gently. "Don't laugh at me and don't take this lightly."

"You don't know what you're saying." Irrational, unexplained panic threatened within her.

"I know exactly what I'm saying."

"Michael." She struggled to find the right words. "You're caught up in the emotion of the moment. You're going off to fight for your country. You're just—"

"Don't treat me like I'm some green seventeen-year-old whose voice has just changed." Anger flashed in his eyes. "I'm an adult. Twenty-two years old. College educated. For crissakes, Katie, I'm a damned officer. I know what I want when I see it."

"You don't know anything." She jerked out of his grasp. "We're in the middle of a war. This is no time to make commitments or promises or anything else. Besides, you have no idea what happens to the women whose husbands are off who knows where facing who knows what."

She shook her head angrily. "I watch them, Michael, and I refuse to become one of them."

"Katie." Frustration simmered in his voice.

"No, Michael." She shook her head firmly, refusing to give in. It was too important, and too permanent, and too darn frightening. "I will not spend the next year or two years or ten years waiting for you to come home. Or for you to be killed. I will not cringe every time there's a knock on the door. I will not listen to the radio with my heart in my throat. And I will not bury someone I love again."

"It's because of your brother, isn't it?" he said gently.

"Harry?" Immediately the tall, sandy-haired big brother with the laughing eyes and teasing smile flashed through her mind. The thought hadn't occurred to her before, but Michael was right: Harry played a big role in her fears. "I guess so."

"Tell me." His tone was colored with compassion.

She shrugged impatiently. "There's not much to tell. Harry wanted to fly and see the world. He ended up in Hawaii. It seemed like the perfect assignment. Two days before he died we got a letter from him all about parties on the beach and learning to surf."

Michael eyed her intently. "It must have come as quite a shock."

A sharper, bitter laugh broke from her. "It came as a shock to the whole country. I was just a little more personally involved, that's all."

"I have no intention of dying in any damn war."

She shook her head. "Harry had no intention of dying either."

Their gazes locked for a long moment and silence fell between them. A myriad of expressions chased across his face: frustration, doubt, and finally determination.

He pulled her back into his arms. "You haven't said the one thing, the only thing, I'll accept as a legitimate excuse for being turned down."

"What?" she snapped.

He raised a brow at the sharp tone and lowered his head to hers. His voice was low and intense. "You haven't said you don't love me."

"Michael, I—"

His lips claimed hers, stifling any possible protest. A rational, indignant voice, a voice of sanity, a voice of sheer terror screamed inside her head.

You don't love him! You can't love him! Not here! Not now!

But right here and right now, she was in his arms and her treacherous body betrayed her. For a split second she resisted, then her guard crumbled. Instinctively she leaned into his embrace as if to forge the separate into the whole, the two into the one. Her breath mixed and mingled with his as if the very air that provided life was incomplete unless shared. Heat pounded through her veins in a rhythm that ebbed and flowed with the throb of his lips crushed to hers.

He groaned and pulled his mouth away to feather

kisses down to the hollow of her throat. "I knew it, Katie. You do love me."

"No, Michael." Her words were little more than a sigh.

Yes, Michael.

She couldn't answer, couldn't find the words, couldn't focus on anything beyond the glory of his lips on flesh heated with newfound passion.

"I saw a sign down the street." His voice rumbled against her neck. "A justice of the peace. Next door to a little inn."

"Judge Thomas." She struggled for sanity, struggled to remain coherent, struggled to ignore the intoxicating sensation of his hands splayed across her back, pressing her tighter until the clothing separating them seemed nonexistent and the flame of his passion arched between them.

"Marry me." His voice was rough with emotion, heavy with need, and the words shot through her with an icy force that jerked her back to reason.

"No." The word was a sob, wrung from deep inside her as if pulled by force or by necessity or by fear. "No."

A shudder of regret, a sigh of resignation shivered through him and he held her firmly, her cheek cradled on his chest. His broad shoulders sagged slightly as if he had finally accepted her rejection.

"Will you wait for me then, Katie?"

"Forever," she whispered.

He tilted her chin up and her gaze meshed with his. He brushed the flat of his thumb over her bottom lip and tossed her a sad smile that clutched at a place in her heart. "You know, if you'd marry me I'd have something to come back for."

"You'll have something to come back for," she said staunchly, steadfast in her belief that this was the right thing to do. "I promise."

"And I promise too, Katie." His eyes burned with conviction. "I will come back to you."

"I'll be right here." She mustered a smile that quivered in spite of her resolve to show nothing but confidence and conviction. "Waiting."

"Okay." He heaved a heavy sigh. "That'll have to do, I guess."

"I guess," she echoed.

They stared at each other for a second or an eternity. There was so much she wanted to say to him, so much she needed to say. But the words didn't come.

The overhead lights flashed on in the main hall, signaling the end of the evening.

"I have to go," he said simply.

"I know." He took her hand and they walked into the rapidly emptying main room, blinking in the bright light after the dim recesses of the corridor.

Her throat tightened and she bit her lip to hold back tears. "I'll walk you out."

"No." He shook his head. "That's okay. I'd rather . . ." He laughed awkwardly and ran his fingers through his hair. "I don't know what to say."

She pulled a deep breath. "Me neither."

He turned to leave, then swiveled back and yanked her into his arms. His dark eyes bored into hers with a fervor that crept into her soul. "You haven't said it, Katie. You haven't told me."

"Told you what?" Frantically she searched her mind. "I said I'll wait for you."

40

"No." He shook his head and stared. "You never said you loved me. Do you, Katie, do you love me?"

Love?

"I—" The word shivered through her, shadowed with indecision and doubt. Was this love? Could she admit the truth to him? Or more, to herself.

"Lieutenant?" an impatient masculine voice called.

"Coming." Michael threw the answer over his shoulder, then swiftly brushed his lips across her forehead. "Write to me."

She swallowed the lump in her throat and nodded.

His gaze lingered on her for a last second. Then abruptly he twisted and strode toward the door.

"Michael," she whispered.

Across the room, he hesitated beside the Christmas tree. His hand snapped out and plucked a glass ball from the fir. He swiveled to face her.

"Katie," he called, "you do need a present."

With an easy underhand pitch, he threw the ornament into the air. It swung high in a long, slow arch, catching and reflecting the light like a Christmas star. She cupped her hands together and held them out before her. The ball landed with a gentle plop in the center of her outstretched palms as if guided by unerring instinct or pure emotion.

Michael tossed her a quick wave and the crooked grin that had already branded a spot on her heart.

"I'll be seeing you, Katie." Even from across the room she could see the smoldering pledge in his eyes, and she read his lips more than heard his words. It was enough. "I promise."

He joined the throng of uniforms swirling through the open door, and she lost sight of him. At once she wanted to run across the room, into the night and back into his arms. She wanted to hear his laughter and bask in the sparkle of his eyes. She wanted to feel the warmth of his body beside hers, as his wife, as his love.

But she couldn't seem to move. Her feet, her mind resisted the urgent cries of her heart. Her shoulders slumped with the realization: she was a coward, plain and simple. Too afraid of the possibility of loss and pain to recognize the greatest gift a man could offer a woman, at Christmas or any other time.

The door slammed shut and at once the noise in the room quieted to a gentle murmur. The only ones left were the hostesses and the chaperons and the odd assortment of males who made up the makeshift band. Only women and children and old men. It was the same in any war.

She was right not to marry him, not to commit her life, her heart to him. She'd write, of course, and she'd wait and she'd pray for his safe return.

Would a ring on her finger make it any harder?

She sucked her breath in sharply and clasped a hand over her mouth. How could she have been so blind? What a complete idiot she was! Married or not, she was in the same boat as Pamela Gillum. But worse, much, much worse. Pamela at least had her husband's name and her memories.

Katie stared down at the delicate ornament in her hand as if it were a crystal ball that held the true meaning of life. But the revelation of some truths come too late. She'd sent Michael away with nothing beyond a simple promise to wait. She hadn't even told him she loved him, when everything inside her proclaimed the truth. Improbable and unrealistic and downright insane, it was still the truth.

She loved him.

And he was gone.

She fought a rising sense of panic. It will be okay. He'll come back. He has to come back.

He promised.

She wrote to him on Christmas morning. And the next day and the day after that. A flurry of letters winged their way across the ocean bearing a flood of emotion. She poured her heart and soul into every word, every line, every page. She wrote of her hopes and dreams for after the war, for the future, their future together. She wrote of love.

And she waited.

Katie returned to school with her mother's promise to forward all mail. She checked her box every day, sometimes twice. Nothing.

Weeks turned to months without word. Anticipation faded and doubt gnawed at the back of her mind like a voracious rodent. Were Michael's words just routine lines after all? Were they merely quick and easy lies designed to play on the wonder of a single night and the threat of mortality? Did he really mean everything he said? Did he mean anything he said?

I do know you. I've known you forever.

No. She refused to believe, even for a moment, that the tone of his words, the touch of his hand, the look in his eye was anything less than what she knew, deep inside some secret place in her soul, to be real. And right.

Faith kept her strong, hope kept her going, and love

kept her alive. She would hear from him. He would come back to her.

He promised.

It was a frigid winter day when she found the bulky Manila envelope stuffed in her mailbox. She yanked it out with fingers numbed from the cold and icy tendrils gripping her heart. Her hands trembled as she struggled to tear the packet open. Her letters to Michael tumbled out, drifting to the ground. Amidst them fluttered a single, official-looking page.

Dear Miss Bedford,

I must apologize for the unforgivable delay in contacting you. Unfortunately, your correspondence with Lt. O'Connor was apparently held up and not discovered until recently. Your letters were not among his personal effects.

I regret to inform you Lt. O'Connor was killed in a training accident shortly after his arrival in England. I didn't know him well but he seemed like a fine young man. Please accept my condolences.

Sincerely,
Capt. Benjamin Gray

Pain speared through her with an intensity that ripped away her breath and stopped her heart and froze her soul. Her legs buckled beneath her and she sank to her knees. She could neither accept the straightforward words nor ignore them. For a long moment she huddled, numbed, as if by avoiding any movement herself she could somehow halt the world in its orbit, turn back the clock, deny what couldn't be denied. One line from the Captain's letter pounded in her head over and over in a refrain of accusation.

Your letters were not among his personal effects.

Michael never received her letters. He never knew how much she regretted her decision not to marry him. He never knew of her ardent, written vows to spend the rest of her life with him.

He never knew she loved him.

Like a dam swept aside by rampaging waters her defenses shattered. Great racking sobs shook through her and she wept for what was lost and what would never be. She cried for the love of a man gained in one night, destined to last a lifetime, now lasting no time at all. And her tears failed to wash away the one unrelenting truth of war and death and even life itself.

Promises can't always be kept. . . .

. . . promises.

Katherine stared at the aged box in her hand. Even now, fifty-four years later, the pain was as fresh and sharp as it had been on that cold, cold winter day. Somehow she'd always ignored it before. She rarely thought about Michael, relegating him to the dim reaches of her mind the same way she'd stored the hatbox and her memories in the back shadows of the closet. Occasionally a twinge of sorrow would tug at her heart. But only occasionally and always on Christmas Eve.

She had put him firmly in the past and gone on with her life. She finished school and fled to sunny California where the flowers bloomed even at Christmas and no one ever worried about icy roads. She got a good job and managed to hang on to it even when the war ended and the men came home. Every bit of passion within her went into her work, her career.

Every now and then she'd long for the magic she tasted so briefly on that one Christmas Eve. She married, twice, both marriages disastrous, both mercifully short. She never even glimpsed what she'd shared with Michael on a single evening in another lifetime.

Crazy old woman.

Disgust and anger surged through her. She ripped open the frail box and rolled what was left of the corsage onto her hand. Hard and dark and shriveled, it bore only the vaguest resemblance to what it had once been.

Just like me.

She gazed at the floral remains as if mesmerized. There was little of Katie left in Katherine. And no one to blame but herself. Her life would have been so very different had she, just that once, listened to her heart instead of her head.

You've lived your life. Made your choices. You can't go back.

Maybe she really had snapped. Maybe all the lonely years had finally sent her over the edge. It was insane to place all one's hopes and dreams and prayers on a promise muttered by a man in a red suit more than half a century ago. Or an odd quirk of lighting that changed the look in the eye of a department store Santa.

Her hand closed around the withered flower and she squeezed her fist tight. Better to crush this delusion, and all the bittersweet memories, right now and simply blow the dust away and face up to reality.

She opened her hand and her heart thudded in her chest. Blood roared in her ears and the room spun around her. She stared in stark disbelief.

In the center of her palm, the gardenia was as fresh and whole and sweet as the day Michael had pinned it on her sweater.

She couldn't seem to catch her breath. Her eyes blurred. The world around her faded. Only the stark white of the flower shimmered in her vision. It gleamed like a Christmas star or a wedding gown or a . . . snowflake.

". . . Katie."

Snowflakes flurried against the glass, incandescent fireflies flitting through a blue-black night.

"Katie Bedford, would you please stop staring out the window and take this?" Mary Ann Hanson held up a hand-blown glass ball and glared with obvious irritation.

"Snow." Katherine gasped the word. "It's really snow!"

"Of course it's snow," Mary Ann said sharply. "Goodness, Katie, it's been snowing off and on for days."

Katherine couldn't pull her gaze away from the window. "It's beautiful."

Mary Ann's tone softened. "It is pretty, all right. Just like a Christmas card."

"A Christmas card," Katherine echoed. "I'd forgotten how perfect snow was for Christmas"—she sucked in her breath sharply—"Eve. It's Christmas Eve!"

Mary Ann threw her a look of exasperation. "Of course it's Christmas Eve."

Katherine widened her eyes with realization. "And it's 1942, isn't it?"

"Katie," Mary Ann shook her head, "I don't think—"

"Mary Ann Hanson." Katherine stared at the blonde from her lofty perch on the rickety ladder. "You're just as I remember you."

"Remember me? What's with you, Katie?" Mary Ann said with irritation.

"What's with me?" Sheer joy bubbled up inside her. Her excited gaze darted around the barely remembered community hall-turned-canteen, skimming past the growing crowd of young, uniformed men, skipping over Christmas decorations and sharp-eyed chaperons. Everything was exactly as it had been that night.

Katherine clapped her hand over her mouth. Surely it wasn't possible. This must all be a dream. Or maybe she'd died. Dropped dead right in her walk-in closet.

"*Santa always keeps his promises.*"

"Katie?" Mary Ann's tone was cautious.

"You called me Katie." Katherine shook her head in wonder. "I can't believe it. And I don't care if I'm dead or asleep. I have a second chance."

"Maybe you'd better come down off that ladder," Mary Ann said carefully. "I think the height is starting to get to you."

"The height?" Katherine laughed with a surge of exuberance she hadn't known for years. "Mary Ann, the height is wonderful. It's incredible. From here I can see everything. Every inch of the room. Every person, every"—she caught her breath—"Michael."

"Who?"

"Oh, um, nothing." What could she say? What

should she say? If this was real, and everything within her screamed that it was indeed true and tangible and solid, she didn't want to blow it. There was no way of knowing if her second chance lasted for just one night or the rest of her life. But it didn't matter. Tonight would be enough to treasure for a lifetime. One way or another, it had to be. "Never mind. Now"—her tone was brisk and no-nonsense—"hand me that ball and we'll get this tree finished."

Mary Ann eyed her suspiciously, then handed her an ornament. "For a moment you had me worried. What's the matter with you tonight?"

"Nothing, pal, not a thing." Katie placed the ball on the lush fir, nodded with satisfaction, and climbed down the ladder. She hopped to the ground and faced her friend with a grin. "Not one little thing. It's Christmas Eve, 1942, and everything is just about perfect."

"I don't know what's gotten into you." Mary Ann shook her head. "Five minutes ago you were complaining and crabby and not in any kind of Christmas spirit at all."

Katherine shrugged. "Go figure." She nodded at the tree. "It must be this magnificent Christmas tree that's completely changed my mood."

"It is lovely," Mary Ann said. "Those old-fashioned balls make all the difference. Somebody left a big box full of them at the door to the hall tonight. The chaperons found it when they arrived." She studied the tree. "I think they add just the right touch of—"

"Magic," Katherine said softly. "Christmas magic."

Mary Ann grinned in agreement. "You got it." She cast her gaze around the rapidly filling room. "I wonder if he'll be here tonight?"

Of course he'll be here. He had to be. Michael was the only reason for reliving this night. Still, already everything was a little different than she remembered it. What if he didn't come? What if—

"Katie, aren't you going to ask who?"

"What?" Katherine jerked her attention back to her friend.

Mary Ann sighed. "Honestly, Katie, I'd swear you were somewhere else tonight."

"Oh no, Mary Ann." Determination underlay her words. "I am definitely right here."

"Well, you don't act like it," Mary Ann huffed. "I was talking about the love of my life, you know, my Prince Charming."

"This is obviously a great place to find him." Katherine scanned the crowd looking for the one face she'd waited a lifetime to see.

"What?" Mary Ann snorted in derision. "No lectures on the evils of husband hunting? No comments on how we're only twenty and have plenty of time to find a man? No stern talks on the risks of falling in love during a war?"

"Absolutely not," Katherine said firmly. She pinned her friend with a steady gaze. "Mary Ann, if you never pay attention to anything else I ever say, pay attention to this. When you find Prince Charming or Mr. Right or whatever you want to call him, don't hesitate, not for a moment. Ignore sanity and reason and common sense and listen only to your heart. It doesn't matter if you don't end up living happily ever after. Love, whether it's for a lifetime or just one night, is worth anything."

Katherine's voice rang with conviction. "It sounds corny, but there is such a thing as fate. Such a thing as destiny. There really is one special man meant for you and you alone. And if you miss your chance to love him and be loved by him, you'll regret it for the rest of your life."

Katherine grabbed Mary Ann's shoulders and stared into her eyes. "You'll grow old alone and, at the end, your life won't have counted one little bit. And regardless of whatever success you may achieve, no matter what challenges you may overcome or mountains you might climb, nothing, positively nothing will ever compare to what you might have had with him." Her voice softened. "Knowing love, just for a moment, is worth anything. Even the pain of losing someone you love is insignificant compared to the agony of not loving at all."

Mary Ann stared wide-eyed. "Wow."

"Sorry." Katherine dropped her hands and laughed self-consciously. "I didn't mean to go overboard. I probably sounded a little nuts."

"No," Mary Ann said breathlessly. "What you said was wonderful. I never imagined you felt that way. Every time I talk about love and finding the right man you always seemed so—"

"Condescending? Conservative? Cautious?" Katherine wrinkled her nose at the accuracy of her words.

Mary Ann nodded sheepishly. "Yeah, I thought—"

"Girls." An older woman bore down on them in the manner of a veteran war horse and thrust two small, cream-colored boxes in their general direction. "Some of the local florists got together and donated these for the hostesses tonight."

"Gardenias," Katherine said, a wistful note in her voice. Her heart leapt. Events were unfolding much

51

as they had before. It was only a matter of minutes before she'd see Michael again. And this time everything would be different.

"Indeed." The energetic matron nodded sharply and handed them the containers. "Isn't it wonderful how everyone wants to do their part for the war effort?"

"Wonderful," the girls echoed in unison.

"You two have a lovely time this evening and be sure to follow the rules. They're there for your protection, you know." The chaperon cast them a stern glance, then continued on her rounds, spewing orders like a general to the tiny troop of high-school-aged volunteers that trailed obediently at her heels like well-trained recruits or puppies.

Katherine pulled the lid off her box and picked up the corsage. Her hands trembled and anticipation threatened to overwhelm her.

"This might not do anything for the war effort in general but it certainly helps my own personal battle plans." Mary Ann pinned the blossom to her sweater and cast an assessing gaze around the room. At once her eyes lit up. "And I see a likely target right now."

"Good luck," Katherine said absently, barely noticing Mary Ann's comments in her own search of the room.

"Katie." Mary Ann hesitated as if she couldn't quite find the words. "I don't know what's going on with you tonight but"—she sighed—"well, good luck to you, too, I guess."

"Thanks." Katherine grinned and gave her friend a little push. "Now get out there and conquer new worlds."

"You bet." Mary Ann tossed her friend a devilish grin. "See you later."

"Happy hunting," Katherine said, relieved to get rid of her. Oh, it was wonderful to see Mary Ann again but time was slipping away quickly and Katherine didn't know how much she'd have. So far, the evening progressed in much the same manner it had the first time. If that held true, next—

A burst of music from the far end of the hall caught Katherine's attention. It was the motley collection of volunteers they'd called a band. What happened now? Her heart raced and she searched her memories. Of course. She'd been idly looking around the hall. The crowd seemed to part, and there he was.

Her gaze skimmed over the room as she waited for a break in the milling mass of uniforms and enthusiastic young women. Nothing happened. Panic fluttered in her stomach. What if history wasn't going to repeat itself? What if nothing was the same at all? Maybe just being here again changed events. This could be some vindictive cosmic joke. What should she do now?

Perhaps if she went to find him? Again she scanned the room. He'd been standing somewhere in that area when she'd first seen him. She drew a steadying breath and took a determined step. The crowd jostled against her and the gardenia in her hand tumbled to the floor.

"Damn," she said under her breath. "I don't have time for this."

Quickly she swooped down to retrieve the flower before it could be crushed in the crowd. She reached toward it, but just as her fingertips brushed the petals, a large, male hand gently plucked it off the floor.

Michael!

Her heart seemed to stop. Her gaze traveled up the length of his long arm, past hard, broad shoulders to his beloved boy-next-door face. To the cocky grin she'd remembered over and over in fifty years of dreams. To his dark, endless eyes that glittered with promise and burned with a fire she'd never forgotten and never forsaken.

"Do you believe in love at first sight?" His voice was a caress, resonant with deep, unspoken meaning.

Katherine stared in stark disbelief and immeasurable joy. She yearned to reach out and place her hand on his cheek, to feel the warmth of his flesh beneath her fingers, to assure herself once and for all that he was real and she was here.

Her voice was barely a whisper. "Yes, I do. Do you?"

"I didn't." His smile didn't quite erase the perplexed look in his eye. "Until now."

She tilted her head to one side, cast him an appraising glance, and struggled to hide her true emotions. As much as she wanted to throw herself in his arms, she had to remember this was his first meeting with her. He hadn't lived this moment over and over again through more than half a century the way she had. She had to take it slow, with care and caution.

"Was that just a line then?" She flashed him a flirtatious smile.

"Not at all." He laughed, and she nearly wept at the well remembered sound. "Here, let me help you up."

He placed his hand under her elbow and they rose to their feet. Even this minimal contact sent shivers coursing down her spine.

"You flyboys are all alike," she teased.

He raised a brow. "How did you know I was a pilot?"

She nodded toward his insignia. "Your wings for one thing. Also, the only other time I was asked if I believed in love at first sight, the question came from a pilot."

"What did you tell him?" His query was offhand but there was an odd light in his eyes and her pulse raced.

"I said . . . no." Her voice was breathless and she fought to sound cool and blasé. "So, if it wasn't a line, then what was it?"

"I'm a romantic at heart, I guess." His gaze searched her face and his brows pulled together in a puzzled frown. "Have we met somewhere before?"

"That's a good line, too, but no, I don't think so," she said lightly.

Oh, yes. Once. In another lifetime.

"No, seriously, are you sure?" He narrowed his eyes thoughtfully. "Have you ever been to Chicago?"

"No, never." Her heart fluttered.

He can't possibly know. Can he?

"Funny." He shook his head as if to clear it. "I have such a strong feeling that we've met before. That I know you from somewhere."

"Déjà vu?" She laughed casually. "Or fate maybe?"

"Maybe." He grinned. "It's as good an answer as any."

"I feel as if I know you too," she said boldly. She obviously had his interest, now she had to hold it and pray that lightning would strike once again. Just like before. "I feel as if I know all kinds of things about you."

"Oh?" He quirked a dark brow. "And just what do you know?"

"Let me think." She considered him for a moment. "I know you're a lieutenant."

He nodded at the bar on his shoulder. "Too easy. What else?"

"I know you're from Chicago."

He shrugged. "Another easy one."

She cocked her head and eyed him reflectively. "You're headed to England tomorrow."

"Not bad," he said grudgingly. "Still, I bet most of the guys here are heading out tomorrow."

"Okay." She pulled a deep breath. "And your name is Michael. Michael Patrick O'Connor."

His eyes widened in surprise. "Very good. How on earth did you . . ." He grinned his crooked smile, and her heart melted at the sight of it. "Somebody told you, right? One of my friends set me up, didn't he?"

"Nope." She laughed with the sheer pleasure of his company.

"Then how—"

"Magic, Lieutenant." She leaned toward him confidentially. "Christmas magic."

"I see." A twinkle danced in his eye. "Does it only work for you or can anybody try it?"

She crossed her arms over her chest. "Just for me."

"I doubt that." He studied her for a moment. "I bet I know a lot about you, too."

She tossed him a challenging glance. "Really? And what do you know about me?"

"I know you've been decorating Christmas trees." He reached out and plucked a small sprig of fir from her hair. His scent of warm spice and male heat washed over her and her breath caught.

"Doesn't count." She shook her head as much to clear it as to deny his observation. "Too easy. What else?"

"You're an excellent dancer."

She laughed. "What makes you think so?"

"Great legs," he said in a matter-of-fact manner. Heat rushed up her face. Lord, she hadn't blushed in so many years the sensation was almost frightening.

"Good line," she shot back. "Anything else?"

He narrowed his midnight eyes in obvious appreciation. "I know you're the prettiest girl here. I know you wear some kind of intriguing perfume that reminds me of roses and cinnamon at the same time. I know your eyes are dark and bewitching enough to make even a man who can't swim want to dive right in. I know . . ."

"Yes?" She stared into eyes that went on forever and seemed to search for answers to unasked questions. "What else do you know?"

"I . . ." An absent note sounded in his voice, as if he lost track of his train of thought, as if he too was caught up in a moment of connection, a moment of truth. He stared, his expression bemused.

He knows. He must know.

Abruptly he shook his head and the fragile bond between them shattered into reality. He smiled down at her. "What I don't know is your name."

"Katherine Bedford," she said softly. "But everybody calls me Katie."

"Katie." The name tripped off his tongue like an embrace or a prayer. "It suits you."

"Does it?"

"Yeah." He considered her for a second. "You look like a Katie."

"Well, Lieutenant—"

"Michael," he said firmly.

"Well, Michael," she smiled, "I'll tell you a little secret. Tonight I feel like a Katie."

He threw her a speculative glance. "I have no idea what that means but I think I like the sound of it."

"So do I," she said under her breath. "More than you know."

The band launched into an especially raucous version of "Boogie Woogie Bugle Boy." Michael winced, and she laughed at the embarrassed expression on his face.

"Sorry." He shrugged, chagrined. "I didn't mean to be rude. They caught me off guard."

"It's okay. They're not much but they're all we've got." She nodded toward the band. "At least they're enthusiastic."

"Would you like to dance?" The eager light in his eyes matched her own need to be, at long last, in his arms.

"I'd love to. But first"—she pointed to the corsage still cradled in his hand—"I'll take my flowers back."

"Sure."

She reached to accept the blossom from his outstretched palm, fighting to still the tremble in her fingers.

"Nervous?" He quirked an amused brow. "Not about dancing with me, I hope? Although, I must admit, I am a great dancer."

"Don't be silly. Of course I'm not nervous," she said sharply and snatched the flowers from his hand. She fumbled to pin the gardenia to her sweater. "It's just a little cold in here, that's all."

"Allow me." He pinned the blossom on her with a swift, efficient move. His head bent close and she ached to run her fingers through his dark, silken hair. "There."

He nodded with satisfaction and straightened up. How could she have forgotten how tall he was? He towered a good half foot over her and her eyes were at a level with his lips. Lips that had haunted her dreams forever. She could still remember the insistent demand of his mouth. The sensual pressure of his lips next to hers. The surge of passion from the merest puff of his breath against her own.

"Katie?"

"Michael." She stared up at him and his gaze searched hers with the same odd look he'd worn earlier as if he reached for something he couldn't quite grasp. She longed to tell him everything. That they'd been through all this once before. That they were destined to be together. That the love they found on this lone night was real and true and right. "Michael?"

"I just don't get it, Katie, there's something about you . . ." He shook his head. "I could swear I know you from somewhere."

She was tempted to tell him the truth. To spill it all and go on from there. No. Firmly she thrust the temptation away. What on earth would he think if she told him they were caught in a replay of history? There was no possibility he would even remotely believe her. Why, he'd think she was a lunatic or worse. Still, would there be anything wrong with using her knowledge of the future to give him a little push, to help him, just a bit faster, to fall in love? They had so little time.

"I guess I'd better confess, Michael." She cast him a confidential look. "It all has to do with fate."

"Fate?" His brows furrowed in confusion. "What do you mean?"

"Fate, Michael, destiny." She glanced to one side then the other as if checking to make sure no one was listening. "We're soul mates, you know."

"Soul mates?" He narrowed his eyes as if he wasn't quite sure how to take her comment. "Are you serious?"

"You bet." She grinned. Joking was probably the easiest and most subtle method of working her way back into his heart. "Relax, Lieutenant, it's all just part of that Christmas magic we've been talking about."

He laughed and grabbed her hand. "Then we might as well see if any of it will work on the dance floor." He pulled her toward the dancers, then stopped abruptly and stared at her for a moment. "You know, I kind of like the way that sounds."

"What?"

"Soul mates." He tossed her an easy smile and continued on his way to the dance floor.

"Lieutenant," she said, more to herself than to him, safe in the knowledge that the blaring music would cover her words, "that's the best news I've heard in half a century."

She wouldn't have believed it possible. This night was somehow better, brighter, and even more special than the first. Perhaps it was simply that she was relaxed and willing to give in to her emotions. Perhaps it was that she and she alone knew how very important the evening was. Or perhaps it was only the ever-present thought that the memories created in this one night must last a lifetime.

She didn't remember laughing quite this much on that first night, but then it had been a very long time since she'd laughed at all. He was funny and smart and every time he touched her hand or held her in his arms for a dance she had to make a conscious effort to keep her heart beating and her breath from catching in her throat. She'd tried not to think about the future all night, just as throughout her life she'd tried not to think about the past. Only here and now could she admit she had never completely closed away that Christmas Eve, and never gotten over him.

Now, he'd left her standing near the Christmas tree to get them something to drink. Her gaze followed his every move. He walked across the room with a long-legged, athletic stride that spoke of confidence and courage. Confidence in ordinary day-to-day living and courage in the face of extraordinary danger. Something in his step clutched at her soul with a sharp reminder of how little life this man had left. And try as she might, there was probably nothing she could do to prevent his fate.

Pamela Gillum walked past with a determined smile on her face. Her expression didn't erase the tiny lines of worry that even makeup couldn't hide. Maybe she couldn't do anything to change Michael's destiny or anybody else's future, but she could do something to help this woman right now.

"Mrs. Gillum . . . Pamela," she said.

"Yes, dear?" The older woman turned toward her,

a question in her eyes. "Can I help you?"

"I . . ." What on earth could she say now? How could she tell her that all her fears were for nothing? That her husband would indeed return home? Frustration flooded through her. Still . . . she drew a deep breath. "It'll be okay. Really, it will. He'll come home. I know it."

Hope glimmered in Pamela's eye, then softened to a look of sad resignation. "That's what we all hope for, dear."

"No, honestly." She reached out and grasped Pamela's arm. "You have to believe me. He'll be fine."

"Katie." Pamela cast her a chastising frown. "I know you're just trying to help but—"

"It's more than that." An urgent need to convince this woman filled her. She lowered her voice. "Please don't tell anyone, but there are some things that I just know. And I know your husband will survive this war." She shrugged helplessly. "I can't explain any more than that. You have to trust me."

Pamela stared, her gaze searching Katie's face as if desperately seeking something in her expression to convince her of the accuracy of her prediction.

"What deep, dark secrets are you two sharing?" Michael handed her a cup of punch and she dropped her hand from Pamela's arm.

"Nothing." Katie smiled weakly.

"I'm not sure why," Pamela said, shaking her head, "but for some strange reason, I think I do believe you. Lord knows I want to. It's absurd, of course, no one knows the future. Even so . . ." She drew a shaky breath. "Thank you, Katie." She smiled, nodded at Michael, and walked slowly away.

Katie heaved a sigh of relief. With any luck, she'd given Pamela something to hang on to and maybe relieved her anxiety just a bit.

"What was that all about?" Idle curiosity shone in Michael's eyes.

"Oh, every now and then I do a little fortune-telling." She took a sip of her punch. "Chalk it up to Christmas magic."

"I see. Something else to add to your many attributes."

She raised a questioning brow. "Are you making a list?"

He nodded solemnly. "And checking it twice. Let's see now." He ticked the items off on his fingers. "You're almost as good a dancer as I am."

"Thank you," she said dryly.

He pointedly ignored her interruption. "You're obviously intelligent, judging from the way you're quick with a sharp comeback."

"Thanks again."

"Beyond that, you're quite a dish." He tossed her a slightly lecherous glance and she laughed in response. "You believe in fate and destiny, and now I find out you tell fortunes as well." He narrowed his eyes in mock suspicion. "You're a witch, aren't you, Katie?"

She chuckled. "I've been called worse."

He snorted doubtfully. "I find that hard to believe." He stepped closer, cupped her chin with his hand, and gazed into her eyes. "Can you tell the future, Katie? My future?" He stared, and his voice deepened with unspoken meaning. "Our future?"

"Our future?" She could barely breathe with the

Victoria Alexander

nearness of his body to hers and the intensity of the look in his eye.

"It's awfully hot in here," he said softly. "Would you like to get some fresh air?"

"It's against the rules and I . . ." She paused. What did she care about the silly rules and moral barriers of a long-lost era? This was the only night she had and she wasn't going to miss out on one magical moment of it. Besides, her success, small though it was, with Pamela had her thinking. Maybe, just maybe, she could change things a little. And then maybe Michael wouldn't have to die so young and so soon. She nodded. "I'd love to. There's a terrace behind the building. I'll get my coat and meet you there."

"Don't take too long." His smile spoke of promises and passion, and anticipation shivered through her. He turned and strode away and she hurried to the cloakroom where she'd left her wrap.

Katie grabbed her coat and with a forced nonchalance made her way toward the back door. Halfway there, a flash of red caught her eye and she froze in her tracks.

Her gaze meshed and locked with eyes deep and wise and kind. He sat in a huge carved wooden throne across the room surrounded by stacks of brightly wrapped packages. It was a scene straight from a children's book. Was this simply a local man playing a part for a Christmas party or was this a vision far beyond the limits of reality as she'd always known it? It no longer mattered. Whoever or whatever he was, she had to thank him for the chance to live this one night over.

She stepped toward him but he shook his head

sternly, then nodded at the back door. He grinned and tossed her a casual salute. She smiled back and turned toward the door. Surely he already knew how grateful she was for this very special gift. Didn't he? The least she could do was tell him what this night meant to her. She swiveled back and scanned the area he'd sat in only a second before.

He was gone. There was no sign of a chair or packages or any evidence that anything was even slightly different from a moment ago. She chuckled to herself and continued to the door.

It was probably time for him to leave. After all, Santa had already delivered the best gift of all.

"Do you really want to be a pilot?" Katie asked as if the answer were of no importance.

"I've never wanted to be anything else." Michael leaned against the terrace wall. The snow drifted gracefully between them. "I've wanted to fly for most of my life. Funny as it sounds, this war is giving me the chance to live a dream." He cocked his head and studied her. "Why did you ask?"

She considered her words carefully. "It's dangerous, that's all. Especially now. I think you should reconsider flying."

His eyes twinkled and his words teased. "Are you worried about me, Katie Bedford?"

"Yes," she said simply.

"Good, I like that." His tone was abruptly serious. "I know we've just met but I feel somehow as if I've known you forever."

"Me, too."

He eyed her solemnly, his gaze considering. "And I

think there's something you're not telling me. What is it, Katie?"

She stared down at the snow-covered ground. There was so much she wanted to say and so much she couldn't. She sighed and looked up. "My brother was a pilot."

"Was?"

She nodded. "He was in the Navy. Stationed at Pearl Harbor."

"I see." Sympathy shone in his eyes. "Were you very close?"

"Harry was my big brother." She smiled sadly. "He was a great guy and I really miss him."

"Katie . . ." Michael shrugged helplessly. "It's a war."

"I know that," she said, her voice sharper than she intended. She glared with all the emotion stored up in a lifetime of regret, and something inside her snapped. "I'm not an idiot. I know all about war. Men have been fighting and killing each other for centuries and for what? In the name of decency or patriotism or God? One war might end but there's always another one sooner or later. Now it's this World War and next is Korea and after that Vietnam—"

"Vietnam?" Confusion shadowed his face. "What are you talking about?"

"Never mind." She waved him off impatiently. There was no way she was about to explain the geopolitical conflicts of the last half of the twentieth century to a man planted firmly in 1942. "The bottom line is that when the smoke clears and the bodies are counted, what difference does any of it make after all? And it's not just men paying the price but the women and children left behind pretending to be brave but really living in constant fear. It's so damned unnecessary to have to sacrifice everything you care for, everyone you love—"

"Do you love me, Katie?"

Did she love him? She'd loved him for most of her life. She gazed into his eyes and prayed for the right words. The words that would draw him closer and not push him away.

"I just met you." Caution underlay her words.

"I think we already established that," he said softly. "Do you love me?"

"What do you want me to say, Michael?"

"It's crazy, Katie, but it's a crazy world we live in these days." He shook his head as if he couldn't believe his own words or his own feelings. "When I first saw you across the room, I thought you were the prettiest girl here."

"You thought I was a dish," she said accusingly.

"You are a dish." His voice was firm.

"And?" she prompted.

"And . . ." He combed his fingers through his hair as if struggling to understand his own words. "And I felt as if I'd been hit by a bolt from the blue. As if someone had reached out and smacked me across the face." He stared at her, confusion battling with wonder in his face. "Does that make any sense at all?"

Joy surged within her. "I think so."

His gaze locked with hers, intense and searching. "You talked about fate and destiny, and, God help me, Katie, I've always believed secretly, in the back of my mind, that there would be only one chance and only one special girl. I was always confident I'd know her when I met her. And I did."

He pulled her into his arms. "What was it you said? About you and me?"

"Soul mates?" she said breathlessly.

"Soul mates." He nodded. "That's it exactly. I feel as if, for the first time in my life, I'm whole and complete. As if there's a part of me that's always been missing until now." He shook his head in amazement. "It doesn't make any sense. It's insane and irrational and—"

"Magic?" She sighed the word. "Christmas magic?"

"No." He brushed his lips against her own and she struggled to keep from melting against him. "This magic isn't just for Christmas. This is forever, Katie."

"Forever." Her voice was barely a whisper and her heart nearly broke at the lie.

He gazed into her eyes for a long, silent moment. "Are you a witch, Katie? Can you tell the future? My future?"

"Yes." She gasped and stared with all the longing of a life lived without him. "I can tell, right now, you're going to kiss me."

The corners of his mouth quirked upward. "You are a witch."

"Then kiss me, Michael."

His lips claimed hers with an eager gentleness that left her aching for more. Long-denied passion flared within her. She wound her arms around his neck and crushed her mouth to his. He hesitated for the barest moment as if surprised by her boldness, then pulled her closer, tighter, until even the clothing between them couldn't hide the aching need of one for the other.

Her mouth opened beneath the pressure of his and his tongue traced the inner edge of her lips in a sensuous path that left her weak with desire. Her hands grasped at the back of his neck, her fingers tunneling up through the thick satin of his hair. So long, she had waited so very long for the heat of his lips on hers.

"Katie." He pulled away and stared down at her. Snowflakes danced between them. "You still haven't answered my question."

She traced the line of his jaw with a trembling finger and marveled at the mix of rough texture and warm flesh. "I told you you were going to kiss me."

"Not that question. The other one." He gave her a tiny shake and her gaze jerked to his. Urgency, desire, and a touch of apprehension lingered in his eye. "Do you love me?"

She stared and a million thoughts flew through her head. Once before he'd asked the very same question. But confusion and fear and downright stupidity had held her tongue. She'd sent him off to war, off to die, without saying the one thing he wanted, no, needed, to hear. And she'd lived a lifetime of regret because of it. She would not make the same mistake again.

"I've loved you forever." She held her hand against his cheek. "And I will always love you. That's a promise."

For a second he simply stared, amazement coloring his face as if he could not believe his luck.

"Did you doubt it, Lieutenant?"

He grinned. "Never, Miss Bedford. Not for a moment."

He let out a whoop of elation, picked her up off the ground, and twirled her around until she laughed with sheer delight and they both tumbled to the snow-covered ground.

He leaned on one elbow, gazing down at her. Snow-flakes swirled around them and she wondered vaguely why they didn't sizzle just a bit when they hit the heat generated between the two of them.

"I love you, too, Katie." His expression was once again serious, his eyes somber. "I almost wish I didn't."

"What?" She struggled to sit up. "Why?"

"You said it yourself a few minutes ago." He shrugged. "Men go off to war. Women stay behind and . . . wait and worry. They go through their own private brand of hell. I'd hate to do that to you."

"It's too late, Michael." She laughed softly. "No matter what happens from here on out, I love you. I will die a little every time there's a news report on the radio or a headline in the paper or a knock at the door. And that's okay."

She reached out and took his hand in hers. She studied his long fingers, his firm palm, and wished she knew which tiny crevasse was his life line. She pulled a steadying breath.

"Loving you, right here and right now, just for tonight is worth anything, any price, any sacrifice. I don't care. This is enough." She gazed straight into his eyes. "I wouldn't trade one single, solitary moment with you for an entire lifetime without you."

"We can have a lifetime." His tone was intense, his eyes deep and compelling. "Marry me, Katie."

"Marry you?" She could have wept with joy at the question. At long last she could do what she always should have done, to make up for her mistake, to have her second chance. "When?"

Astonishment swept his expression. "Is that a yes?"

She laughed. "You seem surprised, Lieutenant."

"Not surprised, baby, more like stunned." He turned her hand over and placed a kiss in the palm. "I can't believe I can be this lucky." He narrowed his eyes and searched her face. "To have found you here and now."

"Christmas magic, Michael?"

"Fate, Katie, destiny." He drew her closer against him and crushed her lips with his in a kiss hard and swift and breathtaking. Then he leapt to his feet and pulled her up beside him. "Didn't I see a justice of the peace sign about a half mile down this road?"

"Next door to an inn." Her heart hammered in her chest.

"Then let's go." He grinned and put his arm around her. They took a few steps and he stopped and studied her, his expression somber. "Katie, nothing in my life has ever seemed as right as this does. But if I'm rushing you into this, if you have any second thoughts, then—"

She gazed up at him with all the love stored within her. "I never wanted anything as much as I want this, Michael. I want to be your wife. I want you."

Concern creased his brow. "Are you sure, Katie? I didn't give you any time to think about it."

"Time?" She laughed softly. "I've had all the time in the world."

". . . till death do you part?"

"I do." The vow fell from Michael's lips with an intensity that echoed in her soul. Judge Thomas and his

71

wife and everything around them faded to a dull haze. All she could see was the promise in eyes as dark as a winter night.

"Harrumph." Judge Thomas cleared his throat. "I said you may now kiss the bride." For a moment, Katie and Michael just stared. "Go on, son," the judge smiled knowingly, "it's the best part."

"Randolph," Mrs. Thomas clucked at her husband, then threw Katie a confidential glance. "He's right, you know."

Katie choked, Michael laughed, and the judge chuckled. Michael kissed her quickly, a brief brush of his lips that left her knees weak with what was to come. Mrs. Thomas produced mugs of hot cider from somewhere and the gathering toasted the newlyweds.

"I wish you the best of luck." Judge Thomas raised his cup in a salute. "You'll need it. I don't mind telling you, these wartime marriages are tough."

"But, Randolph, just look at them," Mrs Thomas said. "Why, anyone with half a brain can see they're obviously in love."

The judge snorted. "Everyone's in love these days. Hardly a night goes by anymore without love-struck kids knocking on the door, waking us up, and wanting to get married." He raised a bushy brow. "Even on Christmas Eve."

Katie and Michael traded swift glances.

"We need to be going," Michael said quickly, shaking the judge's hand.

"Thanks for everything," Katie added, slipping into her coat. "We really appreciate it."

"As well you should," the older man mumbled.

Mrs. Thomas walked them to the door and pulled

Katie aside. "Don't mind him, dear. He's a little cranky when he has to get out of bed unexpectedly. And don't worry about that business about wartime marriages."

She leaned toward Katie and lowered her voice. "I was a war bride, too. Randolph and I were married nearly twenty-four years ago." Mrs. Thomas let out a sigh of contentment. "And look at how well that turned out. We've had a long and happy life together."

Unexpected pain speared though Katie at the woman's words but she forced a smile to her face. This kindhearted soul had no idea that her helpful advice only served to remind Katie of what she and Michael would never share. They had this night and only this night.

"Ready?" Michael said.

"Sure. Thanks again, Mrs. Thomas." Katie threw her a grateful smile.

"You're welcome, dear. And have a wonderful life." Mrs. Thomas closed the door behind them.

Katie and Michael stood silently in the swirling snow. She wasn't quite sure what to say or do next and a surprising awkwardness settled over her. Finally she pulled a deep breath.

"The inn's right next door." The words blurted out and she groaned to herself at her lack of restraint. Lord, she sounded like a sex-starved tart.

Michael's brow rose in amusement. "I noticed."

"Well, do you . . . I mean I thought . . . maybe it would be . . ." This was ridiculous. She was a grown woman in her seventies, no longer young and innocent and virginal. How could she be so uncomfortable on the very brink of what she'd wanted for much of her life?

73

"Nervous?" His expression was serious but his eyes twinkled.

"No." *Yes.* "Of course not," she said loftily. "I am a married woman, you know."

He laughed, hooked his arm through hers, and steered her toward the inn. Aside from a larger building containing an office and the residence of the owners, the inn itself was more a series of tiny cottages than anything resembling an actual hotel. Michael led her to the cottage farthest from the office and grabbed the doorknob.

"Wait." Katie placed a hand on his arm. "Don't we have to check in or something?"

"Mrs. Thomas called and arranged everything when you weren't looking. It's all set." He pushed open the door.

"Well then." She breathed deeply and stepped forward.

"Hold on just a minute." Michael cast her a stern glare. "I believe you're forgetting something."

She pulled her brows together in a puzzled frown. "What?"

"I thought you said you were a married woman." He shook his head with mock disappointment.

She stared in confusion. "I am but—"

"But this." He swept her off her feet and up into his arms. She laughed and threw her arms around his neck. He stepped across the threshold and into the cottage.

"Welcome to the honeymoon suite, Mrs. O'Connor." He glanced around the room and his expression fell. "I wish it could be more."

"It's wonderful." She beamed up at him. He set her

on her feet but she kept her arms wrapped around him. "Don't you know anything yet, Lieutenant? I don't care if it's a shack or a castle. Just as long as you're in it."

Relief shadowed his eyes. "I do have something to make it a little more like a castle." He pulled a bottle of champagne out of his coat pocket. "A little wedding celebration."

She arched a brow. "Mrs. Thomas again?"

"The woman's amazing." He paused and looked thoughtful. "Maybe I should have married her."

She tapped him on the chest sharply. "She's already taken."

He sighed with exaggerated resignation. "Then I guess I'm stuck with you." He laughed. "I'll see if there are any glasses in the bathroom."

He headed to the only other door in the room and she eyed their surroundings. It really was a pleasant little cottage with knotty-pine paneling and cheerful curtains at the window. A big old-fashioned wing chair filled a corner. The room was dominated by a double bed and matching dresser. She shrugged out of her coat and caught sight of herself in the mirror.

She caught her breath and stared, eyes wide with shock. She hadn't looked in a mirror all night. The face that gazed back at her was an image she'd nearly forgotten.

She'd always known that people had considered her pretty in her younger days, even beautiful, but it never really held much meaning for her. In her world, the world of business, a world of men, her looks were always more of a detriment than a benefit. An attractive face and shapely figure meant men typically thought she would be available for mergers that went far beyond the details of a business deal. She'd breathed a sigh of relief when she finally reached an age where she was no longer described as lovely, but "handsome."

Now she stared at dark, shiny hair that glowed with health and vitality instead of the dull gray shimmer she was used to. At a face still untouched by the years with skin smooth and clear and not a line or wrinkle anywhere. And at a body firm and lithe and unaffected by the gravity and infirmity of age.

"You're beautiful, Mrs. O'Connor." Michael stood behind her, his gaze meeting hers in the reflection. He handed her a tumbler of champagne.

"We look pretty good together."

He nodded. "As if we were made for each other."

She took a sip of the wine and gazed at their images in the mirror: a pretty young woman, a handsome young officer. They looked like a photograph or a painting. A wedding painting. Two people in the prime of life with the world at their feet and their whole lives in front of them.

Except that for these two, the future was as much an illusion as the reflection in the glass. A shudder passed through her.

He wrapped his arms around her and she leaned her head against his chest. "Cold?"

She shook her head and her gaze meshed with his in the mirror. "I love you, Michael."

"I love you, too." He kissed the side of her neck and she watched him in the mirror. His lips traversed the sensitive flesh to meet the neckline of her sweater, and she sighed with the sweetness of his touch. His hands found the hem of her cardigan and slipped beneath the wool to caress heated skin, then moved upward to cup her breasts bound by her bra. She gasped and melted against him. His thumbs flicked the hardened tips through the cotton fabric, and need arched through her.

"Michael," she groaned.

She lifted her arms and he pulled the sweater over her head, swiftly unfastening her bra and letting it fall to the floor. For a moment, the two of them stared into the mirror, then all the passion pent-up through a long life alone demanded release.

She turned to him and fumbled with the buttons on his jacket. He struggled with her skirt. Within a few frenzied frantic seconds they stood together with nothing between them except the realization that their joining was as right as destiny and as inevitable as time itself.

They tumbled onto the bed and heated flesh pressed against searing skin. She could not get enough of his touch, of touching him, with hands and mouth and bodies entwined. Together, they searched and explored and discovered a passion she'd only known in the deep recesses of her mind where she'd kept him hidden and whole and alive forever.

At last his body joined with hers in a rhythm of man and nature. And she wondered dimly why she didn't shatter into a million pieces with the joy and wonder and glory of it all. Until finally the ever-tightening spring inside her exploded in a release of fire and flame and scorching desire. She cried out. He shuddered. Her fingers clutched his shoulders, pulling him closer and tighter as if to never let him go. Together they greeted an intensity of mind and body she'd never known and never suspected and would never forget.

And when at last they lay collapsed, side by side, in a dreamy glow of satisfied exhaustion, she leaned on one elbow to study him silently. His eyes were closed and he looked so much younger than she remembered. She tried to focus on every detail, every nuance, every expression on his face, committing them all to memory. To save and savor for the rest of her life.

And no matter what happened, memories of this night and this man would live in her heart always.

In a place reserved for Christmas magic and miracles and promises.

She woke at the first light of dawn, and he was gone. Fear sliced through her like a steel blade. She leapt from the bed, frantically searching for her discarded clothes and throwing them on in a blind panic. How could he have left without saying good-bye?

No! The answer reverberated in her head. Michael would never go without talking to her. He was not the kind of man to sneak out in the middle of the night. He wouldn't do that to anyone but especially not to her, his love, his wife.

She sank back down on the bed and caught her breath. Confidence and faith flooded through her, and her doubts vanished: he would be back. And when he returned . . . it would be to say good-bye. They had so little time left.

Quickly she finished dressing and then cast her gaze around the tiny cottage to make sure she left nothing behind. The minutes slipped past. Where was he? Impatiently she paced back and forth across the room. A radio sat on the table beside the bed and she flicked it on, hoping for distraction. Seasonal music floated through the air. Of course. How could she have forgotten? It was Christmas morning.

"Merry Christmas, baby." Michael's voice sounded behind her. His arms wrapped around her and pulled her close to his chest.

"Merry Christmas, Michael." She leaned back against him, content for a moment to merely bask in the glow of his warmth. "I didn't hear you come in."

"I didn't know if you'd be up yet and I hated to disturb you. I went to pay the bill." His voice was quiet. "I have to leave. Soon."

"I know." She drew a shaky breath. "Why, Michael? Why do you have to go?"

"Why?" Surprise sounded in his tone. "Katie, I'm in the Army. I'm an officer. I don't have much of a choice."

"Sure you do." She didn't want to look at him. Not yet. Her words were slow and measured. "Michael, you don't have to do this. There are places, in Central America and the Caribbean, where a man can disappear and no one can find him. With enough money—"

"Katie." He laughed and twirled her around to face him. "I don't know who you think you married but I'm just a regular joe. I'm not rich. I don't have that kind of money."

"But, Michael, I . . ." She stopped and widened her eyes with realization. She didn't have that kind of money either. Not in 1942. There were no stock portfolios, no investment dividends, no mansion in California. She wasn't Katherine Bedford with wealth and power at her fingertips but plain Katie Bedford. And all she had was love. She shrugged sadly. "I guess I don't either."

"Besides, Katie"—he lifted her chin with his finger and smiled into her eyes—"even if I had the money, I could never do that. I could never run out on my country. I'm heading off to do something that's not going to be pleasant and I don't mind admitting it's a little scary. But"—he shook his head—"when I signed on I gave my word. I won't back down on it now."

"An officer and a gentleman no less," she said with a feeble smile.

"Exactly." He nodded. "O'Connor men might not be wealthy in terms of money but we believe strongly in those things you can't buy, like patriotism and commitment and honor. I could no more abandon my country than I could abandon myself or . . . you."

"I know," she said with a deep sigh of resignation. "I knew before I brought it up. I just thought I had to try."

"You are worried about me, aren't you?" The concern in his eye belied the smug tone of his words. She nodded silently. He gazed at her for a long, thoughtful second. "Katie . . ." He paused as if unsure how to continue.

"Yes, Michael?"

"Do you . . ." Again he hesitated, indecision rampant on his face. Finally his words came in a rush. "Do you have any regrets? About last night? About getting married? Or anything else? Because if you do, we—"

She placed her finger across his lips. "Shut up, Lieutenant. I have a lot of regrets. More than you can possibly imagine. But not about last night and not about today." She bit her lip and fought to keep her voice steady. "I do regret that I didn't meet you a week ago or a month ago or a year ago. I regret that I have to let you leave without me, that I can't go with you like a camp follower from another century. And I regret, more than anything, that we've had so little time together."

"Hey." He kissed the tip of her finger. "We'll have time someday. We'll have the rest of our lives together."

Tears blurred her eyes but she smiled and nodded. He took her hands in his. "We'll have a wonderful life, Katie. And we'll have kids." He stopped and threw her a suspicious glare. "Do you like kids?"

"Kids?" She could barely choke out the word. The tears she'd held in check tumbled down her cheeks. She thought of the annoying little creatures standing in line with her to see Santa and the scorn she'd had for them—only now could she admit that it hadn't been as much disdain as it had been yet another regret. "I've always wanted kids."

"Good." A teasing light shone in his eye. "What do you think? Ten or twenty?"

"Children?" She gasped. "You're kidding, aren't you?"

"Yes, I am. But just about numbers." He stared at her sternly. "I insist only on a boy and a girl." He reached out and brushed an errant strand of hair away from her face, his voice gentle. "A little girl who looks like you."

"And a boy who takes after his dad." Hysteria tinged the edge of her laughter. *Hold on, Katie, don't lose it now.*

"We'll have it all, Katie. I promise." He gathered her into his arms and held her firmly against him.

She closed her eyes, wrapped her arms around him, and savored the solid feel of his body next to hers. Desperately she tried to deny the thoughts crashing around her. There was no time left. There would be no future together. No little girl who looked like her. No little boy who took after his dad. If only they could stay like this always. Capture this one moment and ignore the rest of the world, hide from the inevitable, cheat even time itself.

"Time now for a little change of pace." The tinny voice of the radio announcer broke into her thoughts. "Let's take a break from Christmas music for one of our favorite songs." The first notes of "I'll Be Seeing You" drifted into the room.

Michael released her, stepped back, and held out his arms. "Dance with me, Katie. One more dance and then . . . then I have to go."

She wiped the tears from her face with the back of her hand and nodded silently, unable to trust her voice. She melted into his arms and they swayed together to the bittersweet throb of the music.

"I love this song," he murmured.

She sniffed and snuggled closer. "That's because you're a romantic."

He held her a little tighter. "There are certain benefits to being a romantic, you know."

"Really?"

How can I let him go again?

He nodded. "You bet. For one thing, you acknowledge fate when it hits you across the face. And you recognize love when you find it."

"That's . . . swell."

How can I live my life once more without him?

"And you can appreciate a song like this one." He hummed a bar of music. "Listen to it, Katie. It's a love song and—"

"A promise," she whispered.

How can I say good-bye forever?

"A promise." He pulled back and his gaze locked with hers. "A promise that he'll never forget. That everything he sees, everything he does, everywhere he goes he'll be reminded of her."

"And?" She sobbed the word.

"And . . . it's a promise that he'll come back." Conviction shone on Michael's face. "I will come back to you, Katie. I promise."

"I know." The lie slipped out easily. What else could she say?

"Write to me?" The corners of his mouth quirked upward. "Mrs. O'Connor."

"You can count on it, Lieutenant."

A car horn sounded outside.

"That must be my cab," he said quietly. "I thought he could drop me off, then take you home."

"No." She shook her head sharply and smiled. "I'd rather just say good-bye here. I'll get home on my own."

"Okay." An awkward silence settled between them. There was so much she wanted to say but mere words weren't enough. He brushed his lips against hers, turned, and stepped to the door. Her throat ached

83

with the tears she struggled to hold in check.

He pulled the door open and cast one final glance back. He grinned the crooked smile that had lived a lifetime in her memory and tossed her a cocky salute.

"I'll be seeing you, Katie." Her heart shattered with his words and the fervent vow in his eyes. "I promise." He stepped through the threshold and pulled the door closed behind him.

And once more she was alone.

Unrestrained tears coursed down her face and she stared at the door, at the last place he'd stood. And she waited.

She had no idea if she'd return to 1996. No idea if, instead, she was now destined to live her life over. To survive again all the empty years of pain and yearning, all the years without him. She pulled a deep breath. As daunting as the prospect was, it was not too high a price to pay for one special night, for the opportunity to really know love, for a second chance.

She stood and stared at the door for a minute or an hour or forever until there were no more tears left to fall. Finally she gathered her things to return to the home she'd hadn't seen for years and the life she would have to build again. To wait for the inescapable end: the news of his death.

Katie stepped outside into the silent winter. The pale early-morning winter light matched the somberness of her mood. Snow covered the ground, fresh and new and untouched like a canvas waiting for color. Like the rest of her life. She trudged toward the street, calling on vaguely remembered memories to help her navigate her way home.

A sad smile pulled at the edges of her mouth, and

an odd sense of joy mixed with the pain inside her. It was all worth it: every ache, every tear, every wrenching emotion.

Michael had gone to his death and they would never be together again. But this time, he left with the sure and certain knowledge that he took with him her love, her heart, her soul. And no matter what twists and turns her future might now hold, she would never again deny what she'd refused to admit the first time they met.

She would love him forever.

She promised.

She wrote to him later that day and the day after that and the day after that. It was a futile effort, of course, a total waste of time and energy. There was every possibility he would never receive her letters. Still, there was always hope. And who knew just how long her second chance would last?

She didn't tell her family about her marriage. Somehow, given all that she knew, it seemed pointless. She returned to school with her mother's promise to forward any mail. And she waited with a sense of impending tragedy that grew with every passing day.

Weeks stretched endlessly without word. She existed in a strange kind of limbo, checking her mailbox every day, sometimes twice, at once resigned to the arrival of a bulky Manila envelope and terrified by the prospect.

Each day that passed was hopefully another day that Michael lived. She wondered if, because she'd married him, this time there would be no oversized envelope, but instead the yellow sheet of a telegram or a personal visit by an impersonal military representative. But their wedding had been so hasty, it was possible the Army had no official record of their marriage.

And so she waited.

She didn't know what to expect when word came. More and more she was convinced that with official notification of Michael's death, she would learn of her own fate. Would she go back to Christmas Eve 1996, with her life behind her and nothing ahead but a deteriorating body and an empty existence? Or would she be forced to relive a long and solitary life? She didn't especially relish either prospect. But it surprised her to realize that she could calmly face whichever future faced her now. There was a strange sense of peace, of acceptance and serenity within her she'd never known. She'd had her one special night with the one and only man she was destined to love.

And it would indeed last her a lifetime.

It was a frigid winter day when she checked her box for the second or maybe even third time in a span of a few hours. Damn. The mail still hadn't come. It seemed that erratic mail delivery was the one constant from generation to generation. At least when she knew the mailman had come and gone she could breathe a little easier. Each day without word was at once a frustration and a relief.

She turned away from the boxes with disgust and froze. The world around her spun to a stop. The air grew thick and her breath caught in her throat. Shock widened her eyes and focused her gaze. Disbelief clutched at her heart and she stared in stunned silence.

At a crooked sort of smile.

At blue eyes, dark as the night and just as endless.

At the hero's best friend.

"Do you want to dance, Mrs. O'Connor?"

"Michael?"

He grinned. "The one and only."

In a heartbeat she was in his arms, laughter mingling with tears in a joyous mix of amazement and revelation. She pulled back and stared. "Oh, Michael. I can't believe . . . how can you . . . I thought you were dead."

He cocked a dark brow. "Baby, I'm a lousy letter writer but that doesn't mean I'm not among the living. Actually, I got shipped around a little bit after this." He gestured to the crutches propped under his arms. They'd escaped her notice until now. "Nobody seemed quite sure what to do with me until they came up with the brilliant idea of sending me home to recover."

Her heart thudded in her chest. Was he merely injured this time instead of killed? And if Michael's fate had changed . . . "What happened?"

"It's kind of silly." He shrugged in a self-conscious manner. "A couple of nights after I got to England, well, I was pretty low. It seems I missed my wife." His eyes simmered with a promise of passion and her insides fluttered in response. "I had a few too many one night, and on the way back to the base ran into a flock of sheep."

"Sheep?" She struggled to suppress the exhilaration rising within her.

He shook his head. "Actually, they ran into me. Anyway, I managed to overturn the jeep. They tell me I was in pretty bad shape for a while. I don't remember much."

"Sheep?" Laughter bubbled through her lips. "I have sheep to thank for you being here?"

"Sheep and . . . you."

"Me?"

He pulled her close with one free arm. "If I hadn't been trying to drown my sorrows about not being with you, I wouldn't have had the accident."

She sucked in her breath sharply. "Oh, my."

"Funny thing, too, Katie." His brows drew together in a puzzled frown. "Until the accident, I kept feeling like I was doing things I had done before. As if I was repeating motions over or reliving a life already lived." He shook his head. "It sounds crazy. Do you know what I mean?"

"I have a pretty good idea," she said softly.

"That strange feeling disappeared after the accident. And that's another weird thing. The plane I was supposed to be flying on for a training exercise, the day after the accident, crashed." A shadow crossed his eyes. "Everybody died."

"Good Lord." The revelation struck her with an almost physical force and she resisted the need to collapse against him. At once, everything made sense. This time, Michael survived. This time a little too much to drink, stray sheep, and above all else, the knowledge that she carried his name and would wait for him forever had made a difference. This time, he kept his promise.

He pulled her tighter against him. "I'm not home

for good, you know. I'll be going back as soon as I get the okay. But for now—"

"For now"—she beamed up at him—"you're here and we're together and everything has changed."

Confusion washed across his face. "What do you mean?"

"Never mind. It doesn't matter." She laughed with unrestrained delight. "Nothing matters now except that you're alive and we're both here and—" She caught her breath and stared.

"What is it, Katie?"

"And"—she struggled to swallow the lump in her throat and fight the tears that stung the back of her eyes—"and we'll have children and grow old and spend the rest of our lives together."

He grinned. "That's the whole idea."

"It really is a second chance," she said under her breath and vaguely wondered why her heart didn't break with the miracle of it all.

"Katie." Michael brushed his lips along her forehead. "I don't know what you mean by a second chance and I don't really care. All I know is that the girl I love is in my arms and I'm going to spend the rest of my life making her happy. And that's a promise."

The tears she'd restrained coursed down her cheeks and his face blurred, but the strength of his body next to hers was solid and real and lasting. And she knew without question there would never be a Katherine Bedford who made millions from nothing and had her face on the cover of *Time* magazine. But there would be a Katie O'Connor who'd know all the joy and laughter and love that life could offer.

His lips met hers and she greeted him with the eagerness of a lifetime spent waiting for this one moment. And before passion swept away all possibility of rational thinking she realized the truth of what she'd never even suspected before.

Love is a promise to keep.

Epilogue

December 24, 1996

"I can't stand the thought that she won't be around anymore." The tall, dark-haired young woman wiped a tear from her eye.

The slightly older blonde seated beside her nodded silently.

Their gazes fixed on the front of the church. Winter morning light filtered softly through stained-glass windows and caressed the holiday decorations scattered with joyous abundance throughout the sanctuary. The casket before the altar was at once a sorrowful counterpoint to the festive setting and yet, somehow, appropriate.

"I just never really thought of her as dying," the brunette said. "She wasn't all that old."

"Oh, she was old, Diane." The other girl's voice was

solemn. "She was seventy-four."

"I know but—"

"And everybody in the family kept saying after Grandpa died, Grandma wouldn't last long."

Diane stared at the casket. "Can you imagine loving somebody so much you can't live without them?"

"Sure." The blonde paused and shook her head. "Maybe. I don't know. Do you remember the story about how they met?"

Diane laughed softly. "Who could forget? It was as much a part of Christmas at Grandma's as the tree and stockings." She recited by heart. "Christmas Eve at a community canteen. Right before he shipped out to World War II. It was love at first sight." A wistful note crept into her voice. "It was so romantic."

The blonde chewed on her lower lip for a long moment as if getting her words and her thoughts in order. "I know this sounds kind of stupid but does all this seem . . . well . . . sort of right? Like fate or something?"

"Sandi O'Connor!" Diane's eyes widened with shock. "How can you even think such a thing?"

Sandi wrinkled her nose. "Calm down. I didn't mean it like that." A frown creased her forehead and she struggled to find the right words. "It's just that Christmas was always so important to her. Because of Grandpa, of course, but . . . do you remember what she used to say about Christmas?"

Diane nodded. "She said it was all a matter of believing. Believing in the promises of the season. Believing in the magic . . ."

"And?"

"And"—a smile quirked the corner's of Diane's

mouth—"believing in Santa Claus."

"She really did believe in Santa, you know," Sandi said quietly.

"I know. I always thought it was funny." Diane shook her head in disbelief. "A grown-up believing in Santa like that."

"But don't you see?" Sandi leaned toward her cousin. "The way she felt about Christmas, the way she believed in miracles and promises and Santa"—Sandi shrugged—"it's almost like, at this time of year, with the spirit and excitement and magic of the season, this is when she would have wanted her life to end. What better time to say good-bye?"

"Maybe," Diane said slowly. "I understand what you're trying to say but still"—she released a heartfelt sight—"I'm really going to miss her."

Sandi put her arm around her cousin and gave her a squeeze. "So am I. But she did have a great life."

"She had a wonderful life," Diane said stoutly.

"Look." Sandi tilted her head toward the front of the church. Two young girls armed with violins took their places off to one side of the altar. "Your mom asked Carol and Deb to play today."

"The same song they played at Grandpa's funeral?" Sandi nodded.

Diane sniffed back a fresh tear. "She would have loved this."

The first tremulous strains of "I'll Be Seeing You" echoed through the church. In the last pew, a portly, elderly gentleman slowly rose to his feet and headed toward the door. A slight smile played on rosy lips nearly hidden by a thick white beard.

He paused for a moment and cast a satisfied glance

around the church filled with children and grand-children, family and friends. The end result of a life filled with love and laughter and joy. Bottom-line assets that could be totaled on the only balance sheet that really mattered.

"Merry Christmas, Katie," he said in a murmur so soft no living creature could possibly hear it.

"Santa always keeps his promises."

NAUGHTY OR NICE

SANDRA HILL

When my son Rob was a little boy, he asked, "Mommy, are Santa Claus and God the same person?"

"I like to think they are," I said.

So, this book's dedicated to Rob—my rebel—who tries so hard to be a "bad boy," but will always be a Santa at heart.

Chapter One

Only winos and weirdos shopped at the Piggly Jiggly Supermarket after midnight. But tonight there was also a thirty-year-old desperate woman dressed as Santa Claus.

Correction. A thirty-year-old desperate woman dressed as Santa Claus, *packing a forty-five in her pocket*.

As she waited her turn at the service desk, Jessica Jones grimaced at the ludicrous situation she found herself in. It was the "Christmas Curse," of course. For as long as she could remember, something really awful happened to her during the Christmas season.

She'd thought she was over the bad luck for this year when her fiance, Burton Richards, dumped her two weeks ago, but uh-uh, the fix she found herself in now was even worse. A definite ten on the Christmas Curse Richter scale.

Jessica hitched up the wide belt beneath her sagging Santa stomach with determination. *Like the old song goes, I'm not gonna take it anymore.*

A very tall, broad-shouldered woman walked by, swishing her hips in a red nylon mini-dress—not a good choice for a cold Philadelphia winter. Clearly a male, the cross-dresser was probably a prostitute. She . . . he . . . smiled at Jessica and made a kissy sound through thickly painted lips. Criminey, Santa was being propositioned.

Jessica shook her head vehemently.

The hooker shrugged as if to say it was Santa's loss, and walked over to the cigarette rack.

Good grief!

An old man standing in front of her, waiting to have his welfare check cashed, turned and slurred out, "Wha'dja say?"

His boozy breath almost knocked Jessica over. Her knees were knocking together as it was, and her hands, were shaking so badly she had to stuff them in her wide pockets. She shifted the pillow higher and felt with her right hand for the pistol nestled against her thigh. *Help! This is not happening.* "Nothing. Just get moving, okay?"

"Some grumpy Santa you are," he muttered.

Her eyes darted about the area, casing the automatic exit doors a few feet away. She was the last person in line. The only other person nearby was a gorgeous guy with a light brown ponytail, leaning lazily against the wall, scratching off a lottery ticket. Amazingly, he wore a Santa Claus outfit, too, but his hat, beard, and wig were stuffed in his belt.

He resembled Brad Pitt, but older . . . and better.

The Brad-Santa glanced up, gave her a quick once-over, and winked.

Darn! Caught smack dab in the middle of a leer! Her heated face probably matched her suit. Jessica lifted her chin haughtily and pretended she'd been looking at something else, like the bare wall behind him. *Hah! Who am I fooling? And, Lordy, haven't I had enough of womanizing egomaniacs in my life? I can't believe I'm about to perform a criminal act, and I'm ogling some lech in costume.*

The lech laughed.

She was about to snarl, but it was her turn at the service desk.

Taking a deep breath, she stepped forward. "Put up your hands. This is a stick-out," she yelled in a too-shrill voice to the gum-chewing guy behind the counter whose name badge read "Frank Brown, Assistant Manager." He gulped and swallowed his gum with a squeak.

Brad peered up at her with faint interest through eyelashes that could double for brown feather dusters. "Stick-up, baby. You mean stick-up," he offered helpfully, his lips twitching with amusement.

"This is a stick-up, Frank," she amended, brandishing her gun. *Thank heavens the thing isn't loaded or I'd be in big trouble.* Pointing the weapon at the smiling Santa, she ordered, "And don't give me any of your lip, buster, or I'll wipe you up, too."

"Wipe out, not wipe up," the long, tall Santa laughed.

His ridicule made her so mad she clenched her fingers over the gun, which, to her amazement, went off accidentally. And, holy cow, it shot a big hole in the

Pepsi machine about three feet to the right of the jerk's ear.

Her heart slam-dunked to her throat. *Oh, no! Julio told me it wasn't loaded. I even shot it once in the woods and nothing happened. It can't have real bullets in it. It can't.*

She took another peek at the Pepsi machine. There was an opening the size of a basketball in the glass front. The bullets were real, all right. *Oh, geez!*

Frank screamed.

The hooker called out, "Way to go, big boy! Ho, ho, ho!"

And the Brad-Santa ducked.

Through her peripheral vision she saw a young girl at a cash register, a bag boy, and two customers throw themselves to the floor.

One man cried out, "Oh, God! This is probably one of those maniac postal workers taking us hostage. I'll miss Christmas with my kids." Then as an afterthought he added, "Hallelujah!"

"Do you think we'll make CBS News?" the female clerk asked. "Wouldn't ya just know this would happen on a bad hair day?"

"Shit!" Brad exclaimed, his lottery ticket fluttering to the floor. "Are you nuts?"

Her heart was slowing down to a gallop. *Okay, that was a close call, but I'm okay now. No serious damage. I can mail a check next week. Calm down.* Pretending that her shot had been deliberate, she threw her shoulders back and aimed directly at the shivering assistant manager, being careful not to touch the trigger again. "You're next, Frank, *if* you don't give me my money."

"An . . . anyth . . . anything you want," Frank sputtered. He started to stuff bills in a cloth bag.

"No!" Jessica interrupted sharply. "Just thirty-nine ninety-five."

"Wh-what?" Frank choked out.

Everyone was gawking at her like she was a psycho. She was, of course. "You heard me. Give me thirty-nine dollars and ninety-five cents. And make it quick. I've got an itchy thumb here."

"Trigger finger, sweetheart," the smirking Santa corrected again, snickering. "You gotta get the lingo right if you're gonna follow a life of crime."

She frowned in confusion.

"It's an itchy *trigger finger*, not thumb," he explained patiently.

"Thumb, trigger finger, big difference!" she said, waving her gun dismissively at him. "And stop interrupting me."

"Hey, be careful where you aim that thing," he growled, edging toward her. He probably planned to tackle her. Not a good idea when the curse was in motion.

"Stay where you are," she warned, raising the revolver higher.

He stopped, eyeing her warily.

"Thirty-nine ninety-five!" Frank squealed. "Hey, I know who you are. You're that whacko nun who came in here last week demanding her money back for a defective Buzzy Burp Bear."

"I am *not* a nun," Jessica said weakly.

"Piggly Jiggly has a two-week refund policy," Frank explained to the wino and Brad, "and the damn nun . . . I mean, the nun . . . had it for a month before she brought it back. Said it wouldn't burp. Hah! She'd probably been playing it nonstop all that time and wore out its burp battery."

"A nun?" the wino whimpered, backing away from her as if she had something contagious.

"I am *not* a nun."

"Hot damn!" the Santa-with-an-attitude whistled. "A holy bandit!"

"I am *not* a nun."

"Clara . . . that's your name, Sister Clara," Frank chortled. "Boy, you are in *big* trouble, lady. I'm gonna report you to the police . . . and the Pope."

"I'm not Clara, I tell you. I'm . . . I'm Clara's hit guy." She realized her mistake at once, and before Santa could pipe in, she corrected herself, "Hit man." Then she added, "And I'm not in big trouble, because you owe me . . . I mean, Clara . . . the money for the stupid bear, and that's not stealing. And I'm going to pay for the damage to the Pepsi machine. So there!"

"And here I thought I was gonna have a dull Saturday night. This is more fun than playing the lottery, or doing laundry."

Jessica gave the crud-that-would-be-a-heartthrob a withering appraisal. As if he had any difficulty filling his nights! He probably had women lined up with numbers. He probably drove a Porsche. He probably had a penthouse. He probably posed for centerfolds.

Unfortunately, she knew a few guys just like him; in fact, one of them had been her Christmas Curse six years ago. Except he'd looked like Mel Gibson with a paunch.

The guy's arms were folded casually across his chest and he grinned from ear to ear. Even with the padded

Santa suit, she just knew he didn't have a paunch.

"Give me my money," she demanded, turning back to Frank as she felt the situation deteriorating around her. "I'm not leaving without my thirty-nine ninety-five, dammit."

"Tsk-tsk, nuns aren't supposed to swear," Santa chided.

"Tell it to your reindeer, bozo."

She had no choice then, she had to show she was in control. She aimed for the Little Debbie cupcake stand over to the left. Although she fired two shots, the second one came up blank. That must mean the gun was empty.

But, more important, instead of hitting Little Debbie, she winged the pyramid display of Buzzy Burp Bears. Immediately brown fur flew everywhere as stuffed animals careened to the floor and a chorus of bears began burping to the tune of "Jingle Bells." It was a scene out of the Three Stooges, or her worst nightmare.

Jessica groaned.

Everyone's mouth dropped open in surprise, including the jerk Santa's.

"Now . . . give . . . me . . . my . . . thirty-nine ninety-five," she spat out evenly in her best Clint Eastwood voice, and tacked on in a gravelly rumble, just for effect, "or make my day."

Frank didn't hesitate. With quivering fingers he counted out the bills and coins and shoved them across the counter.

She put the money in her pocket and was about to leave when she saw a flash of dark blue race through the exit door. *A security guard.* Immediately a loud alarm began to ring throughout the store. *Oh, great! What should I do? What should I do?*

Jessica tried to think what a genuine robber might do. *A hostage. I need a hostage.* Quickly Jessica scanned her possibilities: Frank, the wino, the cross-dresser, the sales clerk, the two customers, or Brad Pitt.

"You're coming with me," she yelled at good ol' Brad.

"No, I'm not," he said, backing up.

"Yes, you are. You're my hostage." She leveled her now-empty gun at him—first, at his chest, then lower. Yep, a guy like him would care more about protecting those assets than his heart. Her upper lip curled with disdain. "Listen, Mr. Legend-of-the-Fall, I'm in the middle of my Christmas Curse, and I'd hate to see your dead body be my bad luck this year."

"Curse?" Brad barked with disbelief. "You're pulling a heist because of PMS?"

She blinked at him with confusion. "Oh, you idiot! Not that kind of curse. My Christmas Curse is the real kind—black magic, evil eyes, that sort of thing."

"Give me a break!"

"Really. My parents died in an automobile accident on December twentieth when I was ten. The following yule season, I was in the foster home from hell. I broke my leg on Christmas Eve when I was twenty."

"Coincidences."

"Oh, yeah? Then how about the time my dog Fred impregnated a pedigree poodle at that fancy private kennel five years ago, even though he was fixed? That curse cost me a thousand dollars in legal fines."

"Apparently Fred's fix-job leaked." His hazel eyes twinkled with humor.

She sliced him a sneer of disgust. "I will never forget my Christmas-party blind date last year with the guy who arrived wearing a plaid hunting cap with ear flaps. The wheels of his pickup truck were so high I had a nosebleed for a week."

"I once had a blind date with a girl who had tattoos on three-fourths of her body," he contributed irrelevantly. "Does that qualify as a curse?"

"Quit stalling," she ordered, realizing that he was trying to keep her talking until the police arrived. Even though she knew her bullets were gone, her hand still shook when she raised the gun in a threatening manner.

He said a foul word under his breath as his eyes darted to her trembling fingers. She could practically see the gears grinding in his chauvinistic brain. He was probably worrying about her panicking, or her fingers slipping.

Raising his arms above his head, Brad surrendered. "All right, all right, take it easy, babe. I'm all yours." It was a real Kodak moment.

Actually, there was probably a security camera filming it for posterity. But she couldn't think about that now. With the barrel of her pistol pressed into the back of the guy's neck, she pushed him forward through the doors, yelling over her shoulder, "If anyone follows me, this creep is dead. Do you hear me?"

At first, Luke Carter had been amused by Dirty Harriet. But not anymore. He walked compliantly out of the grocery store, his arms upraised, a gun crammed into his nape, but he was really, *really* pissed. It was humiliating for a man of his background to be kid-napped by a dingbat Santa.

And he just knew that the six o'clock news tomorrow was going to have a stillframe from the security tape of Santa being taken hostage by Santa. The news media would make him the laughing stock of the country.

Luke could have taken the woman down in a flash . . . in the beginning . . . before she'd started ripping out bullets. Hell, he was a bodyguard. And he was wearing a bulletproof vest, having just come off of an assignment. It was his job to disarm potential political assassins or crazy celebrity fans. He'd been trained in the CIA, and had done very well these past five years, thank you very much, operating his own private bodyguard business, "Watchdogs, Inc."

But the worst danger in the security business was a looney-bird. And if a woman—who might, indeed, be a nun—dressed as Santa Claus, wielding a forty-five, ranting about Christmas Curses, and robbing a supermarket for thirty-nine dollars and ninety-five cents wasn't a looney-bird, he didn't know what was.

It was all his sister's fault, and he was going to tell her so, too . . . *if* he was alive after tonight. Since he'd already rented the Santa outfit for his gig protecting Janet Jackson at her concert today at the Spectrum in South Philly, Ellie had talked him into playing the jolly ol' fellow for her third graders' Christmas party afterward. It had seemed reasonable to zip on over to the elementary school where Ellie taught, and it had been fun, too.

Later they'd gone out for pizza and she'd berated him ad nauseam about the dismal state of his personal life. Too many women—"bimbos" was her exact word; no commitments—"How long are you going to mourn Ginny? She's been dead five years"; his biological clock ticking away with no children in sight— "Men don't have biological clocks," he'd pointed out; dirty laundry up the kazoo—okay, she had a point about the laundry piled up in the back of his car; and on, and on, and on. So Ellie was responsible for his present predicament. If not for her nagging, he never would have come out at midnight to do his laundry and met Ms. Psycho Santa.

"Where to, babe?" he asked with a sigh of resignation. "Where'd you park the sled?"

Ms. Santa hesitated, glancing toward a van hidden around the side of the mall behind a dumpster. Emblazoned across its sides was the logo "Clara's House." *Hell, she must be a for-real nun, like that Frank character said.*

He immediately made a mental revision in his strategy. Taking the perp down at the first opportunity had been his original plan. He'd been unconcerned about whether the weird woman got hurt in the process.

But he couldn't in good conscience risk taking out a nun. His sister would never forgive him. The news media would have a field day. His business would be shot to hell.

Besides, she was kinda cute.

"Where's your car?" she asked, biting her full bottom lip—a nervous habit he'd noticed right from the start, which only called attention to her puffy, very kissable mouth. "The van's too easy to follow. And stop jerking around so much. I don't want to shoot you accidentally."

"How about not-so-accidentally?"

"Don't tempt me."

Man, oh, man, she reminded him of one of those "Magic Eye" pictures. Once you saw the hidden image, you couldn't stop looking at it. Her lips were like that. Now that his splintering brain registered how sensual her lips were, they drew his eyes like a magnet. *Maybe I inhaled too many bleach fumes tonight.*

"My car's over here," he said, chastising himself silently for his wandering mind as he indicated a metallic gray Bronco across the empty parking lot, "but, listen, I left all my clothes in the dryer over at the Suds 'n Duds." He pointed to the laundromat down a little ways in the strip mall. "That's why I was in the supermarket. I needed quarters for the machine, and that slimeball assistant manager at the supermarket wouldn't give me any change unless I bought something. So I got a lottery ticket. Hey, I left my ticket back on the floor. Maybe I'm a millionaire. We should go back and check." He was deliberately babbling away in hopes of diverting her attention so he could grab for the piece.

"Forget the clothes and the lottery ticket, buddy. This is more important." She walked him over to the car with the forty-five still imbedded in his neck, too high for his lead corset to protect him.

"I hope you've got the safety clip on that gun," he said.

"What's a safety clip?"

He moaned.

"Don't worry, I'm being careful."

"Yeah, like you were careful with those farting bears."

"Oh, you are so crude. They were *burping* bears."

"Well, that's better, of course. Did anyone ever tell you that you have incredible lips?"

She blinked at him as a current of electricity seemed to ricochet between them. "Ooooh, you are smooth. And the answer is yes. My Christmas Curse eleven years ago."

"Huh?"

"Larry the Lizard told me I had a sexy mouth. That was just before he slept with my best friend, Alice."

"I wouldn't sleep with your best friend," he vowed. "I'd rather—"

"Get serious." They were on the driver's side of the car. "Now, slowly, I want you to take out your keys and open the front and back doors." When he did as ordered, she told him to get in the driver's seat. "I'll sit behind you where I can aim my gun right at your head."

"Puh-leeze!" Luke frowned. *This is not good.* He'd been hoping she would sit in the passenger seat where he could more easily grab for the weapon . . . or his own rod on the floor under the driver's seat.

"What's that thing?"

Oh, damn! Her eyes had homed in on the tip of his revolver peeking out like a beacon.

"Move back," she demanded, training her firearm on his face while she leaned down and picked up his gun gingerly between a thumb and forefinger. For a moment, he saw fear flash in her eyes. "Are you a crook or something?"

He couldn't help grinning. "You mean like you?"

"No, not like me, you jerk. I mean a real crook. A bank robber, or a rapist, or a murderer."

He shook his head. "I'm not a bad guy. Well . . . uh . . . I'm not all that good, either, but—"

"Shut up," she snapped, motioning him into the car. "Testy, are we?"

She slipped into the back seat, immediately positioning her gun with a bead on his unprotected skull, the whole time muttering about Jeffrey Dahmer and Freddie Kruger.

"How 'bout lowering the gun, darlin'? I'd hate to get my hair mussed."

She started to comply.

That's it, honey. Put my metal undershirt in your cross-hairs.

She changed her mind when she realized his back was pressed against the seat. "Just drive."

He was easing the Bronco out of the parking lot when he saw in the rear view mirror a police car, bubblegum light flashing, pull in front of the Piggly Jiggly. The two officers who got out didn't seem in any big hurry. They probably thought it was a routine shoplifting.

"Where to?" he asked, slanting the woman a glimpse over his shoulder. She was biting her bottom lip in concentration.

Those lips again.

"Just head down the highway. I have to think."

That would be a refreshing change. "You could probably take off your disguise now," he advised. He'd like to get a better look at her. All he'd been able to see thus far were high cheekbones, a light sprinkling of freckles over a slightly upturned nose, and big, big brown eyes. She was probably a redhead, if her eyebrows were any indication. He hoped she was ugly, so his wandering lust would come to a halt. Even so, he wondered what kind of body she hid under that Santa costume.

But then he immediately brought himself back to reality. *Why the hell should I care? I know my personal life is going down the toilet lately, but this is the pits. I'm having impure thoughts about a nun with PMS?*

"Geez, watch the road," she shrieked as he almost drove onto the berm. Luckily there wasn't much traffic. "And I'm not taking off my disguise . . . yet."

Yet? "Why not?" he asked suspiciously.

"Pay attention and drive faster," she commanded, ignoring his question. When they'd traveled a few miles, she told him to turn right onto a rural road. After a prolonged silence, she added, "So if you're not a crook, how come you have a gun?"

"I'm a bodyguard."

"A bodyguard!" she exclaimed. "Like Kevin Costner?"

"Yep! Except that women say I favor Brad Pitt." He cast a sidelong glance at her over his shoulder and jiggled his eyebrows. Women loved it when he did that.

"You're too old to look like Brad Pitt."

"Hey, I'm not *that* old. I'm only thirty-five. How old are you?" *Boy, see if I waste my eyebrow jiggle on you again!*

"Thirty, and believe me, I feel pretty darn old sometimes."

"Thirty? Old? No way! Back to me—" he said.

She made a rude sound of disgust and mimicked, "Back to me . . ."

"What's that snort supposed to mean?"

"Men. Everything always comes back to them. And I don't snort."

"Are you trying to say I'm vain?" She snorted again, and it was a snort, no matter what she claimed. "Just because I'm in my prime?"

"And because you think you look like Brad Pitt. An *older* Brad Pitt."

"You've got a real attitude problem, lady. Anyhow, you *really* don't think I look like Brad Pitt? You called me Mr. Legend-of-the-Fall," he reminded her.

"A slip of the tongue," she asserted. "With all that hair, you could be Michael Bolton."

"Michael Bolton? Are you blind? He's blond, and has a big nose and a receding hairline. And he doesn't even have good hair." Affronted, he gritted his teeth and stared straight ahead. Now that he thought about it, he *had* noticed a few extra hairs in his brush lately. It took iron willpower not to touch his brow, just to check for a receding hairline.

He tilted the rear view mirror so he could see her face, and noticed her smiling . . . at his expense. Was he that transparent? Or narcissistic? Probably.

"If you're really a bodyguard, show me some proof. Do you even have a license for this firearm?" She pointed to his revolver which lay, outside his reach, on the far side of the back seat.

"Yeah, in the glove compartment." He reached over slowly, making sure he didn't make any abrupt moves that would surprise her "itchy thumb." Pushing aside a set of handcuffs and a box of condoms, he picked up his wallet, tossing it back to her. He was hoping she'd drop the weapon when she reached to catch his wallet, but no such luck. She let it fall into her lap while her eyes focused on the glove compartment.

"Oh, God, are you a pervert?"

He grinned.

"A gun and handcuffs and a box of condoms! Boy, oh, boy, this is the worst Christmas Curse ever. The Midnight Ride with Paul the Pervert."

"Call me crazy, but I can't for the life of me see the connection between a gun, handcuffs, condoms, and perversion. Do you know many perverts who use condoms?"

"I don't know any perverts at all." She riffled through his wallet, checking his driver's license, muttering, "Lucas Carter," then studied his gun registration and his business card for Watchdogs, Inc. "So you really are a bodyguard, huh?" she commented with curiosity.

"Damn straight."

"For how long?"

"Five years."

"What'd you do before that? CIA? Ha-ha-ha!" she mocked, leaning forward and picking up his handcuffs, examining them idly, even clipping one on her left wrist.

When he didn't answer, she gasped. "Oh, great! Don't tell me I've kidnapped a CIA agent."

"Ex."

"Golly gee! That makes me feel better."

Then, before he could blink, she reached over the seat, locked his right wrist to her extended left, and pocketed the key.

"Sister, you are driving with your lights on dim."

"I am *not* a nun."

Cursing silently, he berated himself for his carelessness. Never underestimate the enemy. Never. How could he have forgotten that golden rule of the security business? His biggest mistake was treating this Santa/bimbo/nun like less than the threat she posed.

"So, Luke, do you know any Mafia?"

Her totally off-the-wall question floored him for a moment. "No, do you?"

"Uh-uh. But I need to find some bad guys to rob. Real quick."

This Mother Teresa clone was not playing with a full deck. "Let me get this straight. You're going to pull another robbery, and you'd like to target the mob."

"I did *not* rob the Piggly Jiggly. I was just getting back my money. That's not a robbery," she declared vehemently. "I would never rob honest people, not that I think Piggly Jiggly is all that honest. But I need cash, *desperately*, and that means I've got to find some bad guys."

He groaned. This was turning into the most bizarre nightmare. "Why do you need the money?"

She refused to answer.

"How much? I've got about fifty dollars in my wallet."

She sniffed indignantly. "That would be robbing."

He crossed his eyes with frustration. *How do I reason with a lunatic?*

"Besides, it's not enough. I need about five hundred dollars. And, take my advice, you don't resemble Brad Pitt when you cross your eyes. If fact, you look downright homely."

Don't react. Be cool. She's just a dumbbell pretend nun. What does she know about good-looking men?

"We could stop at an ATM machine to get more money. My bank will let me take out three hundred dollars at a pop."

"I told you I'm not going to steal from innocent people. If Julio hadn't stolen my car and purse with all my credit cards, I wouldn't have any problems at all. I could have cashed a check or used my own ATM or Visa card. Nope, I need bad guys."

He shouldn't ask. He really shouldn't. "Who's Julio?"

"Some teenage miscreant whose life won't be worth beans when I get a hold of him."

"Well, that explains everything. Listen, Ms. Claus, or Sister Claus . . . what's your name, by the way?"

She hesitated for a long time, and Luke practically heard her devious mind whirring sluggishly.

"Tiffany," she announced finally. "Tiffany Blake."

He let out a hoot of laughter. "Sister Tiffany?"

"I told you, I'm *not* a nun."

"Okay, Ti-fan-ny. Now that you've done your 'Tiffany does Piggly Jiggly' routine, what next?"

"Pull over here," she said abruptly. "That's where I'm going to pull my next job. Oh, this is perfect. Surely the people who run this place qualify as bad guys."

Luke swerved into the parking lot with a screech of brakes and gaped at the flashing neon sign in front of a corrugated metal building: "Sam's Smut Shop." A handmade posterboard next to the red door listed a menu of "triple X-rated videos, sex toys, peep shows." Then, "Body piercings and nude massages, by appointment."

"You're going to rob a porno palace?"

"Yep," she said with a bright burst of enthusiasm. "Good idea, huh?"

Oh, Lord! "Do you think the Christmas Curse is contagious?"

Chapter Two

"Trust me, this is not a good idea," Luke said, shutting off the car and turning in his seat to face her. "I don't think you realize the seriousness of what you're doing. Armed robbery is a felony."

"Only if I get caught," she boasted bravely. *Prison? Me? The worst thing I've ever done is overcharge a customer for an almond creme wedding cake.*

"Maybe you could convince a judge that the supermarket owed you thirty-nine ninety-five, *if* you hadn't been carrying a loaded gun."

"I didn't know it was loaded."

"You didn't?"

"Of course not. I'm not an idiot. And stop looking at me like that."

"How am I looking at you?"

"Your eyes are crossing again. You'd better be careful, your face might freeze like that. Aunt Clara told us once about—"

"Aaarrrgh! Stop changing the subject."

"Listen up, you lunkhead. I didn't know the gun was loaded because Julio told me it was empty."

"Julio again? Never mind." He inhaled deeply. "The bottom line is that you haven't done anything *too* serious yet, providing I don't press charges against you for kidnapping, terroristic threats, auto theft, personal assault—"

"Don't forget 'loss of lottery ticket,' " she snickered. "And 'hair and age insult.' "

He let out a whoosh of exasperation. "You . . . can't . . . go . . . in   this . . . store . . . with . . . a . . . loaded . . . gun," he said through clenched teeth.

"Okay, I'll unload it." She turned the gun over to see how that might be done. Every movement she made jerked his arm along with her, like a puppet, because of the handcuff, but that couldn't be helped.

"Stop!" he cried. "Geez, don't ever point a gun in your face."

"Oops."

"Oops? Lady, you oughta be restrained for your own good." Shaking his head incredulously, he then told her, step by step, how to release the remaining bullets.

There were none.

"Damn! You've been ordering me around like a fool with an empty weapon."

"Whew! I don't know about you, but I'm relieved. I wouldn't have wanted to hurt anyone."

"You're smiling," he accused. "You knew all along

that there were no bullets in the gun, and you let me shiver."

"Were you shivering? Good." She beamed with supreme self-satisfaction. *Put that in your macho pipe, Brad baby.* "Remember when I shot at the Little Debbie cake rack and accidentally hit the Buzzy Burp Bears?"

He was gaping at her as if she'd flipped her lid. "You were aiming for Little Debbie?" he sputtered.

"Yeah. Anyhow, I actually shot twice, and only the first bullet came out. So, *voilà*, I knew the bullets were all gone."

His face turned purple, and he made a sort of strangled sound deep in his throat. Finally he choked out, "You are a certifiable dingaling. Don't you know that just because one bullet is missing in a chamber doesn't mean the gun is empty? Have you ever heard of Russian roulette?"

"Oh, my God!" She started to shiver herself with aftershocks at what she might have done. "This is the Christmas Curse to beat all Christmas Curses."

"You are dangerous. To yourself. Society. The world."

Tell me something I don't already know. "What's done is done. You're okay, I'm okay." She shuddered suddenly. It was getting cold in the car. "Let's move on here. Maybe I should have you park on the other side of the building while I go in," she said, thinking out loud. She wasn't going to let guilt override her plan.

"You're not taking me with you?"

"Of course not."

"Oh, please, *please* take me with you. Consider it a Christmas present."

"Why?"

"Because I *really* want to see you rob a porno shop."

"Wouldn't you be considered an accomplice or something?"

"Probably 'something.' "

"You're making fun of me, aren't you?"

"A little, but, hell, I've never met a robber-nun-Santa who was about to enter a den of iniquity."

"I am *not* a nun."

"Take me with you. Come on. You need someone to protect you from yourself. And you never know what kind of creeps are in these places."

"Nope, I can't do it," she decided. "You'd call for help, or tackle me. How could I trust you?"

"I promise . . . on my mother's grave."

"Is your mother dead?" Her face softened with sympathy.

"No," he confessed sheepishly, "but it's the most solemn oath I could think of." He studied her for a long moment. "I'd take odds that *your* mother is dead, though," he remarked in a gentle voice.

Jessica cautioned herself once again not to reveal anything to the over-observant lout. And she didn't want his pity or anyone else's. "I think I should lock you in the trunk."

That wiped the pity right off his face. "I don't have a trunk."

"Oh. Well, maybe I could duck-tape your mouth shut and your hands and legs together."

"Bondage now? Wow! Who's the pervert here?"

She made a tsk-ing sound of disgust at his innuendo.

"Besides, I don't have any *duct* tape handy. Are you going to rob a hardware store, as well as a supermarket, before you rip off the sex shop?"

"I did *not* rob a supermarket. Will you stop saying that?"

He just smiled infuriatingly. And, my oh my, he really did resemble Brad Pitt when he flashed that dazzling smile. A girl could be tempted, *easily*, into allowing him to plant those teeth on her neck and inhale about a gallon of blood.

"Why are you licking your lips?" the Brad-Dracula asked, smirking knowingly.

If she had a stake handy, she would have whacked him a good one. She had to admit, though, that even when he smirked, he looked pretty darn good.

"You smell nice," he said irrelevantly, leaning closer and sniffing. "Is that Giorgio?"

"No, it's Eau de Scared Silly."

He sniffed a couple more times, and the brute looked sexy even when he sniffed. "Oh, I see. Sort of a designer ripoff of Eau de Stupid?"

"Probably," she agreed.

In the end, Jessica had no choice but to let Luke accompany her after he practically swore a blood oath to behave, at least until they were back in the car. She didn't trust Luke outside her sight, and the blood oath thing gave her the willies, but . . . well, there was another teensy problem. She'd been digging in both pockets of her Santa suit for the past five minutes and was unable to find the blasted handcuff key.

"You're on your honor, Luke," she pointed out. *Do*

vampires and movie star look-alikes have honor? "I'm accepting your word."

"Right," he said, and grasped her free right hand in his handcuffed right one, shaking. She felt the tingle of that warm touch up to her armpits. And other places, too. *Oh, boy!*

Then Luke jammed his beard and wig on, grinning at her the whole time. Lordy, there ought to be a law against men with killer grins like his.

"Hey, Tiffany, I just thought of something." He chortled mischievously as she crawled clumsily over the gear shift area between the seats so she could slide out through the driver's door with him. He didn't help her at all, watching with delight as her rump hung up in the air for a long moment before she righted herself. "Do you think this counts as a first date for us?"

She mumbled a foul word under her breath in answer as they exited the car and began to walk toward the shop. Snow was beginning to come down steadily, and the temperature had turned decidedly colder.

"Today is December twenty-third," the cad continued teasing. "You'll probably want to write it in your diary. First date. Luke. Porno shop."

This time she said the foul word out loud.

He laughed. "I could even clip off a lock of my hair for you to press between the pages."

She yanked on his chain then, hard.

Luke had no intention of letting psycho Santa babe commit another robbery.

He couldn't explain why he felt this protective urge to help a stranger. He just did.

Maybe it was her huge doe eyes that failed to hide abject terror. The woman was clearly frightened to death, and, even so, she insisted on pulling off a robbery.

Then again, maybe it was her absolutely sensuous lower lip (her upper lip wasn't too bad, either) that tugged at his long-deadened emotions.

He hoped it wasn't because the brave front this screwball put on reminded him so much of that day six years ago when he and Ginny had emerged from the doctor's office. They'd gone in expecting to hear good news—that Ginny was finally pregnant. Instead, the obstetrician had dealt her a staggering blow. She had advanced cervical cancer, and less than a year to live.

The look Ginny had given him when they'd hit the street had been filled with terror, but, at the same time, she'd had a desperate need to put on a brave front. Like this dingbat.

He'd been unable to help Ginny, but maybe he could help the dingbat.

Ginny's desperation had been understandable, but why did this squirrely bubblehead need 500 dollars so desperately?

Well, he'd soon find out.

Twining his handcuffed hand with Dirty Harriet's, he walked inside, inhaling deeply. *And it is Giorgio, I know it is.*

Jessica should have pulled her hand out of Luke's firm grasp, but he gave her strength, somehow. The feel of his pulse throbbing against hers, wrist to wrist, comforted and strengthened her for the formidable task she'd set for herself.

"Okay, let's do it," she said resolutely.

He squeezed her hand in answer, but she thought

123

she heard him mumble, "Dumber than a doornail." She wasn't sure if he referred to her, or himself.

The guy behind the counter, presumably Sam—a gray-haired gentleman who was probably somebody's grandfather—nodded at them and went back to waiting on a teenage boy who was purchasing about a gross of condoms and a magazine titled *Nympho Nurses*.

Hundreds of videos lined one wall, and magazine racks covered the other. There were several aisles of glass-topped counters displaying every kind of paraphernalia from edible underwear to bizarrely shaped vibrators to body oils that heated up on skin contact.

To her annoyance, Luke picked up one of the latter bottles and examined it closely, reading the instructions on the back. "Hmmmm," he said aloud. Then the lech winked at her.

His wink—a mere wink—caused her heart to lurch and her breasts to swell. Even in a ridiculous Santa wig and beard, the guy was drop-dead gorgeous and utterly charming. Quickly she turned her face away, not wanting him to see her heated blush, or her attraction to him.

As her eyes scanned the room, Jessica smiled. If she'd entertained any misgivings about their drawing undue attention, wearing Santa outfits and handcuffed together, she'd worried in vain. A stereo speaker belted out old chipmunk Christmas carols, and the customers went about their business browsing the wares.

To her amazement, two other Santas cruised the aisles, one of them schnockered and the other eyeing a pair of padded handcuffs with a matching velvet whip—probably a Christmas present for his spouse. *Gawd!* There were also a sophisticated-looking yuppie couple—definitely lovers, by the seductive glances they exchanged repeatedly; a young guy in a jeans jacket, cowboy hat, and boots; and two twentysomething women who giggled as they handled a pair of red satin men's bikini briefs that played "Jingle Bells" when a string was pulled.

"Gee, this isn't as bad as I thought it would be," she whispered, tugging on Luke's handcuffed wrist. "We should pretend that we're regular customers until the shop empties out a little, don't you think?"

"Whatever you say, Tiffany. You're the boss."

"Hmmmph!"

She immediately changed her mind about the shop not being so bad when she backed into Rita, a lifesize balloon of a nude, flame-haired woman with breasts the size of cantaloupes and red nipples resembling maraschino cherries. Two of the bimbo's plastic girlfriends, Bridget and Trish, stood next to her—a blonde and a brunette.

Do men really buy garbage like this? When the drunk Santa put his arm around the blond balloon's waist and hauled her up to the cash register, Jessica answered her own question. *Yep, they do.*

"Would you like a Bruce Balloon, honey?" Luke chuckled.

She looked where he pointed his free hand and saw a six-foot tall male balloon whose endowments were impressive, to say the least. Bruce. Jessica's eyes almost bugged out.

"Uh, I don't think so, *honey*," she responded, trying to appear casual.

Luke's devilish hazel eyes crinkled with mirth as he guided her over toward the video shelves and began to peruse the offerings nonchalantly. After flicking through *A-cup Cuties, Breaststroke, Porking Miss Piggy,* and *Hot to Trot,* he turned to the "legitimate" movie section. *Hah! There is no such thing as legitimate in this place.* There he snickered as he read the titles aloud. *Hannah Does Her Two Sisters, Forrest Hump, High Nooner, Close Encounters of the Lewdest Kind, Lord of the Fly, The Breasts of Madison County,* and *Three Days of the Condom.*

"Let's get out of this section," she urged.

"No, no, no." He rebelled as his eyes latched onto something new. "How about this, sweetie?" he asked brightly, shoving a video case in her face. *"Tiffany's Great Adventure."*

She made a gurgling sound of revulsion as her face heated up some more. At a sudden blast of cold air, her eyes darted to the doorway where the teenage boy exited, followed by the plastered Santa and the yuppie couple, who'd bought some assorted lotions and a video.

"Merry Christmas," the proprietor called out after them cheerfully. "Hope you have a great night. Ho, ho, ho!"

The other Santa followed soon after, purchasing nothing.

Okay, only three more to go—the two women and the cowboy. With any luck, there wouldn't be any new customers at this time of night.

"Have you ever tried these?" asked one of the women next to her. Her friend had moved to the register where she was paying for the Jingle Bells jock strap.

Me? Is she talking to me?

She was. "Have you ever tried these?" the woman repeated, holding up two eggs connected by a thin electric wire to a battery-operated controller which began to vibrate when she pressed a button. The woman twittered, and Jessica's mouth dropped open. She refused to look at Luke to see what he was doing.

"What *is* that?" she blurted out, and immediately regretted her loose tongue when Luke answered, "Love eggs."

She and the woman both looked at him, and he shrugged. "I read about them in a magazine."

"Sure you did," Jessica muttered under her breath.

But he heard her. "Hey, I haven't been in one of these places since I was a teenager. Not my style."

Soon after, the two women left the store, and the cowboy headed toward the back of the shop where a weary-looking woman dressed only in a black teddy, garter belt, and stiletto heels emerged through a set of swinging, western-style doors. She was crooking a long painted fingernail toward the cowboy, who shuffled back with a puppy-dog grin. Jessica wasn't sure if it was the dude's turn for a nude massage or a body piercing.

No matter. That left her and Luke alone with the proprietor.

"Can I help you folks?" the old guy asked. "Great handcuffs, by the way."

Jessica was about to pull out her gun when Luke pinched her fingers in warning and handed the owner a bottle. "Yeah, I'll buy this."

She hadn't realized he still carried the warming oil. "That'll be nine ninety-five."

One-handed, Luke fished out his wallet and laid a ten-dollar bill on the counter.

Okay, this is it. Now's the time. Oh, geez, oh, geez! Jessica reached in her pocket for the empty pistol, but in the process accidentally elbowed a display on the counter. To her horror, she knocked over a sort of vibrator thing with a huge wiggly tongue on the end, which began to jiggle madly. With two fingers, she distastefully tried to pick the thing up and turn it off, but it shimmied away from her, right off the counter to the floor. She dropped down to her knees, pulling Luke with her, and tried to catch the obscene object.

Luke and the shop owner were laughing hysterically at her antics. Angry now, she gave the thing a kick, which shut it off.

When she stood up, shaking with mortification, her cap and wig slipped and her long hair billowed out in a flaming explosion midway down her back.

Luke gaped at her as if someone had just handed him a bomb. "I can't believe it! You look like Little Orphan Annie," he exclaimed, fingering one of the corkscrew curls—the bane of her life. At least he'd stopped laughing at her.

The fact that he added, "You're beautiful," came too late. Comparing her to Little Orphan Annie was not a compliment in her book—not now, and not when she'd been a real orphan. And there was no way she was beautiful with her wild mop of red hair. No way!

She fought the tears that filled her eyes. Angry with herself and Luke, she jerked out her revolver and started to aim it at the guy behind the counter, who was holding his sides as he continued to howl. With a quivering voice, she shouted, "This . . . is . . . a . . . stick—"

"No!" Luke roared, and with one swift motion he hefted her into the air and over his shoulder, the gun dangling from her fingers. As he headed toward the door with his free hand clamped over her struggling behind, he informed Sam the Sleaze, who'd just noticed the gun and was making hyperventilating noises, "Don't worry, this is a game my wife likes to play every Christmas."

Sam expelled a wheeze of relief. "Hey, I see this kind of thing all the time. It's the curse of my business."

"I'll give you a curse," Jessica raged.

"Merry Christmas," Luke laughed.

"Ho, ho, ho!" Sam chortled.

"You scum! You slimeball! Put me down. Right now. I can't believe you did this. Oooh, oooh, this is awful. I needed that money. You don't know what this means."

Kicking and screaming and thrashing, she pounded his back with her free hand. She dug her fingernails into the palm of his cuffed hand. She landed a pointed toe on his thigh.

"Ouch!"

Finally he set Little Orphan Tiffany down next to his car, and immediately raised both her flailing arms over her head and held them on the car roof by the wrists with his cuffed hand. He pressed his lower body against hers to keep her from escaping or doing him more bodily harm, not an easy task with both of their pillow-bellies.

Angry himself now and sick of this game which had gotten way out of hand, he tore off his disguise, tossing the cap and beard and wig to the snow-covered ground. Then he yanked off her beard. Finally he got his first good gander at his surprising Santa.

Time seemed to stand still.

An ethereal silence surrounded them as snowflakes as big as golfballs came down, landing with feather lightness on her mane of curly red hair, in her eyelashes . . . on her parted lips.

She no longer struggled. In fact, she stared at him with equal awe.

Tears burned in his eyes for reasons he couldn't explain. All he knew was that the tight knot surrounding his heart—a knot he hadn't even realized was there— began to unravel. And he felt as light as the snowflakes caressing his face. And hopeful.

It was so strange.

"Are you an angel? A Christmas mirage?" he murmured. Lowering his lips toward hers—those luscious lips that had drawn him from the start, he sighed.

Instead of protesting, she arched upward, meeting him halfway. "I'm no angel."

"Thank God."

Against his lips she whispered, "I'm not really a nun, either."

"I know," he smiled, then repeated, "Thank God."

"You shouldn't kiss me," she demurred even as she parted her lips. "My Christmas Curse might rub off on you."

"Rub all you want, babe," he growled, grinding his

big belly against hers. "I'm cursed already."

"What's that hard thing?" she asked suddenly.

He laughed.

"Not *that*. Under your jacket."

"A bulletproof vest."

She raised a brow. "So, you weren't afraid of me at all."

"Oh, I was afraid of what you'd do. I still am."

She smiled enigmatically, as if he'd better be.

But he couldn't think about that now. All he could think about was this tempting redhead in his arms.

Cupping her jaw with his free hand to hold her in place, he slanted his lips over hers, shaping her for his kiss, relishing the contrast of cool lips and hot breath. Hard and demanding, soft and cajoling.

She whimpered.

He groaned.

Powerful, bone-melting sensations overwhelmed him. Suddenly he wanted so many things, and they all seemed to revolve around this woman—this stranger. Pulling away slightly, he studied her face—misty eyes locked with his in question, mouth already swollen from his kisses. Their warm breaths, panting, frosted in the cold air between them. Hearts thudding in unison, they tried to comprehend what was happening.

In that instant, he understood. Blood hammered in his ears as the realization hit Luke like a thunderbolt.

I love her, he thought, disbelieving, at first. Then he smiled, happier than he'd been in ages. *I love her*.

He'd never believed in love at first sight before. He did now. *I love her*. He couldn't stop saying the words in his head.

Should he tell her?

No, not yet. He didn't want to scare her away. Besides, he needed more time to think. He rolled the words around in his mind with a joyous relish: *I love her.*

"I feel weird," she said, as if reading his mind.

"So do I, babe. So do I."

She blinked at him. "It must be the Christmas Curse."

He shook his head vehemently. "No, it's a Christmas Miracle."

Chapter Three

"Are you still cold?" Luke asked the shivering woman next to him as he pulled out onto the highway. Lord, how he wanted to stop the car and take her in his arms, but he didn't have the right . . . *yet*. She already appeared scared to death of him. Instead, he turned up the heat.

Jessie—that was the name of the woman he loved, Jessica Jones . . . she'd just told him so—shook her head and bit her bottom lip in concentration. She was probably planning another heist. Perhaps a cathouse this time, he thought with a chuckle. *God, I love her*.

Or maybe she was having second thoughts about their killer kiss.

Uh-oh. No, he wouldn't let himself think that. Now that he'd found a woman he could love, after all these years, he wouldn't let her go. She would love him. He was determined.

But he was nervous, too, and that was something new for him. For the past five years, ever since Ginny died, he'd had more women than he could handle. But he hadn't cared about a single one of them.

Now that he did care, would he be rejected?

Luke clenched the steering wheel tighter. He had to believe that everything would work out all right. God didn't hand out miracles and then yank them away. Nope, all he needed was a little time.

Luke considered his next move as he drove back to the Piggly Jiggly parking lot. Jessie insisted she had to get the van and return to "Clara's House," mission unaccomplished. Alone.

Hah! Not if I have anything to do with it.

He could barely see through the wildly swinging windshield wipers which couldn't keep pace with the falling snow. It would be a white Christmas this year, after all, if this blizzard kept up. He'd already tried using the storm as an excuse to keep Jessie with him, but she'd refused adamantly, pointing out that the van had snow tires.

Luckily they'd been able to find the handcuff key under the back seat floor mat, after some amusing calisthenics necessitated by their bound wrists. Amusing to him, at least. In the close confines, with all her squirming, he'd gotten a real good idea of what kind of body his Santa babe hid under her suit—tall, curvy, not too lean. Perfect.

So now he and Jessie sat unattached for the first time in hours. And Luke felt as if a mile separated them, not three feet.

He reached over and twined his fingers with hers.

Startled, she glanced first at their linked hands,

then at him, questioning. He hoped she got the silent message he was unable to speak out loud, just yet.

Fear flashed through her wide doe-brown eyes for a moment—of what, he wasn't sure—but he suspected she was about to pull away.

"Don't be afraid of me, Jessie," he said, his voice husky. "I won't hurt you."

"But I might hurt you," she said in a voice laden with regret. "I'm cursed. And it's Christmas. I don't stand a chance. Neither do you. You'll be better off when you're rid of me."

He squeezed her hand. "Maybe the trick is to replace your Christmas bad luck with good luck. You know that saying 'When someone hands you a bag of bones, make soup.'"

"Don't you mean lemons, and lemonade?"

He scowled at her interruption and went on. "Treat our meeting as a miracle instead of a curse . . . oh, hell, I'm not very good with this kind of stuff. I have all these thoughts and feelings inside, but they just don't come out right." He ducked his head in embarrassment. "I'm not very good with words."

She squeezed his hand back, and he thought his heart would explode with happiness. "You're doing just fine," she assured him.

"I still say we should go to my place. It's only fifteen minutes from here. You could warm up, and—"

"No, I've got to get back. Sister Clara will be frantic."

"Sister? I thought she was your aunt."

"I call her aunt, everyone who lives at 'Clara's House' does," she said, waving her free hand dismissively. He was holding on to her other hand for dear life.

He frowned. "You live at 'Clara's House'? An orphanage?"

"No. Of course not. But I used to. Besides, it's not really an orphanage. It's sort of a foster home for incorrigible kids."

Now, that was a revelation. Jessie had been an orphan, and incorrigible. His lips twitched with humor. He could understand the incorrigible part. "You mean juvenile delinquents?"

"They don't call them j.d.'s anymore. Politically incorrect." She smiled at him shyly, and Luke could hardly speak over the lump in his throat. Who would have thought that he'd fall in love so quick, so hard?

"What do you do for a living, Jessie?" he asked finally when he got his emotions under control.

She regarded him mischievously, giving him her full attention now. "So you're finally convinced I'm not a nun?"

"Babe, nuns don't tongue kiss," he replied and winked at her.

He could see a blush bloom on her cheeks. Still, she gave him a slick comeback. "Kissed a lot of nuns, have you?"

How lucky could a guy be? A gorgeous redhead. And a sense of humor, too. He was going to light a few thank-you candles the next time he went to church.

He released her hand and wagged a finger at her. "You're changing the subject. What do you do for a living, besides burglary?" Then he immediately took her hand again. He wondered idly what she'd do if he tried to pull her over onto his lap. Or stopped the car to kiss her again . . . and again . . . and again. And unbuckled her belt, and . . . *oh, brother!* About 50,000 of his testosterone were revving up for the start signal.

"I didn't rob . . . oh, never mind," she said huffily. "I don't suppose you'd buy Avon Lady?"

"Hell, why not? You've hit me with Santa, nun, and gun moll so far. There isn't anything else you could do that would surprise me." *Except maybe jump onto my lap, uninvited. Yeah! I should be so lucky.*

"I'm a wedding caterer."

"Say that again."

"I bake spectacular wedding cakes . . . the best almond creme, ten-tier cake in the country. And I supply gourmet food for wedding receptions."

"Here in Philly?"

"No. I'm from Chicago."

Whoa! Red flag! That posed some logistical problems. Long-distance dating and all that. Well, no problem! He'd skip the dating and get right down to the serious stuff. *Hmmm. I wonder how long I can wait before I propose? Oops! First, I've got to tell her I love her. Then I can ask her to marry me and move to Philly. Betcha I could do that all in one shot. Yep, that's what I'll do. I love you, let's tie the knot, wild sex, wedding. Or maybe I could reverse the order. Oh, yeah! Wild sex, I love you, wild sex, let's tie the knot, wild sex, wedding, wild sex. Whatever.* He could barely wait.

"Why are you grinning?" she asked.

"You don't want to know, sweetheart," he chuckled. *Yet.*

"If you're remotely considering sinking your teeth

into my neck and sucking blood, forget it. I have a twentieth-degree black belt in karate."

He shook his head like a shaggy dog to clear it. Sometimes her train of thought confused him. Then he understood. She was associating him with that movie *Interview with a Vampire*. And he probably had been ogling her as if he'd like to suck a few body parts, except his preference would be a bit lower than her throat.

"You're smirking again."

"I don't smirk. That was a lascivious smile."

"Looked like a smirk to me."

Then he thought of something else and he hooted at her, "So, you do think I resemble Brad Pitt."

"Well, maybe an older version," she conceded with a sniff.

He lifted their laced fingers to his mouth and kissed her knuckles. He couldn't help himself.

Instead of resisting, she sighed. That's all. Just a sigh.

The 50,000 testosterone split and multiplied into an orgy of anticipation. He didn't think he could wait another five minutes before kissing her again.

But then, still another thought occurred to him, and his heart began to race with anxiety. "You're not married, are you?"

"Almost, but not quite."

"Almost? Almost? What do you mean 'almost?' " His chest constricted so tightly he could scarcely breathe.

"I got jilted two weeks ago by my fiance, Burton Richards the Third. Burt and I were engaged for a year, but he just discovered that the trust fund I got on my thirtieth birthday isn't quite as large as he'd anticipated."

Luke let out a whoosh of relief. "That's too bad . . . about you and Burp," he said sweetly. He felt like pumping his fist in the air with the victory sign.

"Burt," she corrected, then shrugged. "It's just as well. I didn't like him much toward the end anyhow. He played golf a lot," she confided.

Luke made a note never to play golf again.

"I should have known better, of course, knowing as I do that all men are scumbags."

"I beg your pardon."

"You wouldn't believe how many men—engaged and married men—hit on me even as I'm making preparations for their weddings. The louses! One bridegroom even cornered me at his reception, offering me a quickie."

I've got a lot of backup work to do.

"Well, I've learned my lesson from Burt. I'm never getting married now."

Yep, lots of backup work.

"Maybe I'll become a nun."

Over my dead body.

"So, how about you?" Jessica asked. "Are you married?"

How could she ask that question so calmly, as if she couldn't care less either way? Luke decided she was just playing it cool. Her heart was probably doing a high-speed tap dance, just like his.

"No, not anymore," he said, and was astonished that the usual pain didn't accompany that statement.

"Divorce?"

He shook his head. "Ginny died five years ago of

cancer." And with those words, a door slammed shut on Luke's past. Oh, it wasn't as if he'd ever forget Ginny. How could he? They'd been sweethearts since junior high. But she was dead, and somehow, someway, his new, fantastic feelings for Jessie suddenly gave him permission to go on living . . . not just in meaningless one-night stands, but with a forever kind of commitment.

"Oh, Luke, I'm so sorry. I shouldn't have pried."

"That's okay. She's been gone a long time. Anyhow, tell me why you're here.

" 'Clara's House' is in the Poconos, and—"

"The Poconos! The Poconos! That's two hours from here. What were you doing in Philly at midnight?"

"I had to go to Aunt Clara's 'mother house' in the city. Clara's a discalced nun; that mean's she's no longer a nun but still has ties to her religious order. Anyhow, after I'd completed my errand, the sisters talked me into playing Santa following their Christmas recital. On the way back, I decided to *handle* Aunt Clara's problem at the Piggly Jiggly."

It should have made sense. It didn't. "I meant, what are you doing so far away from Chicago to begin with?"

"Oh. I came here two days ago when I got an SOS call from Aunt Clara. She broke her leg, and she needed my help to keep her foster home together through the holidays."

"I don't understand."

"Aunt Clara operates a group program under state regulations. If they found out she was incapacitated, they'd withdraw her funding and split up these kids quick as spit. She was especially concerned about them missing Christmas together. Not that it's going to be much of a Christmas now." Her expression drooped dolefully.

"Because you weren't able to get any money?" he concluded, finally understanding.

"Yep. I would have been all right if Julio hadn't ripped me off this afternoon, but now . . ."

He cursed under his breath.

"Julio stole all the money Aunt Clara had for Christmas gifts, as well. It's going to be a mighty bleak holiday for those kids." She straightened her shoulders with resolution. "But they're used to disappointment. They'll survive. We . . . I mean *they* . . . always do."

There was a world of hidden meaning in Jessie's words. How many disappointments had she had as a child? As an orphan? How many bleak holidays?

Well, he'd be damned if she'd have another.

"This is the turnoff for the Piggly Jiggly," Jessie reminded him. "Just a few more minutes and you'll be rid of me."

Warning buzzers went off in Luke's head. He had to think fast. How could he keep Jessie with him? Time. He needed time.

"Duck!" he shouted.

She jerked her head toward him in surprise. "What?"

"Hurry, get down on the floor. The parking lot is loaded with cops. Frank must have reported your heist to every precinct from here to New Jersey."

Jessie dropped down into a curled-up ball in the cramped floor space, and he threw the two pillows they'd taken from their bellies on top of her. Then he surveyed the deserted parking lot with a wide grin.

"Whatever you do, don't lift your head or your butt is gonna land in jail." *And a very nice butt, it is, too,* he noted, glancing down at her.

"Oh, geez, oh, geez! What am I going to do now?"

"I guess I'll just have to drive you to 'Clara's House,'" he said with an exaggerated sigh. "No, no . . . don't worry about inconveniencing me. It's the least I can do for those poor orphans." He patted the pillow over her upraised behind, barely stifling the chuckle of satisfaction that rippled through him.

"But what about the van?" she groaned. "Can you turn down the heater? I'm melting here. Oh, good grief, maybe I should just turn myself in, beg for mercy."

"Nope," he said in a rush, "you can't do that. Philly cops are notorious for being hard-nosed. Mercy isn't in their vocabulary. They'd probably put you in a cell with . . . Mafia hitmen or something. Do a strip search . . . naked, body cavities, delousing, the works."

She groaned again.

"You can come back and get the van after Christmas," he advised. Interpreting her silence for assent, he added, "Is there anything you need from the van? Maybe I could slip in unnoticed."

"I don't know. I can't think here. It's about five hundred degrees under this blower. Yeah, you'd better get the boxes."

"Boxes? What boxes? How many boxes?"

"About fifty."

Fifty? he mouthed silently. "What's in them?"

"Fruitcakes."

*　　*　　*

An hour later, Jessica sat in the car in front of an all-night Uni-Mart convenience store, sulking. "I still don't see the harm in my going inside. I promised Aunt Clara to bring back bread and milk. Criminey, don't you think you're being a mite overcautious?"

"Nope, you can't be too careful," Luke said. "Lots of these convenience stores have police radios behind the counter. There might be an all-points bulletin out for you."

"Sixty miles away from Philly?" she scoffed.

"Just sit tight, toots," he said, chucking her under the chin. "I'm perfectly capable of buying bread and milk." He peered down with disgust at the bills and change she'd shoved with stubborn pride into his hands. "Even thirty-nine dollars and ninety-five cents' worth."

"Don't spend it all on bread and milk, you fool. Buy some peanut butter and jelly, too. I've got to make this money stretch till Tuesday, the day after Christmas. Then I should be able to call my bank."

"Just how many kids are at this house?"

"Four . . . five when Julio is there."

"How old are they?"

"Eleven to fourteen. Julio's the oldest."

"Let me get this straight. You expect kids that age, who suck up food like human vacuums, to live on peanut butter and jelly sandwiches for the next two days? Over Christmas?"

"And fruitcake. Don't forget the fruitcake."

"How could I?" he said with a moan. Despite their both protesting that they hated fruitcake, they were so hungry they'd polished off half of a three-pound ring so far. "Whatever possessed those nuns to send fifty fruitcakes?"

"They had a fund-raiser that fell through. I guess they sold less than they expected."

"Exactly how many of those lead sinkers do they have left?"

"Five hundred."

His mouth dropped open in amazement. Then he burst out laughing. "Tell me a little something about these kids."

"Well, Julio you already know about. He's fourteen, half Puerto Rican, half black, and street smart to the nth degree. He's been arrested for everything from grand theft auto to dealing marijuana. You'd like him, though. He could charm the socks off a snake."

"Sounds delightful."

"Darlene is next. She's thirteen, going on thirty. Sexy as hell and headed straight for a life of prostitution if someone doesn't help her soon." She laughed. "Yesterday she pierced her own navel, and she tried to talk me into doing the same."

"Did you?"

She cast him a rueful glance. "Hardly. Robbing porno shops is as adventuresome as I get."

He grinned. "Who's next?"

"Henry is thirteen, too. The next Bill Gates, or so he thinks. He knows everything there is to know about computers. In fact, you'll soon know what he wants for Christmas—a computer system with a CD-Rom— not that he'll get such a pricey item, unless there's a real Santa Claus."

"He doesn't sound too incorrigible. What's he done?"

"Credit card fraud. Illegal hacking. The last scam he pulled off netted him ten thousand dollars. Not bad for a thirteen-year-old, huh?"

"Is your Aunt Clara a saint or what? No sane person would take on all these hopeless cases."

"They're not hopeless," Jessie asserted defensively. "All they need is help."

"Sorry," he apologized. "Go on."

"Kajeeta is twelve. Poor thing. She's . . . well, she's overweight, but she has this dream of becoming a singer and dancer, like Janet Jackson. No one has the heart to tell her it's probably a hopeless dream. Anyhow, Kajeeta refuses to go to school. The other kids make fun of her. She's continually being called into court by school probation officers. Foster parents don't want her, too much trouble."

He nodded. Sounded like a great bunch of kids so far.

"Then there's Willie. He's eleven." She smiled. "His orange hair and freckles will fool you. He's a compulsive shoplifter. And he's going through this Ninja phase right now."

He raised a brow.

"He does karate moves . . . all the time. Seems like he can't even go to the bathroom without Kung Fu-ing along the way." She stared out the window, deep in thought. Then she seemed to shake herself back to the present. "We're wasting time here. Am I going into the store or are you?"

"I am. But how about soda and snack food for the kids?" he suggested.

She raised her chin. "I can't waste money on junk food. We'll get by. Just buy four loaves of bread, four

145

gallons of milk, a jar of peanut butter and a jar of jelly," she said inflexibly, "or I'll do it myself."

He gave her a condemning glare and slammed out of the car, storming into the store. He'd left the wipers on, so she was able to watch him through the well-lit store window, even through the blinding snow. He said something to the teenage girl behind the counter, and she smiled up at him as if God had just walked into her store. Or Brad Pitt.

She couldn't blame the girl. Jessica felt all warm and fuzzy inside when she looked at him herself. Actually, she'd felt more like hot, hot, hot, especially when he'd kissed her. No one, *no one* had ever made her feel like that.

This night was probably just a lark for him. He was humoring some crazy woman who'd pulled a loaded gun in a supermarket, kidnapped him, then tried to rob a porno shop.

She groaned aloud. It sounded awful when she played it back in her mind. Heck, it *was* awful. Her brain really must have splintered apart to have tried such foolish stunts. But she was desperate. How was she ever going to provide a Christmas for those kids who depended on her? In a way, she was letting them down, just like so many adults had let her down as a child when she was shifted from one foster home to another . . . until she'd found Aunt Clara.

Well, enough maudlin thoughts. Her Brad-savior was returning, loaded down with two grocery bags in each arm. She leaned over to press the automatic rear door release.

Even that short walk from the front door of the Uni-Mart to the rear of the car resulted in his being covered with snow. To her surprise, he didn't immediately enter the car, though. He went back in the store twice more, returning with six more grocery bags.

When he finally slid into the front seat, she lit into him. "I told you to buy four things. What's in all those bags?"

"My stuff," he said, latching his seat belt and backing out of the lot. His jaw squared mulishly.

"Stuff? What kind of stuff?"

"Snack stuff. Food I can eat while all the rest of you are scarfing down fruitcake."

She narrowed her eyes suspiciously. "You aren't going to be at 'Clara's House' long enough to see anyone eat fruitcake. You're turning right around after you drop me off, and going home."

He slanted her one of those "wanna bet?" looks, but said nothing.

"Luke?" she persisted.

He sucked in a deep breath and glowered at her as he drove along the deserted highway. It must be three A.M. by now. "Jessie, you can't possibly think I'm going to return tonight. I'm exhausted. We're in the middle of a blizzard. Do you want me to have an accident?"

"No, but . . ." Little alarm bells were ringing all through her body. She wasn't sure how much exposure she could take to this guy, how long she could resist the attraction.

"Surely your Aunt Clara has a sofa or something where I can crash for the night." He fluttered those feather-duster lashes at her. It was a ploy he'd probably perfected over the years to suck in susceptible women . . . like her.

She immediately felt guilty for her lack of charity, especially since Luke had gone out of his way to help her. And it wasn't as if "Clara's House" didn't have plenty of room. The old gingerbread Victorian had three stories and about eight bedrooms. "Oh, all right. But just for one night."

She could have sworn he murmured under his breath, "That's all I need." But when she scrutinized him closer, he stared straight ahead. Innocent as a cobra. Or a blood-sucking vampire.

The next morning, Luke awakened in a third-floor bedroom of "Clara's House" to a wet tongue tracing his lips. His morning hard-on shot up like a rocket.

Wow! What a wake-up call! He hadn't expected his plan to work this fast. He must have more charm than he'd realized. It appeared as if the wild sex was going to come sooner than he'd expected.

With a growl, he reached up to pull Jessie into bed with him.

And she growled back.

Rather, *it* growled. A huge yellow dog was standing next to the bed with its long tongue hanging out. *Fred*, he concluded immediately. Jessie's randy mutt.

Yech! was his next thought as he realized the dog's tongue had been lapping his mouth. He'd probably get ringworm or something.

He stood and stretched with a loud yawn. The house seemed awfully quiet. Checking his watch, he saw that it was already nine o'clock.

No one had been awake when they'd arrived the night before at four A.M. So Jessie had worried in vain that Aunt Clara would be frantic about her safety.

They'd brought the grocery bags and boxes in from the car without awakening anyone and gone immediately to bed.

Jessie had made a point of putting him on the third floor with the boys. Her bedroom was a floor below. No problem. She didn't stand a chance now that he had time on his side. *Wild sex, here I come.*

First things first. He wasn't sure which screaming body organ needed the most attention, his empty stomach or his full bladder. He opted for the bathroom first, with Fred padding after him like a shadow. "So, Fred, knocked up any poodles lately?"

"Woof, woof."

"You old dog, you!"

After leaving the bathroom, whose antiquated plumbing clunked and sputtered in protest, he headed downstairs where he heard chattering voices coming from what he assumed was the kitchen. He was about to push open the closed door when he paused.

"Where did you get those Frosted Flakes?" he heard Jessie's voice ask shrilly.

"They were in the grocery bags," a small-boy voice answered.

"Well, don't eat them. They belong to our guest, Luke Carter. And he's leaving."

"But I already put milk on them," the kid whined. "And there's three other kinds of cereal, too. How's he gonna eat all this stuff himself? Is he fat?"

There was a long silence, for which Luke planned to punish Jessie later, before she answered simply, "No."

But the kid didn't give up. "Besides, how's this Luke dude gonna leave now? There's three feet of snow covering his car. And I'm not shoveling that driveway again. It's a mile long."

Three feet of snow? He smiled. God, or someone, was on his side.

Jessie groaned. Apparently she didn't consider the snow a heavenly blessing. *Yet.*

"Do you think he knows anything about karate?" the kid went on to the accompaniment of slurping noises.

It must be Willie, the eleven-year-old Bruce Lee clone Jessie had described.

"Oh, you are such a toad," a girl's voice said. "Karate, karate, karate . . . that's all you think about."

"Yeah, at least I'm improving my body. You give yours away like lollipops, Darlene. You are a slut. S-L-U-T."

"I'm gonna kill you, you little twerp."

"Put down your knife, Darlene," Jessie cautioned.

Well, enough eavesdropping for now. Luke pushed open the kitchen door and saw four stunned kids gaping at him, and one not-so-pleased adult woman.

"Oh, my Gawd!" a young girl wearing enough makeup to plaster a wall exclaimed. *Darlene.* "It's Brad Pitt. Aunt Jessie brought home a movie star."

On the other side of the table, a fat black girl with buck teeth was inhaling Pop Tarts as if they might disappear. *Kajeeta.* She scrutinized him from head to toe, found him not so interesting, and went on eating.

Another boy, wearing wire-rimmed spectacles and a condescending expression, was reading the back of the Frosted Flakes package, reciting the ingredients. He wore a catalog picture of a computer taped to his forehead probably as a Christmas hint. *Henry, aka Bill*

Gates. He swept Luke with an appraising look, taking in his well-worn jeans and ratty black T-shirt, before asking, "How many credit cards do you have?"

Luke stifled a laugh.

Then a skinny little kid with orange hair, about two zillion freckles, and ears that could propel an airplane—*Willie*—piped in, "Wanna see my num-chucks?" He waved a hand in the air, holding a pair of foot-long black sticks connected by a small chain—*nunchakus.*

Jessie glanced with horror at each of the kids, then him, before laying her head down on the table in resignation.

He plopped down in the chair next to Jessie, patted her shoulders, then beamed at the kids. "Hi, I'm Luke. You can call me Uncle Luke. Your Aunt Jessie and I are gonna get married soon. You're all invited to the wedding."

Chapter Four

A half hour later, Luke was outside helping Willie and Henry and Kajeeta shovel the driveway, which indeed seemed about a mile long and three feet deep in snow. And the flakes continued to come down steadily. *Thank you, God! I'm trapped.* Darlene was inside, probably painting her toenails or something equally important. Fred was rolling in the snow like an orgasmic lunatic. He probably smelled female dog scent in the buried grass.

After Luke had made his amazing wedding declaration in the kitchen—it had amazed even him—Jessie had sputtered at him unintelligibly for several moments before hissing, "We have to talk . . . in private. You dolt!"

He was pretty sure she didn't have wild sex in mind. So he took his cue and hightailed it outside to shovel his butt off. With any luck, Jessie would cool off before he went back inside.

"Do you have a computer?" Henry asked him, jolting him back to the present as he pushed his foggy glasses up on the bridge of his nose for the umpteenth time. The colors from the computer on his forehead were bleeding down his nose and onto his cheeks from the wet snow. He looked ridiculous.

There were teenagers in the world today buying guns and drugs, Luke thought. All this boy wanted was a lousy computer.

Luke felt like crying.

Or hugging the kid.

Or driving to the nearest Computer World and buying him whatever equipment he wanted. Which was impossible with the roads blocked by the storm. Not that Jessie, with her raging pride, would ever allow him such an extravagant charity.

"Yeah, I have a computer," Luke finally answered. "Nothing fancy. Just an IBM home system."

That was all it took. Henry spat out one question after another about megabytes and rams and high-tech software programs, none of which Luke was able to answer. He scarcely knew what a cursor was.

"Hie-yah!" Willie yelled as he attempted a flying side kick, landing with a thud on his well-padded bottom. The Karate Kid he was not. Slack-jawed, Luke watched as the youngster dusted himself off, then waddled over, wearing so many layers of clothing he looked like a roly-poly bear, with only his eyes and mouth visible under a wool cap and scarf. "I'll show you my moves if you show me yours," Willie said right off.

Luke choked.

"Give me a break!" Henry said, and tramped away to the other end of the driveway to shovel, muttering, "Not that again!"

"I beg your pardon," Luke squeaked out to Willie, who was staring up at him, avidly awaiting his answer.

"I'm plannin' on getting my black belt in karate, but I'm havin' trouble with some of the moves," Willie explained, meanwhile poking out his tongue to catch snowflakes in little-boy fashion.

Oh! The boy is talking about karate moves. Whew! I shoulda known. Luke caught himself poking out his own tongue to catch snowflakes.

"So, are you into karate? Do you have a black belt? Huh?" Willie persisted. "Betcha you do, lookin' like Brad Pitt and all. Betcha you learned all the moves early on, to impress the chicks and all. Like Chuck Norris."

Oh, my God! More like the Ninja turtles.

"How come your eyes are crossed? You look really weird when you do that. Aunt Clara says your face might freeze forever and ever if you make faces. You're not gonna teach me any karate moves, are you? Grownups never have the time for kids," he grumbled. Throwing down his shovel, he stalked toward the house.

Kajeeta huffed up the slight incline from the bottom of the driveway, and Luke braced himself. What was this? Trial by kid?

When the girl drew near, Luke got his licks in first.

"I've got to make a telephone call. Can you finish this small section?"

"Phone's disconnected," Kajeeta panted out. If Willie had looked like a roly-poly bear, Kajeeta resembled a huge, mutant peach in her oversized, pale orange, one-piece snow suit.

"Huh?"

"Willie was makin' so many 900 calls to one of those karate hotlines, he ran the bill up to two hundred dollars. Aunt Clara refused to pay, and Ma Bell cut us off."

Oh, great! Good thing I have a cellular phone in the back of my car. I can't let Jessie know about that, though. Nope. She'd probably call a helicopter service to air-evac me out.

"I want to be a dancer someday . . . and a singer," Kajeeta informed him out of the clear blue sky.

Her comment had no relevance whatsoever to anything, not that Willie or Henry's questions did, either. Hell, were these kids so lonely for company that they'd spill their guts to any stranger?

Yes.

"Do you think I have a chance?"

"Everybody has a chance," he assured her, and he meant it.

She beamed at him as if he'd handed her a million bucks.

These kids of Clara's, who clearly had emotional problems, tugged at Luke's heartstrings. "If you don't dream big, it's not worth dreaming at all," he continued with a catch in his voice. "And there isn't anything in the world a person can't have if they want it badly enough."

He kept his fingers crossed behind his back as he spoke because he sure as hell wanted Jessie. And he didn't want to believe there was any chance he couldn't get her.

But how did he convince her?

Wild sex, he decided with sudden, pure male insight. Yep, that made sense. He was great in the sack, if he did say so himself. All he had to do was seduce Jessie into his bed. Then he'd convince her that he was her Christmas Miracle, not her Christmas Curse.

He handed his shovel to Kajeeta, who was still rambling on about her dreams and Weight Watchers and dance lessons and menstrual cramps and God only knew what else. He started toward the house, a determined glint in his eye.

A little niggling voice in his brain suggested that perhaps he ought to try convincing Jessie of his love first, but another part of his body, down a lot lower, moved. It actually moved. And he could swear it said, *wild sex, wild sex, wild sex.*

Who was Luke to argue?

No sooner did Luke hang up his coat on a wooden peg in the kitchen than Jessica grabbed the infuriating man by his ponytail and dragged him into the small, closet-like pantry, locking the door behind her.

"Ouch!" he complained.

She released him and planted a hand on each of her hips, clad in a pair of skin-tight jeans. Her suitcase was in the car Julio had stolen, so she'd had no choice but to wear a pair of Darlene's jeans and a T-shirt that read "Born To Be Wild." It was all part of the Christmas Curse, of course.

Luke was grinning at her.

She shoved him hard with a palm against his chest. "I could kill you for telling those kids such an outrageous lie about our marrying."

He didn't budge an inch. "Now, Jessie—"

"And stop looking at my hips. I know they're too big. You don't have to . . . oomph!"

He hauled her flush against his body and leaned back against the counter top. "Your hips are perfect," he rasped out. Then, before she could react, he spread his long legs and pulled her even tighter into the cradle of his thighs.

Jessie saw stars as the most incredible sensations shot like wildfire through her instantly attuned nerve endings. She forgot why she was so mad at Luke, why she'd shanghaied him into the pantry, why she wanted him out of her life. Heck, she forgot her own name.

He gripped her head in both hands. "How do you feel about wild sex?" he growled just before his mouth swooped down and captured her lips, silencing any protest she might have made.

Wild sex? She would have said, "I hate it" or "How dare you!" or "Huh? What's that?" or "Yesyesyes," but she was incapable of coherent speech. She couldn't talk at all. She was reduced to a whimpering vegetable as Luke devoured her mouth, alternately hard, then soft, pressing and sucking.

She barely recognized the mewling, guttural words of encouragement emitting from her. And when he forced her mouth open with his thrusting tongue, he filled her with such exquisite longing that she drew deeply on him.

He made a raw sound deep in his throat, and she exulted.

The smell of spices surrounded them—cinnamon and basil and cloves. From outside, she could hear the muted, distant laughter of the children. Upstairs in Darlene's bedroom, a Madonna tape blasted out suggestive lyrics in a thrumming rhythm. But all Jessica could think of was the delicious feel of her body pressed up against Luke. Of his lips nuzzling her neck, whispering sweet, sinful things.

Like magic, his fingers slid up under the back of her T-shirt and deftly, with a mere flick, released the catch on her bra. She pulled back to protest, or was she arching her back in invitation? It must have been the latter, because it felt so right when his big hands moved around to the front and cupped her breasts high, from underneath, so that his mouth could take first one aching nipple, then the other through the thin fabric, and suckle deeply.

Her legs trembled all the way down to her wobbly ankles, but he held her firmly in place with his powerful thighs. His hands framed her hips, then moved in a wide caress to palm her bare buttocks.

My bare buttocks!

When had the brute unbuttoned her jeans and pulled down the zipper? When had he slipped his devious hands inside the back of her panties?

Had she lost her mind completely, letting herself be seduced by a too smooth Brad Pitt clone? Had the Christmas Curse totally blindsided her this year?

She tore her lips from his.

Chest heaving, Luke looked down at the precious woman in his arms, who was stiffening with resistance by the minute. His foggy brain fought through the blistering arousal that consumed and disoriented him.

"No," Jessie said in a small voice, but her fingers still dug into his shoulders. Luke also noticed the sexual glaze that misted her honey eyes and the deep pants that came from her parted, kiss-swollen lips.

He hadn't lost her yet.

Wrapping his arms tightly around her waist, he walked her to the opposite counter, sitting her rump on the edge. Before she could blink, or even think of saying "no," he swept her jeans and panties down her parted legs and pulled them off her sneakered feet, which dangled a foot from the floor.

She looked down at herself, naked from navel to calves, with obvious incredulity. Before she could bolt, Luke tilted her chin upward and held her eyes in a coaxing caress. He fished a foil packet from the back pocket of his jeans just before dropping them and his boxers to the floor.

"Please," he whispered and guided her hand to him.

She didn't resist. Instead, in a daze, she ran her fingertips over him lightly, in awe, before taking him in both hands.

He closed his eyes as an explosion of bright lights went off in his head. When his pulse slowed down to breakneck speed, he gently grasped her hands and placed them on his shoulders.

"We shouldn't," she said softly, even as she pulled him closer and spread her legs wider in welcome.

"We should," he insisted, nipping her neck and looping his hands under her knees, dragging her tush even farther out on the edge of the counter.

"I'll be sorry later . . . you'll be sorry," she moaned, and wrapped her legs around his waist.

"No . . . never," he grunted as he eased himself into her tightness. She clenched him spasmodically, and he feared he'd come, way too soon. For long, long moments, forehead to forehead, imbedded fully, he waited out her first orgasm.

When she sighed, finally, he smiled and pulled away to examine her blushing face.

"Oh, Jessie, I love you."

Her face paled with shock.

He hadn't meant to say the words yet. They just came out.

"No. No, you don't. You're just like all men. You think you need to say . . . o-o-oh!"

To stifle her protests, he'd pulled out, then stroked back in. Once, twice, three excruciating times.

"I love you, Jessie. Believe that." This time when he filled her, he twisted his hips, side to side.

She began to keen with the beginning of another climax, but he wanted to slow her down. "Look at us," he urged her. Her half-lidded eyes moved in the direction he pointed, and widened with the same wonder he felt. Highlighted by the winter sunshine streaking through the single window in the pantry, fine red curls blended with his dark, crisp pubic hairs where they were joined, creating an erotic picture, like silken threads in a tapestry.

A tear slipped down her cheek. "We're beautiful together," she whispered.

"Yes," he agreed thickly, and allowed himself to succumb to the overpowering need he had for her. This time when he withdrew and plunged into her, she rippled around him. And each time he stroked, and stroked, and stroked, he repeated, "I love you."

She no longer protested his love words. Maybe she believed him now. Then again, maybe she was as swept away as he was by the most explosive orgasm of his life. With blood roaring in his ears, and bells ringing, he reared his head back and cried out his release, pummeling into her one last time.

Jessie shuddered from head to toe and hung onto him fiercely, crying out, "Oh, oh, oh, oh, oh, oh. . . ."

Even when the racking shudders no longer shook them both, Luke still heard bells ringing. He had to give himself a mental pat on the back. When he'd planned *wild sex*, he'd never imagined that it would happen so soon or that it would be as spectacular as what he'd just experienced . . . bell-ringing and all that. He must be even better than he'd always thought.

"Oh, my God! It's Aunt Clara," Jessie said with horror.

"What about Aunt Clara?" he said, bemused, giving her luscious lips a quick kiss as he eased himself out of her body.

His first clue that he was in big trouble came when she punched him in the stomach, just before she slid to the floor and jerked on her panties and jeans.

"Ooomph!" he said in delayed reaction to her punch, although it didn't really hurt. "Why'd you do that?" He decided to pull up his own pants, as well. Odds were against a repeat performance anytime soon.

"Because you seduced me, you creep. Because you made love to me in Aunt Clara's pantry, for heaven's sake. Because Aunt Clara's bell has been ringing for-ever, and I've been down here engaging in a world-class wall-banger."

Well, at least she has the good taste to recognize world class when it hits her like a ton of testosterone. Then, *so that's what the bell ringing was?* But he didn't voice his thoughts. Instead, he remarked, "I wasn't the one who dragged you into the pantry by the hair looking for wild sex. You seduced me, babe, not the other way around. Not that I wasn't willing."

He reached for her and she slapped his hands away.

"Wild sex! That's what you mentioned when we came in here. Yes, you did, you said something about wild sex just before you kissed me. I heard you. Don't deny it. You deliberately seduced me."

"Whatever." He was in too good a mood to argue. "When can we get married? I mean, will you marry me?" *Oh, boy, I'm getting this love stuff all out of order. Probably because I'm horny again. Just looking at all that wild red hair makes me hot. I wonder what she'd think if I suggested . . . oh, boy. Slow down.* "Jessie, honey," he started over, "I love you. Will you marry me? Tomorrow. Or the day after that?" *And can we go have wild sex again? Now? Maybe in that antique bath-tub on the third floor.*

"Love? Love?" she sputtered. "You are driving with two bricks short of a full load. And stop leering at me. You're not touching me again."

Wanna bet? "Leering? I don't leer, babe. That look you see in my eye is a promise." He jiggled his eye-brows at her and reached around to unlock the door. Aunt Clara's bell was jingling to beat the band.

No sooner did he open the door than he saw Willie,

openly eavesdropping. Willie took in the appearance of both of them, then did a little victory dance, karate style, around the kitchen.

"Oh, Lord!" Jessie said and scooted away, down the hall and toward Aunt Clara's incessant bell-ringing.

He looked at the freckle-faced twit and knew that Jessie had deliberately abandoned him to the adolescent Bruce Lee. Probably her idea of just punishment.

"So, did you boink Aunt Jessie in the pantry?" the kid asked unabashedly.

Luke looked down to make sure he hadn't left his zipper undone. Everything was in order. He sliced a glare at the curious boy, warning, "Willie, that's enough."

He started down the hall, following in Jessie's tracks, but Willie bird-dogged right after him, throwing in a few side kicks and an occasional grunt of "Uut" along the way.

"I need a bong pole. How big is yours?"

Luke's step faltered.

"Will you help me make one out of Aunt Clara's broom? A bong pole's supposed to equal your height, but I think a broom handle will do for me. Don't you? Huh? Willya help me? Huh?"

"No." Luke was already climbing the stairs, and Willie padded after him doggedly. No, that padding sound was Fred. Somehow they'd picked up Fred along the way.

"No?" There was a long silence following his disappointed question, and Luke walked down the second floor hall toward a bedroom where he heard voices. He'd thought he lost the kid until Willie asked, "How old were you the first time you did *it* to a girl?"

Luke stopped suddenly, and Willie and the dog ran into him with a yelp and a bark.

"Listen, Willie," he said, hunkering down. "You can't ask those kinds of questions of complete strangers."

Willie's face and big ears flushed bright red and his eyes filled with tears. "I don't feel like you're a stranger."

And Luke felt like a rat. Hell, the kid was asking a normal question for a boy his age. But usually it was addressed to a parent . . . a dad. Which Willie didn't have.

"Okay," he said, taking a deep breath and wondering how he'd gotten himself into this predicament. "I was fourteen the first time."

"Fourteen! Fourteen!"

Luke stood, laughing, and rumpled the boy's hair as he continued toward Aunt Clara's bedroom. He heard Willie mutter as he skipped back down the stairs, "Did you hear that, Fred? Fourteen! Uncle Luke musta been retarded or somethin'. Guess lookin' like Brad Pitt doesn't mean everything."

Aunt Clara took one look at him when he entered the bedroom and exclaimed, "Thank the Lord! He sent me a miracle."

Luke cast Jessie a knowing smirk that said clearly, "See, I am so a Christmas Miracle."

Jessie was sitting on a straight-backed chair next to the bed, talking to a sixtyish gray-haired woman with one leg encased in a white cast from toe to thigh.

"Aunt Clara, this is Lucas Carter, the man I told you

about who helped me last night when the van got stuck in the snow."

Luke arched a brow at Jessie as he moved around to the other side of the bed. *Lying to a nun now, are you, Jessie? Tsk-tsk!* He leaned down and ignored the hand Aunt Clara extended to him, giving her parchment cheek a light kiss.

It was the right thing to do, he could tell immediately. She literally glowed as she took his right hand in both of hers and drew him down to sit on her bed. "I'm so pleased to meet you, Aunt Clara . . . I hope you don't mind my calling you Aunt Clara . . . I feel as if I know you already."

"Of course not, my boy." Still holding his hand, she studied him intently before nodding, as if answering one of her own silent questions. "So, Darlene tells me that you plan on marrying my sweet girl, Jessie."

Jessie gasped and turned greenish. Probably all that fruitcake she'd consumed.

"Yes. Yes, I do," he said firmly before Jessie could say different. "Jessie doesn't think I'm serious, but I am."

"I am *not* going to marry him," Jessie told Aunt Clara when she finally regained her voice. "We hardly know each other." With that, she shot Luke a glare, daring him to contradict her. At the same time, her face turned from green to a pretty shade of pink—a nice contrast to all those unruly red ringlets—as she remembered just how well they did know each other.

"Well, I don't know if the length of time two people know each other is a true indicator of feelings," Aunt Clara opined.

I love this old bird. "Right," Luke intervened quickly.

"Look how long she knew Burp, and they were a mismatch from the get-go. Why, he even played"—he made an exaggerated shiver of distaste—"golf."

"His name is Burt," Jessie stormed.

Aunt Clara snickered behind her fingers.

"And you and I are the mismatch," Jessica railed. "Geez, Brad Pitt and Little Orphan Annie!"

"Who's Brad Pitt?" Aunt Clara asked.

Luke and Jessie both gaped at her, wondering what world she'd been living in the past few years.

"I'd like to get married real soon," Luke went on, ignoring Jessie's hiss of warning. "How soon do you think it will be before you're out of that cast, Aunt Clara?"

"Well, the doctor said I could have a soft cast next week," she said tentatively.

"Gol-ly," he said contemplatively, tapping his chin. "I don't know if I can wait that long." He turned to an outraged Jessie. "What do you think, honey? Can you wait for a whole week?"

"Lucas, I just knew when I saw you walk through that door that you were the answer to my prayers," Aunt Clara said, smiling at him.

He'd like to be the answer to someone's prayers, although not a nun's. But Jessie didn't look much like she was in the mood for praying. In fact, her eyes were crossed. Someone ought to tell her about faces freezing and stuff. Perhaps he should call Willie.

"You are the worst Christmas Curse I've ever had," Jessie gritted out at him.

Aunt Clara gasped at her harsh words, and Luke felt a little twinge of hurt, as well.

"Jessica Jones, what an awful thing to say! I brought

you up better than that." Then Aunt Clara's frown melted away as she confided in a softer voice, "I was praying this morning for a Christmas Miracle. Who are we to question the answer God gives us? A miracle is a miracle."

Aunt Clara and Jessie looked at him then—him, the miracle.

Aunt Clara beamed.

Jessie's honey eyes threw sparks of disbelief.

Luke wondered how soon till he could have wild sex again.

Chapter Five

Later that afternoon, they were all in the living room, decorating a huge blue spruce tree that Luke and the kids had dragged in from the woods behind the house. Christmas carols played on the radio in the background, interrupted repeatedly by storm warnings.

Aunt Clara was reclining on the sofa in front of the fireplace where Luke had carried her two hours ago. She gave them gentle instructions as to which ornament went where while her knitting needles clicked away at one of her perpetual afghans.

"Are you still mad at me, honey?" Luke said close to Jessica's ear, causing her to jump about two feet.

"Criminey, do you have to sneak up on me all the time?" she snapped.

She'd been avoiding the rascal all day, along with his knowing looks, his disarming smiles, and "accidental" touches. Luke had laughed, and stalked her just the same.

She couldn't believe she'd actually made love with a man she'd met the night before. She hadn't been thinking. It had happened too soon. It shouldn't have happened at all.

She had to get rid of the tempting hunk soon or lose her sanity. Or something worse. Her heart.

"What do you call a nun with one leg?" he asked with a glimmer of humor in his flashing eyes, slanting a glance at Aunt Clara to make sure she didn't overhear.

A joke? She tried to look at him disapprovingly.

"Hopalong Chastity."

She giggled reluctantly, and Luke used that opportunity to put an arm around her shoulder and squeeze her close.

Despite the trill of excitement engendered by that slight embrace, she ducked and escaped, putting several feet between them.

He chuckled.

"Maybe you can still leave tonight . . . if the roads get cleared," she suggested.

Why did her heart constrict at the possibility? He'd have to leave sometime. If not tonight, then tomorrow. Everyone she'd ever loved left eventually. He would, too.

Not that I love him.

And there he went again, looking at her with such hurt, and longing, in his beautiful eyes. He did it every time she rebuffed him.

It's not as if he really loves me.

But what if he did?

"No way!" Willie protested. "Uncle Luke can't leave tonight. He's makin' Philadelphia cheese steaks for dinner."

That was another thing that made Jessie mad. No one would eat her peanut butter sandwiches. They were scarfing down all the junk food Luke had bought, including minute steaks and rolls for a Christmas Eve dinner. He must have spent a hundred dollars in that Uni-Mart.

And Aunt Clara wasn't even protesting that they would miss *Vilia*, the traditional Slovak Christmas Eve dinner she always prepared, where everyone must taste at least twelve of the many dishes assembled, presumably in honor of the twelve apostles. The merry meal always included, at the least, the core items of *oplatky*, the Christmas communion wafers dipped in honey; *bobalky*, braided homemade bread; red wine; *pierogies*, the little cheese-stuffed pies; several kinds of fish; mushroom soup; poppyseed rolls; sauerkraut; nuts; and fresh fruit.

Well, she had to give Luke credit. In the spirit of improvisation, he was putting together a new-age *Villa* supper, complete with Philadelphia cheese steaks, Frosted Flakes, Fruit Loops, peanut butter and jelly sandwiches, Hawaiian Punch, and fruitcake, of course. And everyone—all the kids and Aunt Clara—acted as if everything was hunky-dory.

Was she the only one worried to death about the Christmas Curse, and the kind of holiday disaster that loomed this year?

"You can't make Uncle Luke leave. He's gonna show me how to dance the Philadelphia Stomp later tonight," Kajeeta said, interrupting Jessica's dismal thoughts. Kajeeta peered up shyly at Luke for confirmation.

"Yep," he told Kajeeta, and then caught Jessica's skeptical frown. "And if you're real good, sugar, I'll do the two-step with you." He winked suggestively and whispered *sotto voce*, "Re-e-eal slow. After the kids have gone to sleep."

"In your dreams!" she said haughtily. But already he'd planted some tantalizing pictures in her mind. The Christmas-tree lights flickering in the darkened room, fireplace roaring, soft music . . . *Get a grip, girl*.

"And Luke said he would French braid my hair," Darlene added, having just condescended to join the group.

Everyone gawked at Luke, astounded.

He shrugged with a sheepish grin. "Hey, my sister Ellie made me do her hair when we were kids. She was bigger than me *then*, and considered me her personal slave."

Everyone laughed at the image of Luke being forced by his sister to be her slave.

"Aunt Jessie, you oughta hang onto this guy," Henry added in the end. "He's a lot better than that Burp fellow you brought here last year."

She started to tell Henry that his name was not Burp, but all the kids were having such a good time. And besides, the name Burp suited the jerk much better than Burt, anyhow. So she joined in the good-natured ribbing.

"Tell us about your work," Aunt Clara asked Luke, her nimble fingers moving the knitting needles in an intricate pattern as she spoke.

Luke was on a ladder putting a star atop the tall tree.

"Yeah, did you ever bodyguard anyone famous?" Henry asked as he helped to brace the shaky ladder.

"Sure. All the time," Luke answered, tilting his head this way and that until he positioned the star just right. "Even Bill Gates one time," he told a flabbergasted Henry as he descended the ladder and folded it, preparing to take it out to the kitchen. "He hired me and four other guys to accompany him to Japan. It was a time when there was a lot of anti-American sentiment there."

Henry was gazing at Luke as if he were God.

"And I just came back yesterday afternoon from working a Janet Jackson concert at the Spectrum in South Philly," he told a *very* impressed Kajeeta as he passed en route to the kitchen.

When he reentered the living room, all the kids jumped on him with eager questions.

"Do you *really* know Janet Jackson?" Kajeeta wanted to know.

"Well, I wouldn't say we're friends. But, yes, I've met her and worked for her."

"How about movie stars?" Darlene asked.

"Yep. Lots of movie stars, like Bruce Willis, Sharon Stone, Antonio Banderas, Kim Basinger. And rock stars. Once I guarded Madonna . . . now, that was a trip," he recalled with amusement. "Even Michael Jackson, though he usually has his own private security team."

"Did you ever bodyguard Chuck Norris?" Willie wanted to know.

Luke shook his head negatively. "Mostly I work for

politicians—those who aren't high up enough to qualify for CIA protection, and corporate bigwigs traveling in third world countries."

"Wow!" the kids sighed.

Luke addressed Aunt Clara then, seeming to give her a special silent message. "Once I even guarded Mother Teresa."

"O-o-oh, Luke," Aunt Clara breathed. Her simple words said loud and clear that she thought Luke was the answer to her Christmas prayers . . . sent special delivery by God, via Mother Teresa, no doubt.

Jessie felt the happiness and Christmas spirit swell around her, filling the room, but it was a sham. Because these kids still believed . . . perhaps not in Santa Claus . . . but in miracles. And there was going to be no miracle when they came downstairs tomorrow and found no gifts.

"Stop worrying, Jessica," Aunt Clara said softly with uncanny perception, sensing her distress. "For once in your life, trust. Especially at Christmas time, let yourself believe that good things can just happen."

"Hah! The only thing that ever happens to me at Christmas time is my Christmas Curse," Jessie grumbled.

"Now, Jessica, I have never believed that nonsense."

Henry distracted Aunt Clara then, wanting her advice on some tinsel that had become tangled.

"Have some more fruitcake," Luke urged, pressing a too-big hunk against Jessie's mouth. Lord, the man must be part Indian the way he crept up on her unawares all the time.

"I don't want any more. I hate fruitcake. And I'm not hungry," she insisted, which gave Luke the opportunity to shove the huge morsel in her open mouth. "Glmph."

He kept his fingertips on her lips an intimate second too long, and his smoldering eyes told her he had a hunger of an entirely different kind. Leaning close, he whispered, "Are you ready for some more wild sex?"

She chewed quickly so she could answer him, but he laughed again and moved away.

Willie ambled up with a calculating gleam in his eyes. "So tell me, Aunt Jessie. How old were you when you lost your virginity? Uncle Luke was fourteen."

She began to choke as the blasted fruitcake went down the wrong throat passage. When she finally recovered, after drinking a glass of Hawaiian Punch—another of Luke's purchases—her gaze shot across the room.

Luke threw his hands out hopelessly.

Meanwhile, Willie karate-chopped a fruitcake in half.

Jessica couldn't remember when the Christmas Curse had ever been so bad.

It was close to midnight before all the kids were nestled in their beds. Aunt Clara had retired soon after their absolutely wonderful Christmas Eve dinner—the best any of them had ever experienced. Jessica was about to call it a night herself, but first she had to take Fred out for one last nature call.

"I'll take him," Luke offered, coming down the hall from the kitchen where he'd just gone to put away the last of the leftovers and turn out the lights. "I need to make a few more phone calls."

"Thanks. I'm really beat." Then his words sank in. "Telephone calls?"

"Yeah, I have a cellular phone in my car," he admitted.

She was too tired to be angry with him anymore. "You rat," was the best she could come up with.

"Hey, I have to have a cellular phone in the car at all times, in case of emergency. The nature of my business, you know. Besides, I had to call my sister Ellie to go get my laundry from the laundromat, didn't I? Did you really think I would have gone with you so willingly if I knew I was losing a couple hundred dollars' worth of clothes?"

Jessica wasn't sure what she'd been thinking at the time. Or if she'd been thinking at all.

More important, Luke looked really worried now as he pulled on his jacket with Fred running circles of anticipation around his legs.

"What's wrong?"

"Jessie, I thought I was going to be able to pull off a Christmas surprise for you. I called my sister earlier today, like I said, and . . . well, a few other people. But even with the storm finally stopping tonight, I just don't think I'll be able to get any gifts here by tomorrow morning with the roads the way they are. It looks like there really won't be any gifts when the kids wake up. I'm sorry."

Tears welled in her eyes, and her throat closed over. "Oh, Luke. You did that for these kids?"

"No, Jessie, I did it for you," he said, stepping closer.

She'd been skittish all day every time Luke got near her, but now she opened her arms for him and hugged

175

him warmly. "Thank you. No one's ever done anything so nice for me before."

He smelled like wood smoke from the fireplace, and evergreen boughs, and fruitcake. She smiled against his neck—the brute smelled like fruitcake. And she was developing a compelling taste for fruitcake, darn it!

He pulled back slightly. The fingertips of one hand brushed some unruly ringlets off her cheek, then trailed down to her throat, resting lightly on the pulse point. He gazed at her somberly as his head descended . . . one infinitesimal inch at a time. She angled her lips to meet his kiss.

Unlike their earlier, frenzied touches, Luke acted as if he had all the time in the world now. Gently, gently he laid his lips on hers, exploring, coaxing.

All of Jessica's senses heightened. She felt the heat of Luke's body. She heard a Mormon Tabernacle Choir rendition of "Silent Night" on the radio in the background, more beautiful than the highest heavenly hosts. The fire crackled a seductive lure. The glittering lights on the tree outshone the very stars in the night sky.

Jessica never knew a kiss could be so expressive. And there was no doubt in her mind that Luke was using this gentle kiss to convey all the emotion she refused to recognize. With its shifting, changing textures, its feathery pressures and strokes, Luke's kiss perfected all the nuances that a man's lips could wield on a woman.

He's showing me that he loves me.

Jessica scrunched her eyes closed tight at the wonder of it all.

And, God help me, I love him, too.

Cupping her face in both hands, Luke looked her fully in the eyes. The dog practically crossed its legs, yipping near their feet. "Wait for me, Jessie. We need to talk."

She nodded, too benumbed to speak.

"I'll be right back," he said huskily over his shoulder.

His hand was on the doorknob when a car horn blasted loudly, coming up the drive. Luke turned to her in question.

She shrugged, unknowing.

They both stood on the porch, shivering, watching the red car come barreling up the drive at breakneck speed, way too fast for the snowy conditions. It fishtailed in the turn-around area before the steps.

"Oh, this is too much!" Jessica exclaimed as a tall, lean teenager in a black leather jacket and cowboy boots emerged from the driver's side, grinning smugly.

"Is it . . ." Luke began to ask; ". . . could it be . . . ?"

"Julio."

"*Feliz Navidad*, everyone," the witless kid called out, as if he hadn't disrupted the lives of a whole bunch of people . . . in fact, ruined their Christmas. Jessica clenched her fists at her sides, counting to ten before she ripped him limb from limb.

That's when Luke tugged on her sleeve, pointing incredulously at the armloads of gaily wrapped packages Julio was grabbing from the back seat of Jessica's car.

"I'm gonna kill him," she gritted out.

Luke wrapped both arms around her from behind,

locking her in place. "Slow down. Give him a chance to explain. Then let me kill him."

"Hi, Aunt Jessie," Julio said breezily as he walked by them, big as you please. "Don't just stand there like an icicle. Bring some packages in."

"Now, Jessie. Now, Jessie," Luke cautioned, "he's only a kid."

As Luke dragged her by the hand down to the car and started loading packages in her arms, she pointed out, "That *kid* let me think I was carrying an empty pistol. That *kid* stole my purse and"—she glanced at the dozens of gifts piled in the back seat—"oh, damn, he must have maxed out my credit cards."

Julio was back, beaming up at both of them as if he were a teenage Hispanic Santa Claus. "I did good, didn't I, Aunt Jessie?"

Luke jammed a package on top of the pile in her arms, blocking her face before she could answer.

"I even got a laptop computer for Henry. Boy, are those things expensive. You really should get a larger maximum on your Visa card, you know."

Jessica walked stiffly into the house, counting to ten, then twenty, trying to avoid her inevitable explosion. Behind her, she heard Julio ask Luke, "Who are you? Aunt Jessie's new boyfriend? Man, I hope you're better than that dweeb she was shakin' the sheets with before. Think his name was Burp."

"I think I'm gonna like you, Julio," Luke chortled. "What'd you get for Kajeeta?"

They'd entered the living room and were arranging the gifts under the tree.

"Ballet and tap shoes. And dance tights. But, man oh man, was it hard to find them things in an extra-large chunky size! I got Willie a bong pole, one of those stupid karate pajama outfits, and a Ninja turtle tape. And I bought that bad-ass Darlene a Walkman and a big carry-case of Revlon makeups. Now she can be a high-class slut instead of a low-class bad girl." He grinned at Luke, then fake-punched him in the arm to show he was teasing.

Then Julio added the topper. "Hey, anyone ever tell you that you look a little bit like Brad Pitt . . . except older?"

Jessica did laugh then. The whole situation was so ridiculous. But there would be a Christmas after all. She was still angry with Julio—furious actually—but he'd delivered their Christmas miracle. And for that she had to be thankful. So she couldn't kill the messenger tonight, but tomorrow, *tomorrow* she would give him holy hell.

"I'm starved. I don't know how women do it. Shoppin' their booties off all the time. Man, it wipes a guy out. Is there anything to eat?"

"Fruitcake," she and Luke said at the same time.

A short time later, Jessica exited the bathroom and was shuffling along in her furry bunny slippers and flannel nightgown toward her bedroom. The house was silent now, except for the occasional creak of its aged "bones" and the whistling wind outside. Pleasantly exhausted, she mused that it had been one of the best Christmas Eves of her life, despite that misguided brat, Julio. And she had Luke to thank for it all.

So she shouldn't have been surprised when she opened her bedroom door to see him lying on her bed.

The light of the bedside lamp reflected on his sensually posed, half-reclining body propped against the headboard with two pillows, arms folded behind his neck.

Shirtless and barefooted.

Wearing a pair of jeans that were already enticingly unbuttoned at the top.

Every hormone in her body began to tango.

"Luke," she squeaked out, "you can't come in here. Aunt Clara's in the next room."

"So I guess you'll have to be extra quiet when you—"

"Don't say it," she hissed.

"Nice slippers," he remarked as she stomped closer. Then he gave her voluminous nightgown a sweeping assessment. "Sexy negligee, too."

"Oh, get out of here."

"What? You don't want my Christmas present?" He held out a small package wrapped in Frosty the Snowman paper.

She eyed the gift suspiciously, trying hard not to notice the corded sinews ridging his extended arms, the hard tendons ridging his abdomen, the bulge ridging his . . .

Luke chuckled, and she averted her blushing face, taking the gift he tossed into her hands. He was sitting up now, watching her intently.

"God, I love your hair," he said in a husky voice.

She put a hand to the unmanageable curls, which she hated, and her knees felt weak and buttery under his hungry gaze.

"Can I brush it? *Later?*"

Her knees did buckle then. She had to hold on to the bedpost for support.

"Open your gift, Jessie," he urged.

"But I didn't buy you anything," she said with a moue of embarrassment.

"No problem! This gift's for both of us." A twinkle of mischief, not to mention dark, hard-core arousal, in his deep hazel eyes turned her suddenly alert.

That's when she began to suspect what the rogue had given her. A flutter of excitement teased across her skin as she unpeeled the paper. "Oh!" She put the tips of one hand to her parted lips as she gaped, open-mouthed, at her gift.

The bottle of skin-warming oil.

Chapter Six

"Oh, my!" she gasped, the bottle feeling sinfully hot in her hand.

"I'll second that." He threw his long legs over the side of the bed and stood. Then, boldly holding her eyes, he unzipped his jeans and let them fall to the floor. He wore no underwear. Stepping out of the pant legs, he drawled in a thick, thick voice, "It's peppermint flavored. Do you like peppermint, Jessie?"

She couldn't speak at first, overwhelmed by the beauty of this man . . . this man she'd come to love in such a short time. "I love peppermint," she whispered.

He stood statue-still, five feet away from her, exuding virility. Chiseled bones created stunning curves and planes in his marvelously sculpted face. His hair was clubbed back at the nape, as usual, with a dark rubber band. Not an ounce of excess fat marred his well-toned body, from wide shoulders, to rippled abdomen, to narrow waist and hips, to flat stomach, to . . .

Something primal quickened deep inside her.

. . . to his erection, which stood out in rampant declaration of his need for her . . . his carnal intentions.

Breathlessly she waited for his next move.

There was none. Except for a slight tilt of his head.

And she understood what he wanted.

Jessica was not used to this kind of foreplay. Oh, she'd had lovers before . . . not a lot, but a few. And she'd enjoyed sex some of those times, though the men she'd known were usually the aggressors, and she a docile participant. Willing, but never the seducer. Always the seducee.

Luke was insisting on more from her. Much, much more.

Do I want to make love with him?

Oh, yes!

Do I want to please him?

Definitely!

It would only be this one night.

Of course.

Then he'll leave.

They always do.

One night.

"Jessie," Luke hissed. A single word. Raw and soul-wrenchingly impassioned.

She kicked off her bunny slippers.

He smiled.

She released the ribbon of her ponytail and let her hair spill out over her shoulders and down her back.

He sighed.

Clutching the fabric of her nightgown, she began to draw it slowly upward, exposing first her calves and knees and thighs.

His smoldering eyes followed the hem.

She paused at the juncture of her thighs, took a deep breath to overcome her innate shyness, then drew the nightgown up to her waist.

His lips parted as his eyes locked on that part of her. His ragged breathing was loud and heavy in the silent room.

Licking her dry lips, she gathered courage and pulled the garment the rest of the way upward, over her head.

"Oh, Jessie."

Hunger. His eyes devoured her with a primitive hunger that almost frightened her with its magnitude. His erection was even larger than before, turgid.

He crooked his fingers, coaxing her closer.

She moved halfway.

He closed the distance, still not touching her. Just looking. Then he held a hand out, palm upward, and she realized she still held the warming oil clenched in her hand.

Already, before he'd even touched her, Jessica was fiercely aroused. She didn't know if she could stand to wait. She might splinter apart, way too soon.

Taking the bottle in his hand, he unscrewed the lid and sniffed deeply, grinning at her—a teasing grin of anticipation. Then he winked with wicked promise.

For the first time in her life, Jessica felt like swooning.

Shaking a drop of the slick oil onto his forefinger, he traced her lips, parting them. The pungent odor filled the air, and the flavor of candy canes teased her taste buds. Almost immediately, she forgot about the taste and smell, however, as her lips and tongue grew warm, throbbing with an odd heat.

He kept his body a good foot away from her. When she reached out to embrace him, he shook his head, pressing her arms to her sides. "No, sweetheart. Not yet. I want the sensations to center only on the oil. And the erotic places I touch."

Places? She groaned.

"How does it taste, Jessie?"

"Wonderful."

"How does it feel?"

"Tingly."

He laughed. "Can you feel the heat?"

"Ye-e-es," she breathed.

"Are you sure?" he said, his neck craning forward. "I'd better check." With the tip of his tongue, he traced the outline of her lips, then the seam. "Open for me," he demanded, and, before she'd barely complied, his tongue was filling her mouth, exploring. Stroking, in and out. Stroking. "Ummmm, delicious," he murmured against her, his mouth covering hers wetly.

"I can't stand it," she cried at last as her bones turned to jelly with the intense waves of excitement sweeping from her heated lips to her breasts and downward. Yes, downward.

"Good," he rasped out, and turned her so her back was to him, her head lolling on his right shoulder. His steely erection pressed against the cleft of her buttocks. Gently drawing her hair off her face, he anointed the pulse point at the curve of her neck. When it, too, turned warm, he nipped the spot with his teeth, then soothed the abused skin with slow licks of torture.

She tried to turn. "I want to hold you. I want you to hold me."

"Not yet. Put your hands behind my neck," he urged. Then he sketched an oily line from her armpits to her hips on either side, over to the center where he rotated the tip of his forefinger in her navel, then up through the middle of her body to her collarbone. A hot pulse followed wherever he touched, like a line of ignited dynamite powder. He did the same to the backs of her knees, and the insides of her thighs, even the sensitive arches of her feet.

Next he poured a more generous amount of the fluid on one of his palms and rubbed both palms together. He used the wide, callused surfaces to paint her breasts—under, around, the tops, everywhere but on the aureoles or taut peaks where she wanted the heat most. With a mewling cry, she attempted to guide his hands to the aching nipples, but he resisted, chuckling.

"Come," he said, taking her hand and pulling her to the side of the bed. He seated her on the edge and placed several pillows at her waist, forcing her backward. Her elbows were braced on the bed and her breasts were arched high—a continual vibrating thrum in their warm depths. Then he parted her legs and knelt on the floor between her thighs.

"Luke, no. I don't like this. I feel expos—oh . . . oh!"

Finally he was attending to her nipples, drizzling the warm oil around the aureoles, then over the pebbled points themselves. She let out a soft cry as the area turned immediately hot and pulsing.

"Shhh, babe. Just a little longer," he crooned, leaning forward to take her right breast deep in his mouth, suckling rhythmically, while the palm of his left hand drew wide, pressing circles on her other breast.

She tried to rear up off the bed.

He wouldn't let her.

She tried to buck him away with her hips.

He wouldn't budge.

Then he reversed the positions of his mouth and hand.

And she became a keening mass of quivering arousal. Her skin and nerve endings heightened to the point of ecstatic meltdown. She had no control over her flailing hands and trembling thighs.

In that condition, she was scarcely aware that he'd pulled back and was streaming the erotic oil between her legs.

"Oh, no! No, no, no," she protested as she felt the waves of an overpowering climax began to ripple from her womb, down through that hot channel that he was lubricating with the oil on two fingers. When he lowered his head, still with his fingers inside her, and took the nub in his lips, sucking softly, she gave up the fight.

Tears were streaming down her face.

Luke noticed and stopped, sitting back on his haunches. His lips and fingers were slick from the oil, and her.

"Are those happy tears or sad tears?" he asked with concern.

"Happy tears, you brute."

"Good," he growled, standing, and looped his hands under her thighs, lifting her tush off the bed. Then he bent his knees, entering her with a slow, slow, slow upward stroke.

Before he'd fully penetrated, she climaxed around him with violent spasms of pure, shattering pleasure.

When she finally emerged from her delirium of satisfaction, she lifted her lashes slowly to see Luke still poised above her. Perspiration beaded his upper lip and forehead. A muscle twitched at the side of his compressed lips.

"Kiss me, Luke." She strained her face upward.

With a grunt of sheer male surrender, he lunged into her and brought his mouth down on hers, hard and openmouthed. Then, in a frenzy of movement, he tossed the pillows aside, lifted her hips, and slid her to the middle of the bed.

Jessica tried to caress his shoulders and back, to return his rapacious kisses, but Luke was too out-of-control. His hands and mouth were everywhere, caressing, plucking, sucking, biting, kissing, pressing, pinching, licking.

And her body, which should have been confused by all these conflicting messages, filled with the sweetest burn in the world, overflowing with liquid pleasure which moved closer and closer to the boiling point.

Abruptly, he stopped.

Panting for breath, he rolled them on to their sides, and lifted her topmost leg onto his hip. Unbelievably, he filled her even more completely.

"Jessie," he gasped out, waiting till her lashes fluttered open. When he had her full attention, he whispered, "Can you feel my love flowing? From here"—he pressed a palm against his chest—"down to here?"—he touched the place where they were joined, and Jessica almost exploded with utter ecstasy. "And up inside you"—he moved out and then in for emphasis—"to here?"—he breathed, resting his fingertips against her heart."

"Oh, Luke, don't spoil this by speaking of love. I don't need the words. Really." She tried to kiss him into silence.

He tore his mouth away angrily. "It's love, Jessie. Even if you won't admit it."

Then, with an efficient movement, he rolled over and she was on top of him, straddling his hips.

"If you can't say the words, show me, Jessie," he coaxed. "Love me with your body."

And she did. Oh, how she did!

Jessica hadn't known she had the expertise to make a grown man cry for mercy.

She did.

Jessica hadn't known a woman could climax, over and over, and still want more.

She did.

Jessica hadn't known there were so many erotic points on a man's or a woman's body.

She did now.

Jessica hadn't known a man could control his impending orgasm so stoically.

Oh, boy, did she know now.

Despite her protests, Luke kept repeating, "I love you. I love you. I love you . . ."

She never said the words, but her body did. And, for Luke, that seemed to be enough for now.

Later, but not so much later, they lay under Aunt Clara's handmade quilt, caressing each other softly. Luke gazed down at Jessica and considered himself the luckiest man alive. How had this magic landed in his lap? What miraculous power had put him in the same place as Jessie last night?

He clutched her tighter, overcome with emotion, and whispered soft words of endearment. Jessie whispered back. Nice words. Complimentary words, though not the ones Luke wanted to hear.

His heart tightened painfully, but he forced himself not to become grim. He knew she loved him, and he understood his Little Orphan Jessie a whole lot better now. Her insecurities. Her fears. Her Christmas Curse, he thought with a silent laugh.

He could wait.

A woman like her would need proof of a man's staying power—and he didn't mean that in the sexual sense. He was staying, for good, no matter what she thought.

For now, he had other things on his mind.

Putting a forefinger under her chin, he tilted her face upward. Immediately, he saw the wariness in her honey eyes. She thought he was going to pressure her on the love, and marriage, issues.

"So how do you feel about peppermint sticks?" he asked.

"What?" she asked with suspicion.

"Peppermint sticks. Do you like to . . . lick them?"

"Sure, but I don't understand—"

He kicked the quilt off, looking pointedly at his up-raised "stick," then over to the bedside table where the bottle of peppermint warming oil stood in waiting.

They both laughed then.

But not for long.

* * *

"Why do you and Uncle Luke smell like candy canes?" Willie asked Jessie the next morning, peering up for the first time in an hour from his Ninja turtle tape. Scraps of Christmas wrapping paper surrounded him and were scattered across the living room.

"Who has candy canes? I want a candy cane," Kajeeta whined as she pirouetted across the room in her new flame-red tights.

Even from across the room, Luke saw a rush of pink stain Jessie cheeks. And her eyes—her soulful eyes—met his reluctantly, then darted away in embarrassment.

Was she embarrassed by Willie's impudent question, or about the incredible things they'd done to each other last night?

He'd left Jessie's bed near dawn, not wanting her to be caught in a compromising situation by any unexpected visitors. She'd been asleep when he slipped out, and he hadn't talked to her in private since then. Surely she didn't take his considerate departure as a mark of abandonment.

He felt hurt by the distance she was putting between them. Last night was special. To them both. He wanted to shout his love aloud . . . to the kids, to Aunt Clara, to Jessie. He wanted to hold hands. To kiss under the mistletoe. To hug. And make plans.

But she was as skittish now as a cat on a hot tin roof.

"Candy canes! Oh, you dweeb!" Julio snorted to Willie, pulling Luke back to the present. Julio was sitting on an easy chair with his feet propped on a hassock, basking in the glow of his benevolent charity, albeit at Jessie's expense. "It's probably skin warming oil, like they sell in porno shops," Julio explained.

"Porno shops?" Willie inquired.

Everyone turned to look in question, first at Jessie, then him. Luckily, Aunt Clara was in the kitchen having a cup of tea.

Before he and Jessie had a chance to turn crimson with telling humiliation, Darlene piped in, "Julio, you are such a jerk. You think you're so hot. You think you know everything. You think—"

"Hah! I know a slut when I see one."

"Eff off!"

Julio flicked a middle finger at her.

"That's enough!" Luke roared. Really, someone needed to lay down the law with these kids. They all looked chastened as he continued to glare at them, hands on hips. Eventually they grumbled and went back to examining the Christmas gifts that Julio-Santa had brought them.

At least attention had been diverted away from him and Jessie.

That is, until Willie peered up from his tape once again and asked Luke, "Do you wear a jock strap when you practice karate?"

Luke couldn't speak. Only a gurgling sound came out.

"Gawd!" Henry said and left the room.

"I know what a jock strap is," Kajeeta exclaimed with glee in the middle of an amazing pirouette.

Even Darlene blushed.

"A blush from you, Dar-lene-ey," Julio teased. "Well, wonders never cease."

It was obvious to Luke, if not to anyone else, that

Julio had a crush on Darlene. This continual baiting was his juvenile way of showing it.

Darlene was sputtering unintelligible words about cutting out Julio's tongue and sticking it someplace unmentionable.

Jessie fled to the kitchen, muttering something about helping Aunt Clara with the breakfast dishes. The coward! They'd eaten fruitcake and leftover cheese steaks on paper plates.

Well, she wasn't going to escape from him this time. Perhaps he needed a little help, though.

"Oh, Wil-lie," Luke said in a sugary, coaxing voice. "How'd you like to do me a *big* favor."

Early that afternoon, the house had settled down to a peaceful hum, and Jessica retreated to the kitchen where she was singing "Silent Night" under her breath while puttering around with preparations for Christmas dinner. Julio, God bless him, had purchased an already prepared roasted turkey dinner for ten from a supermarket. It had cost him . . . *her* . . . a hundred bucks.

Jessica planned to take every dollar out of his hide, but not today.

A wonderful peacefulness enveloped Jessica. A feeling of family. Darlene was sitting under the tree playing some of her new CD's on a disc player "Santa" had brought. Henry was teaching Willie how to play a computer game. Kajeeta was watching *A Christmas Carol* on TV with Luke. Aunt Clara was upstairs taking a nap.

If only things could stay this way.

"Aunt Jessie," Willie said, padding into the kitchen

193

barefooted, wearing his new white karate outfit. "Can I ask you something . . . um . . . personal?"

Uh-oh. Jessica looked at the red-haired imp and groaned inwardly. There was a suspicious twinkle in his eyes.

"Do girls like guys who do karate? I mean, does it turn them on?"

"Wh-what?" she stammered, backing away from him and looking around blindly for a quick exit or somewhere to hide.

"I know that girls like football players. And wrestlers. But what about karate guys?"

Oh, God! "Willie, why don't you go ask Julio, or Uncle Luke?" She made a couple of crablike sidesteps, hoping she could make it to the hallway leading to the front door before having to answer.

"Julio's the one that told me to start doing karate. Either that or get a tattoo."

"A . . . a tattoo?"

Willie shuffled around, inadvertently blocking her route to the hall. "And I asked Uncle Luke about this girls and karate and sex stuff, but he told me to come ask you."

"Oh, he did, did he?"

"Yep. How's a guy supposed to know what turns a girl's crank? I mean, really, Aunt Jessie, guys like just about anything, but girls are different. Aren't they? Huh? Aren't they?" He was pressing closer, gazing up at her with wide-eyed innocence. Still, there was that suspicious twinkle in his eyes, too.

How could she answer such questions? "Uh, I'm busy right now, Willie. Come back later. I'll tell you then," she promised. And, gutless wimp that she was, she dashed into the pantry.

To her shock, she heard the door close behind her and the lock click from the other side, followed by the sound of Willie's snickering. That shock was followed immediately by another as she discovered the rat who'd planted the cheese—Willie—in her path, diverting her toward this very spot.

Luke stood leaning against the window on the far wall of the narrow pantry. If this was intended to be a joke, he wasn't laughing.

"So tell me, Jessie, what does turn a girl's crank?"

Chapter Seven

"What's going on?" she said shrilly, twisting the knob unsuccessfully.

"You tell me, Jessie. What the hell's going on?"

"I . . . I don't know what you mean." She knew exactly what he meant. She'd been dodging him all morning, ever since she'd awakened, alone, in her bed.

Oh, she didn't blame him for leaving. He'd probably been concerned about her reputation with the kids and Aunt Clara. Still, his leaving had reminded her that he would leave eventually, and she couldn't allow herself to get too attached.

Last night had been wonderful. End of story.

Stepping away from the window, Luke moved closer to her. Bright sunlight reflected off his brown hair, giving it golden highlights. He wore a crisp, pure white T-shirt of Julio's tucked into faded jeans.

And already she felt warm and tingly. It was probably the aftereffects of the warming oil.

"You know, Jessie, when you look at me, your eyes give you away."

She lowered her lashes.

He laughed mirthlessly and tickled her under the chin.

Her head jerked up. How had he discovered that that tiny section of skin was a particularly sensitive spot on her body? *Hah! He knows that and a whole lot more about my body.*

He braced his arms on either side of her head. There was a touch of anger in his clenched jaw, as well as hurt in his hazel eyes, which glittered more gray than green today. Stormy.

"What gives, Jessie?" he gritted out. "Tell me what's going through that quirky mind of yours."

"Luke, let me go. Let's go outside. Then we'll talk." The pantry was very small, no bigger than a walk-in closet. Too intimate. She could smell a hint of coffee on his breath. She could feel the heat of his body. She could imagine a whole lot more.

"Why can't we talk here?" He cocked his head, then a slow grin spread across his face. "Do I make you nervous?"

"No, but . . . but I should keep an eye on the kids while Aunt Clara's sleeping."

"Liar."

She groaned in resignation. He wasn't going to let her escape until they'd cleared the air. "What do you want, Luke?"

"You."

She whimpered.

"Why are you fighting this? Is loving me such a bad thing?"

"Love is never a bad thing," she declared vehemently, angry herself now, "but it's just not in the cards for me."

"You're not going to mention that damn Christmas Curse again."

"No, I'm pretty sure the Christmas Curse is over. Last night just about wiped it out, I would think."

"Damn straight!"

"Oh, Luke, last night was wonderful, for both of us, but I don't want you to make it into something more than what it was."

"Which was?" he asked icily.

"People have a way of getting caught up in the magic of the Christmas season, but the glow rarely lasts beyond the tinsel and mistletoe. It's sort of like vacation romances where lovers forget each other once they go home."

"Bull!"

She winced at his harsh scorn.

"I love you, Jessie."

"You think you do," she corrected.

"Don't tell me what I think. I love you, and you love me, dammit. Deny it. Go ahead. Tell me you don't love me."

Tears welled in her eyes as she tried to tell him she didn't love him. The words stuck in her throat.

"Jessie, honey, have you ever told anyone you loved them?"

She shook her head mutely.

"Because they always left first, right?"

She nodded.

"Ah, sweetheart, don't you know . . . can't you trust that I'm not leaving?"

She shook her head again, but a soft sob escaped.

He bent his knees so he was at eye level with her and pressed his lips lightly against hers, shifting from side to side, as if trying to show her his sincerity. "I'm in this for the long haul, babe," he said in a choked voice. "I've waited too long to find love again. I'll prove to you that my love is for real. I will."

He was lowering his mouth for another kiss when footsteps clamored loudly on the other side of the door, followed by a rattling of the door knob.

"Uncle Luke, your phone is ringing like crazy, and there's a car coming up the driveway . . . a stretch limo."

Jessica canted her head at Luke in question. Giving her a quick peck, he looped an arm around her shoulder, firm notice that he wasn't going to let her bolt again.

Henry was speaking on Luke's cellular phone in the hallway when they emerged. His eyes seemed watery with unshed tears and his glasses were all fogged up.

Jessica's maternal instincts kicked in. "Henry, what's wrong? Is it bad news?" Henry was an orphan, but there might be some distant relative she didn't know about.

He ignored her with a wave of his hand. "Yes, sir. I will, sir. I promise," Henry said into the mouthpiece, a tone of awe in his voice. "A summer school for computer whiz kids? No, I never heard about that. A what? Oh, Gawd! A college scholarship, maybe, sometime down the road?" Tears streamed unrestrained down Henry's face now. "But, Mr. Gates, how did you hear about me? Oh. Yes, Lucas Carter is still here." Henry gave Luke a sideways glance of adoration.

"Bill Gates?" Jessica said, turning to Luke. "You called Bill Gates on Henry's behalf?"

"No big deal," he said dismissively.

"Yes, it is a very big deal," she asserted and hugged him tightly.

And a tiny grain of trust began to build between them. Well, actually, it was more like a rock.

He winked at her. "Hey, if a telephone call turns you on, I've got a really good dialing finger." He jiggled his eyebrows at her.

Lord, she loved it when he jiggled his eyebrows.

Not that she'd tell him that.

Not that he probably didn't know it already.

Oh, this was turning into the best Christmas ever. And it wasn't over yet.

Darlene and Kajeeta stood at the open front door, gaping at the limo which had just pulled to a stop. The two teenagers looked outside, then looked at each other, threw their hands up in the air, and squealed girlishly.

Jessica felt like screaming, too.

Janet Jackson walked in the door. For real.

"Shut your mouth, Jessie," Luke advised her with a chuckle. He squeezed her shoulder before releasing her and stepping forward to welcome his guest.

"Yo, Janet, glad you could come," Luke said, kissing the star on the cheek. Janet wore a skin-tight, red jump suit with a fuzzy white fake-fur jacket. A dozen tiny gold Christmas bells tinkled from her earrings as she moved.

"Which one of you is Kajeeta?" Janet asked, homing

in on the astonished black girl. "You and I have a lot to talk about, girlfriend." Then turning to Darlene, she added, "You must be Darlene. Great makeup!"

The three headed into the living room where Willie stood like a frozen statue watching Janet Jackson approach. The expression on his face couldn't have been more delighted if he'd been handed a karate black belt on a silver platter. Jessica shuddered to think what questions he might ask the sexy rock singer/dancer. Julio put his hands in his pockets, striking a nonchalant pose, and Jessica was pretty sure he planned to hit on the celebrity.

That left her and Luke to follow dumbly after the crowd. Henry was still chattering away on the phone with Bill Gates.

Luke watched her watch Janet with a great deal of amusement.

"Glad you could make it," Luke said to Janet once he could get a word in edgewise.

"Hey, man, I wouldn't have missed this for anything. When you told me yesterday that you'd met your dream girl, I had to come take a look-see."

Luke draped a proprietary arm around Jessica's waist.

"Yeah, you done good, Luke-master," Janet said teasingly, giving Jessica a sweeping appraisal. "Maybe too good. Maybe I should introduce her to my chauffeur. He's studying to be an actor."

Luke stiffened beside her.

But Janet just hooted and tapped Luke on the chin with one of her very long fingernails. "Gotcha, good buddy!" She told Jessica then, "This guy of yours is the best bodyguard I ever hired. Did you know that

Brad Pitt has been trying to convince him for years to take a job as his body double, but he refuses to move to the West Coast? Maybe you can talk some sense into him, honey."

Jessica was too flabbergasted by that news to respond.

"So where's this famous fruitcake?" Janet asked Luke.

Everyone started to laugh, but then a car horn blew outside.

What next? Jessica mouthed to Luke.

"Damned if I know," he replied, peering out the window. Immediately, he exclaimed, "Oh, my God!"

"What's the matter?" Jessica asked with concern.

He gave her a rueful glance. "It's my sister, Ellie. I told her to bring some Christmas presents."

"So?" He'd already told her of his fondness for his sister.

"And my mother, too."

Oooh, boy!

Early that evening, Luke sat on the floor before the fire with his arm wrapped around Jessie. Their backs were propped against the sofa where Aunt Clara knitted away on an afghan—a Christmas present for him. Luke had to chuckle when he saw her latest creation for the first time. Brown and speckled with red and orange and green, it resembled a big slice of fruitcake.

The kids sat around the room playing with their Christmas gifts. Although everyone was tired from the long day and the excitement, they were reluctant to go to bed and end what had been a perfect day for them all.

Janet had left soon after dinner, dog-tired from dancing with all the kids, stuffed from Julio's Christmas feast, and ears ringing with all the questions. She'd brought little nonsense gifts for the orphans, which they would, no doubt, cherish for a lifetime.

Before they'd gotten in the limo—the limo driver had joined them for Christmas dinner, too, and to Luke's annoyance he was way too good-looking—Luke had heard Willie ask Janet, "Do you think girls are attracted to karate guys?"

"Oooh, yes!" Janet cooed with a straight face. "I think Steven Seagal is the number-one stud in the nation. In fact, I'm thinking about using some karate moves in my next music video." That about made Willie's day.

And Julio had somehow managed an invitation from Janet to go to Hollywood for a job next summer. He probably had a strategy mapped out already for taking the town by storm . . . or just taking it.

A smiling Aunt Clara had made a gift of five fruitcakes to Janet. She was struck speechless with gratitude.

Luke's mother and Ellie had approved heartily of Jessie. Well, why wouldn't they? She was wonderful, although she'd appeared half-paralyzed by their exuberance. Ellie, especially, came on like gangbusters sometimes. His mother had started to ask Jessie whether she could help with wedding plans, but backed off, luckily, when she'd seen the sheer panic in Jessie's eyes. He'd given his mom a silent signal that he'd talk to her later.

Now he sat in the afterglow of the best Christmas he'd ever had, with the woman he loved in his arms.

Later, after everyone else sacked out for the night, he and Jessie would talk. Then wild sex again. Or should they have wild sex, and then talk?

"Why are you smirking?" Jessie tilted her head to gaze at him.

In the background, he heard his cellular phone going off. Probably his mother or Ellie. He'd told them to call when they arrived home safely.

"I was *not* smirking. I'm just happy. Aren't you?"

She nodded, and he could see that she was getting weepy-eyed again. She did that a lot when unable to express her emotions. He was a little weepy-eyed himself.

"Uncle Luke, it's for you," Henry called out. "Your secretary. She says it's an emergency."

Uh-oh.

Jessica sat on the floor waiting for Luke to return. Little by little, he'd peeled away the armor of her distrust today. She'd already admitted to herself that she loved him, but she was beginning to actually believe he could love her, too . . . that they had a future together.

When Luke came back a short time later, he'd already donned a jacket. With worry lining his voice, he said, "Come here, Jessie, I have to talk to you."

"What is it?" She jumped up in panic. "Has there been an accident? Your mother and sister?"

"No, no," he assured her quickly. "They're fine, but there has been an accident. One of my employees was shot. Dead." He swallowed with difficulty, then went on, "His partner's badly wounded. I have to get back to Philadelphia right away."

"Of course," she said, rushing to his side.

Luke said all his good-byes to Aunt Clara and the kids, telling them he'd return as soon as possible. Then, a short time later, Luke was kissing her at the side of his car.

"Wait here for me, Jessie," he ordered gruffly.

She nodded, unable to keep her cold hands from caressing his face and shoulders, memorizing him till he returned.

"I'll call you later tonight. I should be able to get back by tomorrow, but I'll know better once I see what the situation is with this job. Okay?" He was nuzzling her neck and giving her little nibbling kisses the whole time he talked.

Jessica tried to keep up a brave front. She was missing Luke before he even left.

"I have to go," he said finally, setting her away from him and opening the car door. "I love you, Jessie."

She started to say the words she knew he wanted to hear, but he put his fingertips over her lips to silence her. "No, I know that you love me. But I want you to say the words on your own, without the pressure of my leaving."

She nodded and watched through a screen of tears as Luke drove away.

Two days later, Jessica hadn't heard from Luke.

The night he'd left, there'd been no call, even though he'd promised. And all the following day, she'd waited in vain.

At first, his lack of communication had stunned her. There had to be an excuse.

Then reality had sunk in.

Despite Aunt Clara's admonitions to trust in her heart, Jessica accepted the truth. Luke wasn't coming back.

By the third day after Christmas, Jessica had her shield of cynicism firmly in place again. And she began packing for her return to Chicago, with oaths of secrecy forced from Aunt Clara and the kids not to divulge her address or phone number if Luke should ever show up again. She suspected that a twinge of pity might strike Luke sometime in the future, if not for her, perhaps for the kids, and she didn't want his damn pity. Or anything else from him, for that matter.

So Jessica traveled back to Chicago alone, except for ten fruitcakes which she intended to dump at the first roadside rest stop, and memories of candy canes and a rogue Santa that would stay with her forever.

Some Christmas miracles weren't intended to last.

On New Year's Eve, Jessica stood in the kitchen of the Shangri-la Inn, arranging Roquefort-stuffed shrimp and crab canapes on an appetizer tray.

The loud rendition of the Jewish folk dance "Hava Nagila" being played by the orchestra at the wedding reception rocked the entire building, but did nothing for her low spirits. The band soon moved on to a fast-paced number, and the shrill announcer encouraged everyone to get up and dance the Chicken. *The Chicken?* She clucked her tongue woefully. What was it about weddings that made grown people behave like imbeciles?

She heard the whoosh of the swinging door from the dining room and grabbed for the meat tenderizing hammer in front of her. The lecherous bridegroom,

Cecil Goldstein, had been making passes at her all afternoon, and she'd had about enough. As it was, she probably had bruises on her butt from all his pinches. Well, time to give the schnockered newlywed a lesson good and proper, where it really hurt.

"Put your hands up, lady. This is a stick-out," she heard behind her. And it wasn't the bridegroom's voice.

Oh, my God! Jessica turned abruptly and dropped her meat mallet to the floor with a clunk of surprise.

Santa Claus stood before her with a raised pistol. Madder than hell, if his flaring nostrils and steely eyes were any indication.

"What are you doing here?"

"I came for something that belongs to me. This is *not* a robbery," he emphasized, parroting some words she'd said once. "And get those hands back up, lady, or I'm gonna have to wipe you up."

A grin twitched the edges of her lips. She couldn't help herself. Was that how silly she'd sounded? And Luke looked so comical standing there with a gun pointed in her face. *A gun?* "You shouldn't aim a loaded gun at anyone. It is loaded, isn't it?"

"You betcha, babe," he said, and squirted her in the face.

Jessica laughed and wiped the moisture away while Luke pulled the beard and wig and hat off, dropping them to the floor. She saw immediately that his teasing words conflicted with the stone-cold fury stiffening his body, flattening his lips into a thin line.

"Why didn't you wait for me, Jessie? And why did you tell everyone to keep your whereabouts from me?" Luke was bristling with anger.

"Why didn't you call?"

"Because I had to go to London to take over for Jerry and Mike." His voice cracked at the end.

"Oh," she said, remembering the accident the night Luke had been called away. She wanted to reach out her arms in comfort, but Luke's stony expression daunted her. "How is he . . . I mean, the one employee, did he survive?"

"Jerry was buried three days ago, and Mike will recover," he said grimly.

Agitated, she brushed some stray curls off her forehead. "How did you find me?"

"Julio," he responded tersely.

She waited for him to say more. When he didn't, she took a deep breath and pressed forward. "Why?"

"He said he'd never met two old fogies as dumb as us," he informed her with a rueful shrug.

She tried to smile, but her facial muscles froze.

"You didn't answer my question, Jessie. Why didn't you wait?" He studied her so calmly and coldly that Jessica's heart began to splinter.

"When you didn't call, I figured that . . . well, you changed your mind. That you didn't really . . ."

". . . love you?" He shook his head sadly. "Dammit, Jessie, why couldn't you have trusted me?"

"But you didn't call," she accused.

"I did call, Jessie."

She waited for an explanation, puzzled.

"Did it ever occur to anyone to recharge the battery on the cellular phone, or plug the thing into a wall outlet?"

"Battery?" she squeaked out. Then, "You called?"

He nodded somberly.

Jessica understood then how foolish she'd been. And she understood something else, too. This was good-bye. Luke hadn't come to woo her back.

Without trust, a relationship was nothing. And she'd proven they had nothing . . . no foundation to build on, not even the love she'd failed to profess to him. But Luke was an ethical man, and he would have felt a responsibility to explain himself.

Could he possibly doubt her love?

Of course. Hadn't she doubted him, with even less reason?

"Good luck, Jessie. I hope someday you'll find what you want. I hope you'll let yourself," Luke said, about to turn and leave. "I really did love you."

Did? Jessica's heart was beating a mile a minute. She had to do something, but things were happening too fast.

"Since you've traveled all this way, wouldn't you like to go back to my place? We could . . ." At the disbelieving scowl on his face, her words trailed off.

"For what?" he scoffed.

"Fruitcake?" she proffered weakly. She was in such a panic she couldn't think clearly.

"No, thanks. I've had enough."

He'd had enough. Was there a double meaning there? Did he mean her, too?

He stared at her for one long, excruciating moment, then spun on his heels.

"I bought something for you," she blurted out to his back as he walked stiffly toward the door. Then she put a palm over her mouth to stop herself from saying more.

"You bought something for me?" He turned. "What?"

Heat suffused her face. "Some peppermint oil," she mumbled.

His eyes widened. "What did you say?"

She gulped. "I bought some damn peppermint warming oil. And, believe me, it took all my nerve to go into one of those places by myself. I was going to mail it to you with my address on the package. And then if you contacted me, I figured . . ." She had to stop because tears flowed down her face and she was blubbering.

"You figured what?" He came back to stand in front of her.

She closed her eyes for a minute to collect her nerve. "I figured it would mean that you might still love me then, like . . . like . . ." She couldn't go on.

"Say it, Jessie," he insisted. His hazel eyes locked with hers, no longer in anger or despair. There was hope there now.

". . . like I love you," she whispered.

Luke let out a loud sigh of relief and roughly pulled her into his arms, kissing her face and neck as if he couldn't get enough of her. "Geez, Jessie, I thought you were really going to let me go. You had me scared to death. I thought maybe I'd been wrong all along, that maybe you didn't love me."

"I love you, Luke," she said on a sob, framing his handsome face with two hands. He made her say it ten more times before he stopped grinning like a silly idiot.

When the bridegroom stomped into the kitchen demanding to know what the hell was going on, she shoved the appetizer tray in his hands and announced, "I quit, Cecil."

"You can't quit," Cecil sputtered.

"Wanna bet?" Luke stepped in.

"What am I supposed to do with all this food?" he whined.

"I'd suggest you serve it yourself. Unless you want me to tell your bride how you offended me," she threatened.

"How did he offend you?" Luke narrowed his eyes and began to advance on the cowering lech.

"Never mind," Jessica said and pulled on Luke's arm, dropping her apron to the floor. Nothing else mattered now that she had Luke back. Nothing.

"Don't forget to serve the almond creme wedding cake," she added. "It cost you five hundred dollars."

Cecil stammered incoherently. She wasn't sure if it was over his being forced to serve at his own wedding, or the price tag she'd just quoted.

Laughing, she and Luke emerged from the back exit of the restaurant moments later.

Stopping abruptly, Luke asked, "So, Jessie, where's this present of mine?"

"In the trunk of my car," she said, leaning her head into the crook of his neck and shoulder.

"I hope you bought a gallon," he growled.

"I did," she laughed. "And I also bought some in peach. How do you feel about peaches?"

He never answered.

But he showed her a short time later.

Noel Carter was born ninth months later, having been conceived on Christmas Eve.

Some might say that Lucas's faulty birth control had been a Christmas Curse. But Lucas and Jessica Carter believed they were blessed with a Christmas Miracle.

SANTA READS ROMANCE

DARA JOY

for

WHISKERS
(11/17/81—3/21/96)

*Who stood up on his chubby hind legs and danced
for a scallion,*

*Who unlocked every door and cabinet in my house
simply to prove a point,*

*Who bravely captured tie-wraps and wrestled them
to death with his patented immobilizer,*

*Who slept with me when he thought I wasn't
looking,*

*Who always came when I called his name and
stayed with me in my darkest hours,*

*Who passed on to loving memory the day I
completed this story.*

Chapter One

Writers. They were the bane of his existence.

Unfortunately, they were his bread and butter too.

C. Hunter Douglas slammed the heel of his hand against the steering wheel of the rental car. *What came into their strange little minds that caused them to react so . . . so . . .*

They had to be from another planet. Probably plants of an alien race, put here to slowly drive the sane mad.

He peered through the windshield into the darkness.

A snow squall had sprung up out of nowhere, adding to his rising irritation. The Weather Channel had conveniently left this piece of information out of its travel report this morning. He should have realized. Maine. Christmas week.

It was a trip only a sailor returning home from war

or a desperate publisher would attempt to make.

His hand slammed on the wheel again.

One million dollars.

Of his money.

And no manuscript.

Normally he was not a violent man, but the idea of grabbing the oh-so-talented Rex Stevens by the throat and slowly squeezing the air from his self-indulgent lungs held great appeal. He'd show the horror writer something really scary. A pissed-off publisher.

What was he going to do?

Publicity and marketing had been set in motion, a book tour ready and waiting, appearances on talk shows, tie-ins . . . Shit, the whole thing was going to fall apart!

He had counted on this. Placed all of his dwindling profit-margin eggs in Rex's basket of frightening words. His uncle had made some terrible financial decisions; Hunter had been called in to clean up.

Everything would have been nice and tidy if the "writer"—he grimaced at the word—had delivered as contracted!

When the manuscript had still not arrived three weeks after the deadline, an uncomfortable, nauseous feeling had settled in the pit of his stomach.

It was a feeling he recognized.

Hunter called it his "imminent author sickness."

He had called the man and his agent several times, leaving message after message. The agent was in the hospital for his ulcers (Hunter bet he knew why), and Rex had not returned his calls.

So Hunter had flown up to Maine.

He would've flown to Timbuktu to get his hands on that manuscript.

Only when he arrived on Rex's doorstep in this god-forsaken rural town, the housekeeper had cheerfully informed him that Mr. Rex was not there.

Mr. Rex was in Sri Lanka.

At an *ashram*.

In search of himself.

Hunter's left eye twitched. *Writers*.

Chapter Two

May threw another log on the fire.

She watched the sparks fly up the chimney as if it were the most interesting sight she had ever seen. Unfortunately, the amazing spectacle was over in less than a minute.

She sighed, wondering what else could suddenly capture her attention. Surely something?

Come to me.

Her green eyes began to cloud over at the subliminal suggestion.

You must come to me . . .

Her shoulders scrunched up as she tried to fight off the insistent voice.

Get your butt over here!

The damn laptop was trying to get her attention again. It was the voice of conscience and reason. It was the voice of a deadline fast approaching. It would not leave her alone!

May desperately scanned the room, searching for an important task that needed to be done immediately. Perhaps the ceilings needed vacuuming? Never mind that they weren't her ceilings—anything was better than staring at that empty screen.

This was the stupidest idea she had ever had.

And she had had some whoppers.

When her neighbor Billy had told her about his cabin in Maine, May had practically begged him to let her use it for a few weeks. It seemed the ideal hideaway where she would write, diet, and reflect.

The perfect solution.

She could remove herself from the temptations of everyday life, finish her book, and maybe lose a few pounds at the same time.

Most importantly, she would not be surrounded by well-meaning family and friends who smothered her in sympathy invites at Christmas. The holiday that never failed to remind her: a) she was alone; b) she was alone and; c) *she was alone.*

It was supposed to be "the great escape." After all, she would be working; she had the perfect excuse to turn down all the invitations.

Everything would be accomplished in one swell foop.

Only it hadn't quite worked out that way.

Even though Billy had warned her that the cabin was remote, secluded, and had little in the way of conveniences, she had somehow ignored all that, her inner sights focusing on a new and improved May. A

May armed with a *completed* novel.

After two days here, she was beginning to question the wisdom of the plan.

The one-room cabin with kitchenette was starting to get on her nerves.

Whatever had possessed her to come here equipped with only a laptop, a sack full of frozen diet dinners, a giant box of Cheerios, and ten pounds of Braeburn apples? What kind of diet was that?

Thankfully, she couldn't bear the thought of giving up coffee cream, so she at least had a small carton of Half-and-Half to stare at and dole out like liquid platinum.

Well, enough suffering! Tomorrow she was going to drive into the little village she had passed on her way to the cabin and lay in some writer's survival supplies. Lots of Chippy Nicks, Chocomongos, and Jelly Wellys. Her stomach growled agreement with the fine idea.

Seeking security of another kind, her sights went to the overflowing carton in the corner near the fireplace. At least she'd had sense enough to bring her favorite romance novels. She sighed contentedly at the lovely sight. Food she could live without. Creature comforts she could live without. Romance novels, however, were a different story.

Come to think of it, this cabin was the perfect setting for a romance book.

Her imagination took flight. Yes . . . remote cabin, two strangers thrown together by chance . . .

She giggled to herself. How often had she read that particular story line? Too many times. It was the *plot du jour.* Although she had loved so many of those stories. . . .

A few snowflakes fell softly against the windowpane.

Her brow furrowed. She hadn't heard anything about snow this morning on the radio. Probably just a small snow shower.

Shrugging, she threw another log on the fire and avidly watched the sparks fly up the chimney.

That's another minute down.

Chapter Three

Perhaps if his mind hadn't been wandering along the lines of throttling his favorite author, he would've noticed the man sooner.

He had just turned down the main street of the town. The snow had picked up in the last fifteen minutes, although visibility wasn't that bad. He should've seen him.

Even though it was just past eight in the evening, the streets were deserted. It seemed as though one moment it was clear sailing, and the next a surprised visage materialized in front of his windshield, followed by a sickening thump.

Christ! He had hit somebody!

Hunter slammed on the brakes, sweat breaking out across his forehead. The car skidded to a stop, but Hunter was already out the door while the car was still rocking.

A red lump lay unmoving in the gutter. He ran to the huddled shape, falling to his knees in the shallow snow. Hunter had never been so scared in his life.

The man was dressed in a Santa suit.

Next to him, lying on the pavement, was a large sack full of presents. If possible, Hunter felt even worse. He had run over Santa Claus! Not even a disgruntled publisher would intentionally do that.

"Talk to me!" Gently he placed his hand on the man's shoulder. "I didn't even see you there, pop, I swear it! Hey, buddy, say something, please! Are you hurt bad?"

Leaning over, he worked his palm under the man's shirt to feel for a heartbeat. Something wet licked his hand.

"Jesus!" Hunter fell back in the snow. What the hell was that?

A piteous groan came from under the prone figure. It did not sound human.

Hunter blanched. He had read too many of Rex's books lately—they always seemed to involve horrific happenings in the backwoods of Maine . . .

"Don't just sit there gawking at me, boyo! Help me up!"

The acerbic words penetrated Hunter's fog-brain. He let out a sigh of relief. At least the man was conscious and speaking.

"You okay, mister? Maybe you shouldn't move."

"And how am I supposed to be gettin' up if I don't move? C'mon now, help ol' Santa up. Benny's not happy."

Against his better judgment, Hunter crawled toward the man, helping him to sit up. A wave of cheap gin assailed his nostrils.

Uh-huh. The picture was getting clearer. The old coot had probably fallen into the path of his car in a drunken stupor. Idly Hunter wondered what Benny was supposed to be a euphemism for. As if he needed to know.

"Santa" sat up, swaying slightly, his eyes round and bleary. He shook his head several times, slapped the back of his head twice, and hiccupped.

Hunter viewed him askance. "Are—are you sure you're okay, old-timer?"

"Fit as a fiddle. It's Benny took the brunt of it, poor little fellow."

Hunter winced. Yeah, the old coot had probably landed right on his . . . well, he'd never heard it called a *benny* before. "Ah, yah, must've hurt like hell. Sorry."

The man looked at him reproachfully. "And him being such a tiny little thing."

Hunter stared at him. He blinked. What could he say to that? He rubbed his forehead. "Hey, you know, cold weather and all . . ."

Santa raised one bushy eyebrow and, shaking his head, muttered under his breath. It sounded suspiciously like "twit."

The old coot seemed okay. Drunk as a skunk, but okay. Impatiently, Hunter looked at his watch. He had a flight leaving from Bangor in a little over three hours and this was one flight he did not want to miss. The sooner he exited this horror-hotel the better; so far the trip had been one long nightmare.

Besides, the chances of him getting another flight

out tonight during Christmas week were probably five trillion to one. Conservatively speaking.

"Well, if you're sure you're all right . . ."

"I told ya, lad, I'm fine."

Nodding, Hunter turned and started to walk back to his car, missing the old man's surprised look. He had just reached the driver's door when an ear-splitting yell pierced the night, shattering Hunter's eardrums.

"Me leg! I can't move me leg!"

Hunter raced back to him, face pale. "You are hurt! Don't worry, I have a cell phone in the car. I'll go call an ambulance. Stay put—I'll be right back—"

"I ain't getting into no meat wagon!" the voice wailed indignantly.

"But you—"

"You'll take me then, won't ya, sonny?" Santa looked at him slyly.

Hunter sighed. He was being sucker-punched and there wasn't a damn thing he could do about it. "All right."

The old coot grinned. "Put your hands out so I can give ya Benny."

Hunter's eyes widened. He stepped back. Three steps.

"Now, there's nothing to be afraid of. Benny's real friendly. I'm sure you're going to be very fond of him—"

"The hell you say!" Hunter took another step back.

Santa clicked his tongue and rolled his eyes heavenward as if asking for divine interference. Reaching into his voluminous velvet shirt, he extracted a small reddish-brown bundle of fur with floppy ears. A blue bow was tied around its neck.

A puppy. Benny was a puppy. I've been living in New York too long, Hunter concluded. He tentatively reached down and took the little guy from the man.

The puppy immediately licked his hand. Then, wagging his wispy tail, he looked up at Hunter with big brown eyes.

Cute little tyke. Unconsciously, he petted the dog's head. "Nice puppy," he murmured distractedly. He had never been around dogs much. "What kind of dog is this?"

"That there's a genuine long-haired dachshund. Don't see too many of them dogs about. Kinda special, they are. Benny's being relocated."

"Relocated?"

"His old family didn't treat him none too well, poor mite. And him being the fine dog he is."

Hunter stroked the soft little head. "Too bad. How old is he?"

"About a year old."

Hunter was surprised. "I thought he was just a puppy."

"He is; always will be. That's the magic of some dogs," he confided before hiccupping drunkenly.

Hunter looked at him askance. "Ah, yah. Do you need a hand up?"

"Probably. But ya need to take me bag first." He nodded to the sack lying near him on the snowy pavement.

Hunter quirked his brow. "Let me guess, gifts to be dispensed?"

"Right ya are, boyo. I was headed to the children's home before ya ran me down like some no-account slug in the gutter." He speared him with a pointed look from beneath bushy brows.

"Now wait just a minute, old-timer, you—"

"The bag, sonny."

Letting out a hiss of disgust, Hunter retrieved the huge sack of wrapped gifts, throwing it onto the back seat of his car. Then he helped the old coot into the front seat, almost passing out from the alcohol fumes.

He wondered if it would affect him like secondary smoke in the closed confines of the automobile.

The way his day had been going? Absolutely.

He could see it now. He would get pulled over by the Maine police and get arrested for secondary drunk driving, and while he was hauled away, he would babble pitiful phrases about million-dollar advances and an *ashram* in Sri Lanka.

Hunter decided he definitely needed a vacation.

"You'll just have to do it, boyo!"

"Santa" lay on the hospital bed, propped up by three pillows and surrounded by four pretty nurses. Never mind that the ER doctor could find nothing wrong with the old coot. For a man supposedly in pain, he seemed remarkably comfortable. And smug.

Go figure, but the young women couldn't do too much for the guy. Even his white beard looked as if it had the snarls combed out of it.

Hunter's brow furrowed. Odd how the man had seemed to sober up as soon as they entered the emergency room. Even the noxious alcohol fumes had mysteriously disappeared.

In response, the corner of Hunter's mouth lifted in

a semblance of a sarcastic grin. "I don't think so, pop. I got a plane to catch."

A screech of utter despair filled the room. "Aw, the children! How will they get their gifts? *The chi-i-l-l-dren!*"

The pitiful wail of anguish bounced off the green walls, causing the four nurses to cross their arms over their ample chests in unison and level looks of utter disdain at Hunter.

He felt like a first-class heel.

He tried to explain. "Look, I have to get back to New—"

Santa stopped in mid-wail to pin him to the spot. "Ya can still make yer plane! Won't take but fifteen minutes! Ya told me on the drive ain't no family waitin' home for ya anyway. Think of the children . . ."

"Well, I . . ." Hunter could feel himself caving in. How could he refuse? And live with himself. Just because he was alone and didn't have anyone to share Christmas with was no reason to be a Grinch. As long as he still made his plane, that is.

The old codger knew the instant he had won. He pointed to the red velvet suit draped over the chair next to the bed.

This was where C. Hunter Douglas drew the line. "Absolutely not, pop."

A petite red-haired nurse joined in. "Oh, but you can't deliver the gifts to those poor children not dressed as Santa! That would be even worse than no gifts at all."

Santa nodded vehemently in agreement.

Dammit. He might as well just do it and get it over with. Maybe then he could get out of this godforsaken town! Anything was better than those five sets of dog-eyes staring at him. Make that six including Benny, who had started up a soulful whine in chorus.

He stormed over to the chair and grabbed the velvet suit.

"What about your beard?" the red-headed nurse asked.

"What about it?" he snapped.

"Well, you don't have one! The hat will cover your hair, but the beard . . . I've got it!" She snapped her fingers. "I'll make you one from some cotton batting and surgical thread."

"Good idea, Rudy." Santa praised the nurse's ingenuity.

She smiled broadly. "I'll be right back."

"I can hardly wait," Hunter muttered under his breath.

Hunter started to put the mangy outfit on over his Armani suit, came to his senses, and headed for the cubicle bathroom. When he exited all in red, his business suit was draped carefully over his arm.

"I never realized how fine I look in that suit." The old-timer on the bed grinned wickedly at him. He was really enjoying this.

Hunter narrowed his silver eyes. The daunting effect was somewhat spoiled when the pom-pom at the end of the hat smacked into his nose.

"Here we go!" Nurse Rudy raced back into the room with a fluffy wad of cotton attached to a string. "Bend down and I'll tie it on for you."

Hunter knelt his tall frame so she could tie it behind his ears. She began stuffing his wavy dark brown hair under the rim of the hat. "Can't let the kids see this.

You know, I have some scissors in my pocket; I could trim it off . . ."

"No!" Hunter abruptly stood.

Walking over to a small square mirror on the wall, he peered at his new high-powered image. "I look like a cross between a sheep's butt and a horse's behind."

The nurses giggled.

Santa stroked his beard. "I will admit ya don't carry it off with quite the same flair I do."

Hunter faced him. "You can have the job back any time, pop."

The man's eyes twinkled. "Right ya are, sonny! Now, here's the directions to the place; I wrote them down for ya." He handed him a heavily scrawled piece of paper.

Hunter scanned it. "Are you sure this is close by; it seems—"

"Country roads. Don't worry about that none, just follow those directions exactly and ya won't have no problem."

Hunter stuffed the note in his pocket. Then he hoisted the heavy sack over his broad shoulder. "Well, see ya later, Santa. It's been . . . interesting."

"Wait a minute!" Hunter turned around. The codger held the puppy out to him. "Ya forgot Benny."

Hunter sighed resignedly, putting out his hand for the dog.

"He don't like the cold much!" Santa yelled after him.

Hunter waved acknowledgment without turning around.

Before he left the hospital he scooted the dog safely inside his shirt.

Chapter Four

Turkeyfoote Road.

Where in the hell was Turkeyfoote Road?

It seemed as if he'd been driving for hours, although his watch claimed it was only about thirty minutes.

He had left the outskirts of the village twenty minutes ago. The snowfall had picked up considerably; his wipers were just keeping up with it. If he didn't find the turn-off soon, he was going to turn back, drop off the gifts and Benny. The small dog was still nestled next to his chest, refusing to leave the warmth of his shirt.

At this pace, he might miss his plane. And he still had to drive to Bangor. These dark country roads were—

A small wooden sign staked to the ground seesawed in the wind to his left. It was placed next to—not a road exactly, more a trail.

On the front of the wooden sign someone had drawn in red paint what one might assume was a turkey foot.

It was a good enough indication for him.

He swung the car to the left and followed the narrow rutted pathway. After ten minutes of bouncing and sliding on the dirt track, he wondered what had possessed him to take that turn.

The snow was falling fast and furious now.

He had just decided to turn back when he rounded a bend and spotted some lights in the distance. About 300 yards up the road a house sat on a hill. It was too dark and snowy to see much of its shape, but Hunter had no doubt that it was the children's home. He had followed the directions exactly.

Unfortunately, at that point the road became steeper and rougher. In this snow, without four-wheel drive, he didn't think he'd be able to drive much further. The surface was slick and pitted with ice.

Deciding it was best to walk the remaining distance—he wasn't going to take any chances of getting stuck here—he stopped the car, grabbed the sack from the back seat, tucked Benny's head back in his shirt, and headed up to the house.

Chapter Five

The lights flickered and went out.

May peered out the window. The storm was really picking up. Earlier she had tried to tune in a local radio station on her Walkman but all she got was static. Reception hadn't been the best these past few days, and she supposed with this snow . . .

The firelight cast eerie shadows on the walls.

She swallowed. This was creepy. She had never done anything like this before. *Why, oh why, had she come here by herself?*

The wind howled outside. An eerie sonata.

Billy had told her there was a generator in the cellar, but she didn't have the foggiest idea how to use it. And even if she could use it, there was no way she was going down in that dirt cellar by herself in the dark! It was a *Tales from the Crypt* waiting to happen.

She would just scrunch close to the fireplace all

night and hope she didn't freeze. It seemed to be doing a fairly good job of keeping the room warm. And she had plenty of firewood.

Tomorrow she was going to go back home.

May had had all she could stand of the little hideaway.

She wanted TV, phone, CD-Rom, and home delivery.

This was the last time she would . . . She leaned closer to the window. *Was something moving out there?*

A fuzzy blur of staggered movement seemed to weave its way through the snow. May gulped. *Something was out there.*

Oh, God.

Her rapid breath fogged up the glass. Quickly she wiped the pane with a circular motion of her palm. She did not want to lose sight of it!

Squinting, she tried to get a better view through the heavily falling snow.

It was big, whatever it was.

It—it seemed to have a . . . huge *hump* on its back! *Oh, God.* A thin film of sweat dotted her brow.

As the figure got closer, she could discern the shape of a man. This was not necessarily comforting.

May stood on tiptoe to watch his progress through the storm, taking solace from the fact that he seemed to be having considerable trouble negotiating the pathway to the cabin. He kept slipping and sliding on the icy walkway.

When he got close enough so that the firelight from the window illuminated him better, May put her hand to her throat in utter terror. It was all she could do not to scream out loud. *He was wearing a Santa suit!*

There was no doubt in her mind now that he was a homicidal maniac. There had been a very popular slasher movie where the killer had done the exact same thing. What better way to sucker in your victims than dressing as kindly old Santa?

May thought she was going to be sick.

He was making his way to the front porch now. She could hear the heavy fall of his uncoordinated feet dragging across the wooden planks.

Thinking quickly, she grabbed a hefty piece of firewood and stood behind the door. Her best chance would be in taking him unawares. She knew this because she was an author who was very good at plotting.

Carefully she inched over and unlocked the door.

And waited like a spider.

Chapter Six

Hunter hefted the sack on his shoulder and went to knock on the door. He had been surprised at how small the house—no, cabin—was when it came into better view. How many children could live here? It seemed kind of primitive . . .

The door creaked slowly open.

Placing the sack down on the porch, Hunter gingerly stepped forward. "Hello?" No answer. He crossed the threshold. "Anybody here? I'm deliver—"

Something whacked him hard on the back of the head.

Hunter went down like a ton of bricks.

He was thinking he was the biggest fool of all time just before the world went black.

Chapter Seven

Got him! May slammed the door shut. No sense letting out the warm air.

She ran into the kitchenette looking for the ball of twine she had spotted when she first arrived and was putting away her groceries. Grabbing it off the nail on the inside of the sink cabinet, she raced back into the main room, hoping the maniac hadn't come to yet.

There he was! Lying on his stomach just where she had left him—looking like a beached red whale.

May made short work of tying his hands behind his back. Then she wrapped the twine around his feet, which surprisingly were not clad in black Santa boots, but in rather expensive-looking brown leather shoes. His socks were soaked through, but she didn't feel the least sympathy for him or his wet feet.

May had him trussed up like a Christmas turkey in no time flat.

Now that he wasn't going anywhere without her approval, she felt confident enough to roll the scoundrel over.

She first noted that his dark lashes (which were rather long for a man) framed cheeks that looked rather pale even through his tan-colored skin. He appeared younger than she originally thought. At first glance in that suit, she had taken him for a man in his fifties. Now she saw that he was probably only in his early to mid thirties.

Which made him all the more dangerous.

Removing his stocking hat, she was surprised at the mass of luxuriant wavy brown hair that fell over her hands. It wasn't to his shoulders, but close to it, falling a few inches shorter in a tapered cut.

She hadn't seen his entire face yet, but so far he was exceedingly nice-looking. May shook her head in disgust. *Now, why would a man who looked like this have to resort to being a fiend?*

Maybe he was a moron.

That really had a tendency to turn women off.

His fake beard was slightly askew. Carefully she removed the fuzzy beard, frowning as it fell apart in her hands. It looked like he had just taken some cotton balls and threaded them through a string! What a pervert!

Her mouth parted slightly as she caught her first glimpse of his completely unmasked face.

It held to the original promise, revealing a strong chin—which no doubt indicated a pugnacious streak—a classically straight nose neither too large nor too small, and well-shaped lips. The bottom lip, she noted absently, was slightly fuller than the top;

the indentation below it hinting at a sensual . . . no, she wouldn't even think it.

He looked . . . familiar somehow.

Now that his whole face was visible, May noted that his tan skin did have a palish cast to it.

Maybe she had whacked him a bit too hard?

Not that she'd had a choice! Still . . . she couldn't stand to see any living thing suffer; even if the living thing was a maniac.

Gingerly she placed her palms on either side of his face, lifting his head a few inches off the floor.

His skin was a bit clammy, too, but he seemed to be breathing fine.

The man gave a slight moan and his lashes fluttered. Slowly his eyes opened, trying to focus on her.

May caught sight of those silver eyes and instantly recognized him.

"*You!*" She dropped his head like a hot potato.

It hit the wooden floor with a clunk.

The man's startled groan was cut off as he passed out again.

Oh, great! She had just beaned and trussed up C. Hunter Douglas, wunderkind and vice-president of Fortuna Books! Should do wonders for her career.

What on earth was he doing here?

Obviously, he had come to see her, but why? May bit her lip. Wait a minute . . . her first book had done remarkably well. There was a rumor going around that Fortuna was looking into starting up a romance line. That's it! Somehow he had found out she was here, probably from her agent, and had come up here to woo her away from her present publisher.

Well, it wouldn't work!

She was very happy where she was. Besides, this was rather *nervy* of him, intruding into her solitude. During Christmas. Publishers!

He would have to stay here until the morning (especially since he was out cold on her floor), but come morning he could just pick himself up and leave!

In the meantime, May thought it best to untie him.

She rolled him over, unwrapped his hands, then flipped him back. It wasn't easy—the man seemed to be six feet plus of solid muscle. Apparently, wrestling writers to the ground like heifers from a shoot on a regular basis did wonders for toning the body.

Better check his breathing. She grimaced, reaching inside his shirt to place her palm over his heart.

Something licked her fingers. May screamed.

"Ahhh!" She fell backward on the floor.

A small furry head poked out of the red velvet, tongue lolling.

A puppy! Her face lit up with a huge grin at the sight of the silly-looking thing. Until she realized that Mr. Douglas had probably counted on such a reaction from her. The nerve! Using a sweet animal to get under her defenses.

Now that she knew his game, she would be totally immune.

The small dog wiggled out from his host's garment, shaking his body in an attempt to smooth out his fur. The action only caused the silky strands to fly in every direction with static electricity. He looked at her and grinned.

Awww . . . May melted completely.

"C'mere, boy!" The dog trotted over to her with a frisky step. "Aren't you the sweetest wittle fellow?"

She rubbed the soft face, and his small, wispy tail thumped on the floor.

He was the cutest little wiener dog! She was a goner; already she was speaking baby-talk to him. When a person did that with an animal, the animal knew he had you. Didn't matter if it was a cat or a dog, they all gave you that same smug look which said quite clearly, "personal sucker."

"Let me check on your owner and then I'll see about you." Leaning over Douglas again, she placed her hand over his chest, feeling the steady thump thump thump of his heart.

Then she opened his eyelids to check his pupils. They were slightly dilated, but he didn't seem too bad off.

In any case, she had no telephone to call for help. There was a radio in the cellar, but she hadn't had any reason to use it before this and doubted she could find and work it in the dark. Besides, the electricity was out.

She figured Douglas would sleep the night through and wake up in the morning with a gargantuan headache and a temper to match.

The best she could do was keep an eye on him throughout the night.

Chapter Eight

May was really starting to get worried.

She had sat on the bed watching the publisher all night. The temperature in the cabin had soon plummeted with the heaters not working.

She had put on her heavy coat and, knowing it had to be freezing on the floor, had rolled him in the bed quilt.

It had not been an easy task.

She practically had to sweep him around the whole floor like a human rolling pin before she could get him situated on the quilt properly.

After that, the dog had sat up near the foot of her bed, and with his stubby paws waving madly, begged her to pick him up. As soon as she did, he dived under her coat for warmth and had not come out since.

Of course, the up side was that he was also acting as a small hot water bottle for her.

Her gaze went worriedly to the windows. It had been snowing steadily all night; in fact, it was a downright blizzard. The wind had picked up at around midnight, shaking the rafters and lending a weird howling sound to the scene.

Even though Douglas couldn't exactly be considered company, especially since he was still out cold, May was almost glad for his bizarre intrusion. At least she wasn't alone in this storm. Not that she would ever admit that she was even remotely pleased with the man's intrusion.

Around dawn, he finally regained consciousness with a loud, protesting groan.

Sitting up, he rubbed the back of his head, silver eyes narrowing slightly when he came across the goose egg on the back of his head.

She must have made a slight sound, because his head snapped up.

The action caused him to wince. He watched her for a few moments silently. When he spoke, his words reflected his anger.

"If this is some type of kidnapping scheme, you can tell your accomplice with the white beard it won't work. I plan on—"

May cut him off. "*Kidnapping scheme?* You've got to be kidding! *You* came here, Mr. Douglas. Completely uninvited, I might add. And you can just forget your little ploy to win me over!"

Hunter squinted his eyes, fighting down a wave of nausea from his throbbing head. "What the hell are you talking about?"

"Don't you remember me, Mr. Douglas? You came here to see me." He examined her face. A little too long. Her black hair was a snarled mass around her shoulders.

"Honey, I'm sure I would remember someone who looked like you."

She made a face at him.

"If you're not trying to kidnap me, why did you hit me on the head? And where are the kids?"

He wasn't making any sense. Uh-oh. Maybe she *had* conked him too hard. "Kids?" she asked tentatively.

"Yeah, the kids. I brought them their Christmas gifts just like your friend asked."

"I don't think so. You came here to see me."

He stopped rubbing the back of his head to stare at her, disbelieving. None of this made any sense. Which meant he was either concussed or he was dealing with a . . . He didn't want to think of the possibility. "I did?"

She nodded. The bump on his head was probably making him foggy. "I'm a writer," she proudly informed him.

Hunter closed his eyes and groaned. Better he was concussed. He had to be cursed. He was certainly in the wrong place.

"Look, I don't know how this happened but I ran over Santa Claus last night and—"

May snorted. "Did you skin him before or after you 'bagged' him?" She let her gaze travel insultingly up and down his body, letting him know her opinion of his attire.

Hunter tried to explain. "He made me deliver some gifts for him to the children, so I had to—"

She held up her hand. "Please. Don't embarrass yourself further."

He opened his mouth to respond; she cut him off.

"The point is, Mr. Douglas, you've wasted your time. I'm perfectly happy with my present publisher. I'm really sorry about the bump on your head, but what did you expect? Sneaking up on a writer in the Maine woods was not very smart. I can't imagine you've had much success with the technique."

He stared at her dumbfounded. "Do you actually believe I—"

"After all, this is my retreat, my *ashram* . . . " She stopped speaking because his eyes had suddenly thinned into two silver slits.

"What did you say?" His voice had gone dangerously soft.

"Um, never mind." May ran her fingers through her tangled hair.

"Who the hell *are* you?"

"You know—" she began.

"Humor me."

"May Forrester. Well, that's the name you would know me by."

The name did not register. "Sorry," he said with a shrug.

Hunter threw off the quilt, attempting to stand. The room swirled around him, and he grabbed at the bedpost to steady himself.

"Hey, go easy!" May reached over to steady him. "You've had quite a bang on your head."

He opened one eye and glared at her. "Just what did you hit me with?"

May swallowed guiltily. Not that she believed his fumbling explanation. For what other reason would he be here? "A piece of firewood," she admitted quietly.

"Mmm. Pine or oak?"

"Oak," she mumbled.

He rubbed his throbbing temples. "I thought so."

"Look, I'll go make us some coffee. Maybe that will help your headache. It's not as if we can go anywhere." She gestured to the windows.

He looked at her, then let his gaze travel to the windows. Snow was blowing against the glass. He crossed the room in three strides to see what was going on out there.

The view was not encouraging. It was a real "noreaster." Already drifts were over four feet high and rising.

He turned back to her, an expression akin to horror on his handsome face. "Are you telling me I'm snowbound in a cabin with a . . . a . . . *writer?*"

Like she was a leper or something! May crossed her arms. "As if you didn't plan this! You knew very well what you were doing. I'm not happy about it, but since I'm stuck with you for the time being, I suppose I'll have to make the best of it." With that she turned and headed for the small kitchenette.

It was starting already. He had no idea what she was talking about. And why should he? She was one of *those.* There was no sense trying to reason with her; this he knew from experience. *A writer.* His left eye twitched.

He suddenly remembered something. *Where was the dog?*

Had he somehow dropped him on the porch before she whacked him? *Oh, no.* The little fella never would have made it through the storm last night. "Benny!"

Sick to his stomach, Hunter ran to the front door,

only to stop short when she called over her shoulder, "If you mean this adorable puppy here, he's all right. In fact, he's still burrowed under my coat. But I warn you, he won't help your cause."

Hunter let out a sigh of relief. If anything had happened to the little guy . . .

He shivered, suddenly realizing how cold it was in here. Now that he was up and walking, every part of his body fairly screamed in soreness. Strange, but he felt as though he had been rolled across a rough floor all night, then left to stiffen on it.

"Why is it so cold in here?" he called out in the direction of the kitchenette.

"Electricity went out last night. The cabin's heated by electric baseboard, and even when it is working it's none too hot in here. How do you like your coffee?"

"Black." He walked over to the firewood piled by the fireplace. "Is this all the firewood you have?" There was concern in his voice.

"No, there's plenty of cut wood in the cellar."

"I hope it's enough so we don't freeze to death."

May ignored the "we." "There is a generator down there, but I haven't had a chance to look at it yet." She walked into the room and handed him a mug of coffee. He sipped the brew gratefully, letting the steam hit his face.

"I'll have a look at it when I finish my coffee. Phone out, too?"

"There is no phone."

He stared at her incredulously. "You came out here by yourself, a woman alone, to a secluded place that has no access to a telephone? What if there was an emergency?"

The formulaic expression he wore was one she was becoming familiar with; it said, "writer = alien species."

"I never thought of that—I just wanted some solitude." She gave him a pointed look. "So I could write. I told you, this was to be my *ashram*."

He shuddered, holding up his palm. "Please, not before breakfast."

What was that supposed to mean? May wasn't sure she liked C. Hunter Douglas.

"I have a cell phone in my car. It'll need a charge, but it should be fine."

"And how do you propose to get this cell phone? Have you looked outside lately?"

"As soon as it stops snowing, I'll make my way to the car."

May calmly took a sip of coffee. Typical New York businessman! Ignoring the small matter of four-foot drifts, hurricane-strength winds, and white-out conditions. If she didn't know better, she would have taken him for an agent.

"And where exactly is this car of yours parked?" she asked calmly.

He rubbed his ear. "About three hundred yards down the road."

"Uh-huh." She took another sip of coffee. "I have news for you, Attila, I managed to get a station on my Walkman last night for all of fifteen minutes, but I did hear words to the effect of 'storm of the century,' ninety-mile-per-hour winds, and something in the range of three and a half feet of snow."

Hunter was surprised. "This wasn't predicted."

"They never are. Apparently this baby went out to

sea, picked up a ton of moisture, and headed back inland. The weathermen were going bonkers, from what I heard."

He ran his hand distractedly through his hair. "Dammit! I need to get out of here today. I have to get to Sri Lanka!"

May eyed him strangely. "Uh-huh. Are you sure you're feeling all right? How many fingers do I have up?" May wasn't holding any fingers up.

"Don't be cute. Since it seems we're both stuck here for the time being, how are we set for supplies?"

There was that "we" business again. "There's plenty to eat. More than enough for two." For the amount of time *he* would be here. Wisely, May kept that thought to herself.

Apparently C. Hunter Douglas wasn't going to take her estimation of the subject; he stormed off to the cubicle kitchen and began slamming cabinet doors open and shut. "Where are your food supplies? All I see here is this bag of apples."

"Try the refrigerator."

He opened up the fridge and found a box of Cheerios and a carton of Half-and-Half. He frowned. "Why do you have Cheerios in the refrigerator?"

"Just in case." This was relayed with the utmost seriousness.

Coming from New York City, Hunter understood. One could never be too careful until one checked out the premises. Uninvited surprises rustling over the breakfast cereal had a tendency to remove one's appetite.

He opened the freezer.

A row of Tiny Cuisine boxes greeted him.

He rubbed the bridge of his nose. Great. Midget food.

"There's not enough here for one person to eat. Tell me this is not all the food you have here."

"Okay, I won't."

May reached past him, opening the refrigerator to remove the box of cereal. Getting a small bowl for Benny, she poured the dachshund a bowl, moistening it with a little water and a drop of Half-and-Half. The dog eagerly began consuming, his small tail wagging happily.

"We probably should save the cereal for him."

That left the midget food. Hunter grimaced; his stomach was already growling. He grabbed an apple off the counter. "I'll go check out that generator. See what you can pick up on your radio."

May crossed her arms over her chest. Why do men feel they can barge in anywhere and start giving orders? As if she would pay heed to a man talking to her in a red velvet suit! "Excuse me, but there's something you seem to have forgotten."

Hunter paused at the head of the cellar stairs. "What's that?"

"This is *my* rental cabin—*you* are the intruder."

He raised one eyebrow. "Meaning?"

"Meaning I'll give the orders around here."

He exhaled. "I see." He leaned against the door jamb and, imitating her, crossed his arms over his chest.

May had to admit that, of the two of them, he probably looked the more authoritative.

"And what, pray tell, are your 'orders'?"

She notched her chin challengingly in the air. "I'll go check the generator and you listen to the radio."

She wanted to slap her own face. *Why had she said that?* She *really* did not want to go in that creepy cellar. She tried to look brave.

Hunter grinned slowly. It was clear the woman did not want to go down there. She was rather cute . . . If only she weren't one of *them*. "Okay, green eyes, I'll check the generator while you listen to the radio."

"Right." She nodded briskly as if that were what she had actually said.

He whistled all the way down the stairs.

Which made May realize that C. Hunter Douglas was going to prove to be the irritating type.

Chapter Nine

It had taken him a couple of hours, but C. Hunter Douglas had gotten the old generator working, which moved him up considerably in May's estimation.

He had also managed to drag up the cumbersome radio from the cellar, placing it on the countertop in the kitchen. He had worked on the radio as well, with some rusty tools he had found down there.

May was impressed. She had figured him for a man who never saw the outside walls of an office and therefore assumed he would have no mechanical ability.

When she jokingly told him this, he smiled faintly. "I sometimes suffer from insomnia and often turn on a do-it-yourself cable station in the middle of the night, hoping it will knock me out. It hasn't cured my insomnia, but I have learned how to plant an asparagus bed, put up dry wall, wire an enclosed porch, decorate with style on a shoestring, and cook a Cornish game hen."

He paused, then added, "I hate Cornish game hens. They look like diminutive pigeons."

May chuckled, the word "diminutive" reminding her that they hadn't eaten the Tiny Cuisine yet. She offered to heat up their meals in the small microwave she had brought with her.

Hunter continued to fiddle with the radio. They both were surprised when a burst of static blasted the kitchen.

"It's working!" May beamed at him.

Douglas wore the expression most men wore when they'd managed to repair something. It was a look of demure caveman cockiness. May had often considered the look just short of a gorilla beating its chest.

Women never displayed that look when they did something considered traditionally "female"! Like managing to feed a family of five on a blue-collar budget. Now, there was an accomplishment!

She could just imagine a woman taking her masterpiece of a tuna casserole out of the oven, placing it on the table, only to throw back her shoulders and beat her chest with her fists while letting out a victorious Tarzan yell.

Her humorous fantasy was interrupted by a now familiar male voice angrily yelling into the radio receiver.

"What do you mean, a week? I can't stay here that long! I'm a publisher!"

Apparently Douglas had reached the sheriff's office in town.

The radio crackled and a tired-sounding voice responded, "Look pal, haven't you been listening to me? It's still snowing out there! And it's going to be snowing for the next two days. The whole Northeast has been paralyzed by this storm. We can't even keep up with the emergencies."

"This *is* an emergency! I have to get a manuscript!" Douglas started ranting about a million dollars and Sri Lanka, and May was sure the guy on the other end had chalked him up as New York City looney-tunes.

"Hey! Hey!" the guy was getting really irritated. "You have shelter and food and you're in no immediate danger—that's all I care about. I know where you are. In order to get you out of there, we're going to need some heavy equipment which I can't supply right now. I've got people in desperate situations all over the county. The roads are impassable. So you can just sit tight and wait." The man ended the transmission.

May banged Hunter's tray of food on the table.

"Congratulations, Mr. Congeniality. We should be dug out of here by next spring!"

Hunter roughly pulled his chair out, seating himself. "It wasn't my fault! He . . ." His gaze went to the food in front of him. A spoonful of rice. Two half-dollar-size slices of turkey swimming in a cup of brown water meant to be gravy. "Where's the rest of this?"

Even though she secretly agreed with him, had even been planning on getting some real food, there was no way she was going to admit the deficiencies of the meal to him. Better he think she was a woman with an agenda who stuck to her plans! Otherwise there would be no end to the complaining.

"That's it," she loftily informed him, making her voice sound slightly disdainful as if there were nothing lacking in her choice of fare. "And since it looks like we're going to be stuck here together for a week, we have to go easy on this stuff."

She licked the edge of her fork. "Eat up."

She remembered a cartoon in which Mickey Mouse, Donald Duck, and Goofy all sat down at an elegantly dressed table, complete with overhanging chandelier. Unfortunately, they had nothing to eat except one bean, which Mickey made a great show of slicing into see-thru-thin slices, placing one slice on each plate. Donald Duck watched Mickey silently, his temper slowly reaching the boiling point until suddenly he erupted. Pulling the feathers out of his head, he squawked his head off as he swung upside down from the chandelier.

C. Hunter Douglas had that same look on his face right now.

So she was surprised when, after he clenched and unclenched his fists several times, he quietly picked up his fork.

He took a bite of rice. "Not only is there nothing to eat here, but it tastes lousy."

May shrugged off the critique. "Dieters can't be choosers."

Hunter's silver gaze skimmed her figure. "Why are you dieting? You look fine to me."

She put down her fork in exasperation. "I have a deadline!"

Hunter stared at her unblinking for several moments. "And A is to B as C is to . . . ?"

"Oh, you wouldn't understand."

"Try me." He swallowed both slices of turkey in one gulp.

"It's sort of all tied in with a sense of accomplishment."

Hunter gestured at her with his fork. "It shouldn't be. I have never understood why women feel they have to starve themselves scrawny to feel good about themselves."

"I hardly starve myself, as you can see!"

Hunter's eyes twinkled. "Which makes it all the more confusing as to why you only brought these minuscule dinners with you."

Her cheeks flamed. She thought he might be insulting her but she wasn't sure. "Are you saying what I think you're saying?"

He smiled, revealing two curved dimples. "No, I am not." He let his gaze travel over her again, lingering on her rounded hips and full breasts. She really was a lovely woman. Now that his head wasn't pounding so bad, he was beginning to see some advantage to his situation.

"Just the opposite," he murmured.

Now she did blush. May reached for a glass of water rather shakily. He had better behave himself or he was going to get locked in the fruit cellar with Norman Bates's mother.

Hunter tossed his plastic dinner tray onto the floor for Benny, who gratefully licked up the soupy gravy.

"That won't upset his stomach, will it?"

"Nah. Dogs can eat anything."

"Are you sure? I now he's your dog, but—"

"He's not my dog. He was one of the gifts I—"

"Uh-huh. And how did you know I would even want a dog?"

Hunter sighed. There was no sense trying to explain that to her again. He stood, grabbing two apples off the table. "I'm going to scoop out a place for our friend here. I'm sure he needs to go. The back stoop isn't too bad because of the overhang; it'll have to do. C'mon, Benny." The dachshund trotted after Douglas, something akin to hero worship in his eyes.

C. Hunter Douglas might say that dog does not belong to him, May thought, but the wiener believed otherwise.

Chapter Ten

By late that afternoon May wanted to murder him.

In fact, she began to think up ways to do it.

She closed her eyes as he paced by the back of her chair for the thousandth time. He had been pacing for hours. Admittedly, there wasn't much for him to do—there was no TV, her radio wasn't picking up any stations, and there was no phone for "business chats." It was obvious that C. Hunter Douglas was completely at a loss.

She clenched her jaw at his next pass. "Mr. Douglas, *please!* I'm trying to work here."

"It's Hunter." He stopped pacing suddenly. "Hey, do you have any games on that laptop?"

She gritted her teeth. "No. Just word processing. As in manuscript."

He groaned, clutching his stomach. "Don't mention that word to me, it's making my stomach hurt."

"You don't think it could be the six apples you ate?" she said wryly.

He paused to look at her. "You think?" he asked seriously.

She smiled at the boyish expression. "It's a distinct possibility. You better lay off them, Hunter."

"I'm starving!"

"Oh, stop complaining! You'd have to pay a spa three thousand bucks a week for the same treatment you'll be getting here for free, and all they would add to the plate would be a little raddichio."

He threw her a dirty look.

"Don't think about it."

"And what would you suggest I do to take my mind off it?" His glance ran suggestively over her again. If he had met her under other circumstances he would have asked her out to dinner. And more.

May had no trouble reading his look. "*Forget it.* Men in moldy, baggy red velvet are not a major turn-on for me." She wondering if her nose was growing. Hunter was an extremely attractive man. Even in the Santa suit.

"If it'll make you feel better, I'd be happy to remove it." He grinned wickedly at her.

She exhaled. "You're just trying to annoy me because you're bored. Why don't you read?"

"*Read?* You've got books here? Why didn't you say so hours ago?"

She gave him an exasperated look. "What do you think has been staring at you in that open carton over there by the fireplace?"

He shrugged. "Oh, well, those are *romance* books. I thought you meant you had—"

That deserved a glare. "Don't say it if you value your red velvet hide."

"I didn't mean it like that. It's just that I've never—I mean they are women's books—"

"It's not like you have anything else to do—why don't you pick up one, you might be surprised."

He speculated on that, then walked over to the box of books. He knelt down, shuffling through the titles. "Is your book in here?"

"Why would I bring my own book?"

Hunter shrugged. "Why not? Is May Forrester your real name?"

"May is; Forrester is a nom de plume."

Hunter picked up one of her favorite books, opening the step-back cover. His eyes widened. "This guy doesn't have anything on but a towel!"

"Best towel I've ever seen," she agreed with a smile.

He threw her a look. "So what is your real last name?" He sat down on the floor near the fireplace, opening the book.

"Bea."

He read a few paragraphs, then stopped, capturing her in his gaze. "Your real name is May Bea?" Rich laughter filled the room.

"Stop that!"

"That must have been real interesting in high school—'May Bea she will and May Bea she won't.'" He chuckled, shaking his head. "No wonder you took a pen name."

May snapped the lid of her laptop shut. The man was not going to let her work! And he was too close to the mark; the kids had teased her mercilessly when she was young. Which was probably why she had become a writer; she had often run off by herself and daydreams had been her constant companions.

She placed her hands on her hips. "And who are you to talk? I can just guess what hideous first name is hidden by the initial C, Mr. *C.* Hunter Douglas!"

A dimple showed in his cheek. "Go ahead." His silver eyes flashed challengingly at her.

She hesitated, leery of the look on his provocative face. "Go ahead what?"

"Try and guess."

She narrowed a distrustful look at him. "You'll tell me if I guess correctly?"

"Sure."

"All right." She tapped her foot against the wooden floor. "Cecil."

"Nope."

"Clem."

He grinned. "Uh-uh." He went back to reading his book.

"Don't you worry, I have a whole week to come up with it."

"It's enough to give one pause," he said without looking up. Which was a good thing, because his eyes were definitely twinkling with humor.

And something else.

Chapter Eleven

"By the way, what *was* the name of your book?"

It was late evening. Hunter had moved up to the bed. The floor was drafty and, with the winds still howling from the unabated storm, May guessed, downright cold.

It was going to make sleeping difficult for him.

She had already decided to offer him the one and only quilt. She would have to try to keep herself warm with her jacket.

"You know very well what the name of it is."

He quirked his brow. "Let's pretend I don't."

"*Love's Loose Canon.*"

He burst into laughter.

May was incensed. "It's a pirate story, so stop that right now! There were *lots* of people who loved it."

He stopped laughing; that had gotten the publisher's attention. "By 'lots' what are we talking about?"

"Romance is *very* popular." Translated for him, it meant profitable.

He suddenly became serious. "I know; I've been looking into it, actually. My uncle has some old-fashioned notions about what Fortuna should and should not publish."

"Well, this could turn out to be a very good opportunity for you! You have the time, I've got the books, not to mention my knowledge of the genre, which I am willing to let you pick at—you could make good use of your time here."

A tiny line formed across his brow as he considered it. "Mmm . . . that's not a bad idea."

"Just remember, I'm off limits."

He looked her questioningly.

"I—I mean as far as writing for your company," she stammered.

He smiled rather sexily, enjoying her discomfort. "Does that mean you're 'on limits' for anything else?"

"Don't be cute."

He batted his thick lashes at her. "I can't help it; I'm a publisher. We're naturally alluring to writers."

"You have a warped mind."

He winked at her. "I'm going to take a shower. Any chance of finding a razor?" He rubbed the dark shadow on his cheeks.

While May thought the shadowy beard very attractive, giving him a brooding, dangerous look, she also recognized the wisdom of removing it from her sight. Hunter was starting to look tempting.

"Check the medicine cabinet; I think Billy left some stuff in there."

"Billy?"

"My neighbor—this is his place."

Hunter nodded, whistling off to the bathroom.

Surely she had misread that brief flash of relief in his eyes?

Hunter lathered his thick hair with some shampoo he found. Along with razor, shaving cream, deodorant, and best of all, a new toothbrush, he didn't feel half bad. Good ole Billy. He'd have to thank the man personally for the supplies.

Earlier, Hunter had noticed a box of condoms on the top shelf behind a large bottle of mouthwash. It remained to be seen whether he would be thanking the man for those as well. Ms. May Bea was looking mighty tempting to him.

In fact, she had from the instant he had first seen her.

Admittedly, he had been momentarily turned off when he discovered she had almost cracked his skull. But once he found out she was a writer, he realized he couldn't hold the outlandish behavior against her.

She couldn't help it. The poor kid.

The hot water sluiced over his head.

It felt great. The cabin was drafty as hell, and the heating system didn't keep up with the nightly drop in temperature.

When he came out of the shower, he eyed the red velvet outfit distastefully. He was going to have to see what he could rustle up in the way of clothes. And he wasn't going to put on that moldy red suit again until he washed it.

Donning his T-shirt and boxers, he padded out of the bathroom.

May was leaning over the bed, and he had a very good view of her backside. She had changed into a heavy flannel nightgown; inexplicably the old-fashioned garment looked sexier than a lacy negligee to him.

Her derriere wiggled under the loose flannel as she tried to pull the quilt free from the top mattress. Hunter crossed his arms over his chest and, leaning against the fireplace mantel, considered the scenery. It was . . . picturesque.

And it worked for him.

He felt himself begin to harden.

When she turned around and saw him standing there, she jumped a little. Seemingly against her will, her sights drifted to his paisley boxers, hesitating slightly. He wasn't really erect but he was . . . bulging. A becoming blush stained her cheeks.

Which made him bulge more.

He stepped forward. "Ready to go to bed?" His voice held the slow drawl of suggestion.

May sucked in her breath. *He was gorgeous.* Even the wretched red suit had not been able to disguise that fact, but when he appeared fresh from his shower in a V-neck white T-shirt and silk boxers, May was nonplused. He had an exquisite physique. Perfectly toned.

Real contemporary hero material, she acknowledged to herself.

However, the heated look in his silver eyes said he had more on his mind than sleeping. Therefore, May did the only thing a romance writer could do in this situation: she stuffed the quilt into his arms and showed him the floor.

To say that C. Hunter Douglas was not a happy camper was an understatement.

He was even less happy when she allowed the wiener dog to get into bed with her.

The floor was hard, cold, and drafty. Hunter heard the dog rustling close to her under her jacket. He bit off an expletive.

For a dog, Benny was one lucky bastard.

Chapter Twelve

Sometime in the middle of the night, May felt the bed dip.

Sleepily, she opened her eyes to the sight of Hunter crawling into bed with her.

She was instantly wide awake. "What do you think—" He placed a finger against her mouth.

"It's freezing on that floor. I'm sleeping here and I don't want to hear one word." That said, he covered them both with the quilt.

Then he turned his back to her.

May's lips curved in amusement. And didn't that sound just like a hero in a book? She'd have to remember that line.

The bed shook slightly and she realized he was shivering. So he really had been cold. Unaccountably, she felt bad for him. His T-shirt and boxers couldn't be providing him with much protection.

Turning her back to him, she scooted a little bit closer to give him some of her body heat. May heard a faint sigh of contentment coming from his side of the bed.

Benny wiggled under the quilt like a sand worm, heading to the foot of the bed. He covered Hunter's cold feet with his long, puppy-warm body, giving his ankle a little lick before settling in to sleep.

Hunter got the strangest impression that he had just come home.

It didn't make sense, but he was too comfortable to care.

Chapter Thirteen

"He threw back his head and roared with laughter."

May looked at the sentence she had just typed on her screen. Something about it bothered her.

She paused, brow furrowed. "He threw back his head and roared with laughter"? She read it again, this time picturing the strange scene in her mind. May wondered if the gesture didn't indicate a silent plea from her hero for Prozac . . .

What's the matter with me? Everyone loves it when the hero does that! I love it when the hero does that . . .

May sneaked a peek at Hunter, who was sitting on the floor by the fire, engrossed in one of her books.

Well, if Hunter started throwing back his head to roar with laughter she was going to radio that sheriff to have them parachute down some medication for him!

She shut off her laptop.

When this kind of stuff happened, May knew it was useless even to attempt to write. Yawning, she stretched her hands over her head to loosen stiff muscles, her mind going to that morning and how she had awakened in Hunter's arms.

He had been wrapped all over her, and to make matters worse, Benny was tangled up in there with them, too. The three of them lay there like a multi-tentacled lump of snoozing flesh.

The man might suffer insomnia on occasion, but when he did fall asleep, he slept like the dead.

"Hunter!" She jabbed an elbow in his side.

"Nnnn," he mumbled into the curve of her neck. The man was too comfortable.

"Claude?"

She felt him smile against the skin of her throat. "No." He snuggled in and went back to sleep. After a few minutes, May gave up on the idea of untangling herself and fell asleep again as well.

The next time she woke, Hunter was up and making coffee in the kitchenette.

That's when she discovered him draped over the refrigerator drinking the Half-and-Half. *From the carton.*

She let out an ear-piercing shriek.

Stupefied, Hunter stared at her, a mustache of white coating his upper lip.

May made a dive for the carton, rescuing what was left of her cream. "You fiend!" She clutched the carton to her bosom.

"What in the world is wrong with you?"

"I'm a writer; I have to have coffee! It's our life-blood; our adrenaline!"

Having had a great deal of experience with the breed, Hunter calmly inquired, "Can't you drink it black?"

"No!" She clutched the carton tighter. "It's my one weakness. My God, you drank almost half the container!"

He gave her a patient look. "Your *one* weakness," he said dryly.

"And you were drinking right from the carton!" She screwed up her face. "Eew! I hate it when men do that! What is it—something genetic with you guys?"

She ranted on until he poured her a cup of coffee, pried the cream lose from her, plopped some into her cup, and brought it to her lips, forcing her to drink.

Those silver eyes flashing all the while in amusement.

She was fine after the first cup.

May glanced to where he was sitting by the fire. What was he reading that had him so engrossed? He hadn't lifted his nicely shaped nose from that book in hours.

She squinted her eyes to read the title. No wonder. It was one of her favorite authors and the woman wrote steam heat. Her love scenes could blister paint from a wall. Smiling, she went back to her own story.

Hunter closed the book and leaned his back against the wall of the cabin.

He had just had an incredible revelation.

He had just realized that all these years he had known next to nothing about women. Not according to these books, anyway.

Like most men, he had always assumed that women wanted the same things men did. Now, he realized, they wanted something *else*. Something completely different. Something more.

Did they really go for the swaggering, drag-them-by-the-hair, boy-next-door type? And what did that mean? How could one man be all those things?

Did a man with a heavy-lidded expression—whatever the hell *that* was—turn them into . . . He tried to recall how the last author had phrased it. "A bowl of mush."

And those love scenes.

Mama mia.

They were beyond even his imagination. Since Hunter had always prided himself as a man with an excellent imagination, especially in bed, he was impressed. *I've discovered something here.*

It was a blueprint! A set of directions. Waiting in every bookstore, supermarket, and airport for any man smart enough to find it.

His sights rested on May. Luscious, soft, sweet-smelling May. Totally-oblivious-to-her-own-appeal May. Who had made him stone hard with one sweep of those sexy green eyes.

Hunter smiled wickedly. The theory was at least worth a test run.

Chapter Fourteen

That night Hunter came out of his shower wrapped in the quilt.

He sat by the fireplace and pretended to read. Making doubly sure the quilt slipped over his shoulder and down one side of his chest.

May finished the last sentence in her chapter and gratefully closed down her computer. "Well, that does it for toni—"

Hunter was sitting by the fire dressed in nothing but that fluffy comforter. May swallowed. *Is he naked under there?*

Firelight bounced off the highlights in his rich brown hair, gilding his shoulder and chest. May noted that said shoulder was plenty muscular and said chest was nicely delineated.

Hunter shifted his attention from his book to her, gazing at her with a carefully constructed, boyishly sweet, totally innocent expression. Like the book said. "Were you saying something?"

She quaked a bit under that intense regard. "N-no, just that I'm finished working for the night."

"Oh. Were you going to take a shower? I washed all my clothes and hung them up over the tub, but I'll take them down if you need to use it."

"Thanks." Her voice cracked a bit. She was right; he was naked under there.

It was sweet of him to offer to clear the shower for her . . . although, she didn't want him to move just yet. He looked awfully cute sitting there quietly reading a book.

Naked.

But for the quilt.

"It'll just take me a minute." He stood up, clumsily gathering the quilt about him. A section accidentally parted, revealing a tantalizing glimpse of tanned, muscled thigh before his fist clenched the material closed.

May forced herself to look away. Unfortunately, the picture must have seared in her brain, for she could not seem to shake it.

Hunter exited the bathroom, his damp clothes draped over his arm.

"You *washed* the velvet suit?" she asked incredulously.

"Uh-huh. Why? Is something wrong?" He looked at her earnestly.

She didn't have the heart to tell him. He'd find out soon enough when it dried. And could stand on its own.

She straightened the stack of papers she had

printed out, scanning them for typos. A voice came from right behind her chair and it sounded like a croaking bullfrog.

"You must be stiff from sitting here all day; would you like me to massage—"

She gaped at him over her shoulder. "What happened to your voice?"

He seemed surprised at her reaction. He frowned. "I'm speaking to you in a husky murmur."

"Well, don't. You sound like a foghorn at low tide."

Hunter stroked his freshly shaved jaw. "I must be doing it wrong. Can you demonstrate it for me?"

She put her hands on her hips. "Where did you ever get such a crazy idea? And why do you want to talk in a husky murmur?"

"I'm . . . testing out something. Go with me on this, okay?"

She expelled a gust of breath. The man was strange. "All right. Try this." She lowered her voice to a throaty, intimate drawl. *"The shower's ready and waiting . . . "*

Hunter's eyes glazed over. His heart kick-started. He leaned toward her . . .

"Your turn," she said in her normal voice.

Hunter pulled up short. Well, it sure worked on him! Positive that he could give as good as he got, he cleared his throat to try again.

Resting his forearm on the back of her chair, he bent close to her, whispering softly, "Your . . . shower is *ready* and I'm waiting . . ."

May's eyes widened. "Th-that's good." More than just good. Drooling good.

The corners of Hunter's mouth curved. He decided

to move in a little closer to her. He wanted to kiss that little curve on the corner of her mouth that had been fascinating him since he met her.

May bounced out of her chair. "Guess I better take advantage of it then, huh?" She dashed to the bathroom.

Just before she closed the door, she called out, "Cedric?"

"No," he yelled back, smiling. *It was working.* He could feel it in his . . . bones.

The thought made him laugh. Huskily.

Chapter Fifteen

"My underwear is still damp. I guess I'll have to sleep like this."

Hunter gestured to the quilt covering his bronzed skin and gave her an apologetic "it's beyond my control—what can I do?" look which didn't quite pass muster.

May's black brow notched. The man was getting decidedly frisky. And if he thought he was crawling into bed with her buck naked, he had another think coming. There was no chance she was going to wake up in the morning wrapped up with an *in-the-raw* Hunter.

She marched to the bathroom, where he had slung the clothes he'd washed over the shower rod. Hunter followed behind warily. May looked like she meant business.

Spotting the paisley silk, she whipped the shorts off

the rack and grabbed her blow dryer. Adjusting the heat setting to low, she held the very edge of the garment up between two fingers as if it might bite her at any moment and blasted the dampness right out of it.

Hunter's lips parted slightly. Now, why hadn't he ever thought of that? His second thought was: foiled.

May turned to him with his boxers dangling from her index finger. The arrangement of her features was definitely smug. "There you go—nice and dry."

Sheepishly, Hunter reached for them. "Ah, yeah. Thanks."

Once again, when they got into bed they turned their backs to each other.

Just before May drifted off, she asked him in the darkness, "Chester?"

Hunter smiled, drowsy. "Nope." He rubbed his silk-covered backside against her flannel-covered one before falling into a restful sleep.

Chapter Sixteen

Hunter tossed a piece of apple to Benny, then crunched into his fourth apple of the day. And it was only late afternoon. He was getting mighty sick of apples.

Well, beggars couldn't be choosers. Desultorily he wolfed down the fruit. He was starving.

Those frozen meals were not enough for him, even though May had been giving him two of the tiny cuisine meals every night.

His silver gaze wandered to the windows. It had stopped snowing this morning but it was a real mess out there. There was no chance of getting to his car. Not without boots and a plow.

He looked down at his wardrobe. May had dug out a pair of her black sweat pants this morning after he discovered that the red velvet suit was now a free-standing sculpture. They fit him like a second skin and only came to mid-calf on him, but he had been determined to ram down into them.

There was a faint floral perfume to the pants which evoked May. The fact that he was *inside* them, surrounded by the scent, made him . . . bulge. A situation made more blatant by the stretchy material.

He rubbed the bridge of his nose, wishing it were something else. Something May.

This morning she had been been draped over his back, her cheek using his shoulder as a pillow. One of her small hands had found its way around his waist to rest flat against his lower stomach, just above the band of his shorts.

In his sleep his hand had come over hers, making sure she didn't leave the needy spot. He was uncomfortably aroused and had a hell of a time disengaging himself from her without waking her up.

The memory of it alone was enough to get him going again.

Frustrated, he grabbed up another book. *Rough Possession* was the title. Hunter quickly threw it down and picked up another. *Day for Knight*. That sounded innocuous enough.

He began to read.

Across the room, May furtively eyed Hunter.

He was engrossed in his book and he didn't seem to be paying any attention to her.

Good.

Her hand inched slowly to the stack of papers on her lap. The stack that was hiding the half-eaten package of M&M's she had found in the bottom of her purse this morning.

She was starving.

In desperation she had tackled her pocketbook for booty and had come up with a small treasure trove.

Covertly she rooted around in the little bag, her finger snagging the small candy-coated jewel. Glancing his way one more time to be certain the coast was clear, she secretively brought the nugget of heaven to her mouth where she sucked on it for five minutes, savoring every molecule.

When it was over, her eyes were dilated with chocolate satisfaction.

Hunter was still engaged in the book. And looking damn fine, she thought resentfully. Those black sweat pants had been a mistake. Instead of covering him up and removing temptation from her sight, they seemed to be doing the opposite. The clingy material delineated every muscle in his strong thighs.

Every muscle.

May fanned herself with a sheet of paper. Hunter was packing.

She rummaged around for another M&M.

"What are you eating?"

May's head snapped up, her face flaming guiltily. "What?"

Hunter's silver eyes narrowed. "Don't what me—you've got something stashed away under those papers. What is it?" He tossed his book down. Rising to his feet, he began stalking her.

She didn't know why she did what she did.

There must have been a little devil on her shoulder.

She looked the publisher square in the eye and, parting her lips, she stuck out her tongue and flaunted the yellow M&M at him.

It was like waving a red flag at a bull.

Hunter charged her.

Squealing, May bolted out of her chair and took off. The papers and the candy package which had been on her lap toppled to the floor.

Hunter stopped briefly to grab the empty M&M wrapper. Then he turned and sets his sights on her.

"Last one," May taunted around the candy in her mouth.

Hunter lunged for her.

If she hadn't backed herself against a wall she might have escaped.

His palms came down on either side. He pinned her in place with the lower half of his body. Even through her jeans, May had no trouble feeling the hardness that pressed against her. Her breath caught in her throat.

She looked up into his face. A lock of mahogany hair had fallen over his forehead, giving his face a definite rakish cast.

As he bent his head, May noted that he didn't seem to be thinking about candy anymore. By the glint in those silvery eyes, it appeared that Hunter had decided to substitute one gratification for another.

May squeaked, the sound distorted by the candy in her mouth. "Hunter, you shouldn't—"

His mouth sizzled over hers.

There really was no other way to describe it.

A hot flame shot down the center of her body to her toes. Which began to wiggle.

May moaned into his mouth. There was only one other man who had ever made her toes wiggle . . . and not nearly this much.

Hunter removed one of his hands from the wall and cupped the back of her head, holding her to him. He strengthened the kiss, probing between her slightly parted lips with his tongue. Sinking deeper and deeper with every delving thrust, he forced her to open her mouth wider, to accept him . . .

He plunged into her with rough expertise, neither too naive nor too practised. His movements were honest and raw. He explored her thoroughly, leaving her totally breathless and wanting more Hunter.

May thought he tasted sweeter than any candy, and she clutched at his shoulders to bring him closer.

This time it was Hunter who groaned. His other hand left the wall to capture her waist, clasping her tight against him.

She didn't know how long the kiss went on but when they came up for air, May was feeling somewhat disoriented. She placed her palm against his chest to steady herself.

He was breathing heavily, but was curiously silent. Warily she glanced up at him.

His eyes glimmered with heat and . . . something akin to mischief. He quirked his brow in a cocky way, then slowly opened his mouth.

The yellow M&M dangled impudently from his tongue.

"Hunter!"

He grinned roguishly at her.

"That was a dirty trick!"

"Mmm . . . best M&M I ever had," he drawled. He made a great show of savoring the candy, even to the point of licking his lips when he was done.

May's face flamed.

He chuckled, leaning back into her. "Seconds?" he asked innocently.

"No!" She shoved his chest, pushing him away.

"You mean you don't like the heated press of my masculine lips against the soft fullness of your ripened mouth?" He spoke from behind her.

"Don't you dare!" she gritted out, refusing to look at him.

"Surely you felt the savage intensity of my raging hunger as I claimed you with the brand of my desire?"

"You are horrible!" She walked to the bathroom and slammed the door behind her.

His low laughter followed her.

May winced. The truth was she had felt all those things.

She splashed cold water on her face.

Chapter Seventeen

"What's wrong with Benny?"

Hunter had just come out of his nightly shower and when he bent down next to her, May caught a whiff of soap and after-shave. Old Spice. Billy's choice, she knew; Hunter was definitely not the type to buy Old Spice.

For some reason, the spicy scent reminded her that it was Christmas Eve.

She delicately inhaled more of the scent. It brought her back to her childhood when she had lived by the coast in a small New England fishing village. A lot of the men had worn Old Spice back then, and she rather liked the old-fashioned scent.

The word old-fashioned brought to mind how gentlemanly Hunter had been these last few nights, letting her shower first, giving her best crack at the hot water, which had a tendency to suddenly give out.

She adjusted her nightgown as she sat cross-legged on the floor.

"He has a tummy ache." She continued to rub the dachshund's belly.

Benny lay on his back, short feet up in the air, in what May was beginning to think of as his dead cockroach position. The wiener dog's expression was a carefully balanced blend of ecstasy at what she was doing combined with the sad "I'm a poor puppy" face which instantly produced a feeling a guilt in humans.

"How did he get an upset stomach?" Hunter had the nerve to ask that seriously.

May threw him a look. "How many pieces of apple did you give him today?"

A dull bronze colored his cheekbones. "I . . . ah . . . don't remember."

Benny gave a little whimper right on cue.

Hunter was consumed with remorse. "Hey, there, fellah." His hand joined hers on the dog's belly, rubbing. "Will he be all right?"

With all the attention, Benny was in puppy heaven and trying hard not to show it, while the man leaning over him had an expression of concern which only comes from an owner of a beloved pet. May smiled inwardly. Hunter was as good as gotten.

"Yes, but you shouldn't keep tossing him food; he probably can't eat so many strange combinations."

Hunter nodded, continuing to rub the dog's stomach with her. Every now and then their hands brushed against each other.

"How come you didn't do this for me when I had a tummy ache?" Hunter murmured next to her ear.

"Because you don't keep my feet warm at night,"

she replied without thinking.

May realized her mistake as soon as she saw those dark lashes lift languorously and those silvery eyes met her own.

There was such a frankly sexual look in them that her breath stopped in her throat.

"I'd be happy to keep you warm at night."

He did it. He spoke in a husky murmur.

And it sounded exactly the way she had imagined a perfectly executed husky murmur would sound. It even sent shivers down her spine.

He leaned toward her just a bit, and May knew he was going to kiss her. Instinctively she moved her head back a few inches.

His hand came over hers on top of Benny.

His other hand cupped the back of her neck, bringing her up against his descending mouth in a seamless move. She opened her mouth to attempt to object, but Hunter was already there.

His lips covered hers in a gentle press that was somehow persuasive at the same time. The tender act turned May into. . . . a bowl of mush.

Her mouth softened beneath his, returning his kiss.

Like any red-blooded man, Hunter took this as encouragement. He went from softly coaxing to "seize-the-moment fire" in the blink of an eye.

May gasped. What were they doing? She began to pull back.

"Hunter, stop!" She tried to speak between the molten imprint of his ongoing kisses. It was almost impossible; the man was definitely charged up.

"We shouldn't be doing this," she managed to croak just before he swept inside her mouth, staking a devastating claim. She moaned in response.

"Why not?" he whispered a few seconds later, not stopping in the least.

The question had been rhetorical, but May attempted to respond any way. "Be-because . . . you're only doing this because you're hungry! You're substituting—"

He chuckled, a low rumble against her lips. "I'm *hungry* all right." His mouth moved along her jawline to her throat.

May sucked in her breath. That was a very sensitive area. She closed her eyes, desperately trying again. "You see? You admitted it. You've been complaining how starving—"

He stopped. Raising his head, he looked at her, desire and something akin to amusement lighting his features.

With his lips a mere heartbeat away from hers, he purred, "I'm hungry for May."

Then his mouth seized hers and that was the end of that objection.

How did the man kiss like that? May was devastated and knew it. Especially since her toes were wiggling like mad under the hem of her nightgown.

His lips moved back to her throat, and May actually arched her throat to give him better access.

Hunter breathed in her flowery scent and went as hard as a brick.

Earlier, in the bathroom, he had opened her jar of floral scented cream and had inhaled deeply. It had not had the same effect on him and he realized that it needed the added factor of May. Her personal, sexy scent which had been driving him crazy since that first night.

His mouth closed over the spot of tender skin under her ear and he felt her tremble. She was responding to him.

"*Hunter* . . ." It was the sound of a woman in the throes of desire; however, there was the faintest hint of underlying protest.

He did not want her to stop him. Not now. Not ever. C. Hunter Douglas wanted May "Forrester" Bea.

So, clever strategist that he was, he decided to make absolutely sure of her compliance.

He was going to pull all the stops out and completely test his new theory. He was going to follow the directions that had been handed to him in the books he'd read. He was going to make love to her with *romance*.

He leaned over and, gathering her in his arms, he stood, without breaking the kiss. It was not an easy thing to do from a sitting position, but Hunter was a strong, large man. He hoped the small pop he heard in his back had been the settling of his joints and not a disc compressing.

Benny gave one bark of protest at the loss of his belly rub, then gave up, apparently recognizing when it was pointless for a dog to bid for attention.

Hunter carried her to the bed, gently depositing her in its center. He immediately came over her, his silk boxers sliding against the flannel of her gown.

His mouth fused with hers as he laced his fingers through her hair and kissed her senseless.

May's hands reached for his bare shoulders. They were muscular and hard, yet so very warm. . . . And the way the man kissed should be illegal!

He had carried her to the bed, actually carried her to the bed!

Her toes wiggled.

Hunter's knee wedged between her flannel-clad legs. He rubbed his thigh back and forth in a suggestive slide, inching higher and higher. The flannel of her gown pulled taut with his erotic motions and she gasped into his mouth.

How could she come to her senses when he wasn't giving her time to think?

One of his hands moved to the front of her gown and he cupped her breast, flicking his thumb slowly back and forth across the flannel-covered nipple. It hardened instantly.

He covered the jutting peak with his mouth, capturing it with his teeth.

When May felt the damp heat of his mouth through the material, a strangled sob seem to escape from her throat. Without thinking, she sank her fingers in the rich thickness of his mahogany hair. Drawing him closer.

He began to unbutton the front placket of her gown.

The feel of the tips of his fingers against the soft skin of her breast suddenly made May realize what she was doing. "Hunter," she choked, "what—what are we doing?"

Hunter paused. She was starting to balk. Now what? Time out for following the directions, he realized.

"You feel this, sweetheart?" He spoke against her lips as he stroked his fingers around her breast.

May closed her eyes and nodded.

"I'm stroking my hand against your velvet skin—here. And here." He brushed her lips with his mouth. "Does it feel good?" he whispered.

"Yes . . . oh, yes, Hunter, it does," she whispered back breathlessly.

Hmmm . . . it seemed to be working. "Do you know what I'm going to do next?"

She watched him, eyes open wide. Slowly she shook her head, indicating she had no idea.

"I'm going to dip my hot tongue into your luscious mouth and then . . ." He paused purposely.

May swallowed. My god, the man was dangerous. And he was very good with dialogue. "And then?" she asked faintly.

The corner of his mouth lifted in a roguish grin. "And then, lovely May, I'm going to *drink*."

She gasped, lips parting, and Hunter did exactly as he said he would. He delved into her. And drank. May writhed beneath him, caught up in the sensual storm he was creating.

He reached down and methodically lifted her nightgown inch by inch up and over her head. She wore nothing underneath. When the entire six-foot length of his flesh pressed against her, heavy and hot, she sighed into his mouth.

Hunter ran the palms of his hands over the curves of her body, marveling at how exquisite the touch of her skin was. He hadn't stopped to get a thorough look, but he had seen enough.

May was beautiful.

He expected she would be because . . . well, she had had that effect on him right from the beginning. In his eyes, she would always be beautiful.

He took her breast into his mouth and she arched up against him, a small, sexy moan of pleasure escaping her lips. The feminine sound shook him to his core.

"Hunter!"

"Easy, May . . . I'm just tasting you." He rolled his tongue around the jutting peak. "And teasing you." He flicked the nubbin several times, causing her to clutch at his shoulders.

"And taking you inside the burning dampness of my fiery mouth so I can draw on you with an untold hunger," he improvised.

May blinked. An untold hunger? That line needed a good editor. But then he drew on her voraciously, and in the next instant she didn't care what he was saying.

It was what he was *doing* that held her interest. And what he was doing was sending her over the roof. His hands were caressing her and molding her. Stroking and rubbing and stirring her up with each delicious sweep of his fingers.

Her palms found their way down his contoured back and of their own accord slipped under the elastic band of his shorts.

But no further.

May suddenly comprehended that there was only the thin silk of his boxers between the two of them.

And that item of clothing had a convenient slit in it.

May swallowed nervously. She couldn't do this! There was a very good reason why she couldn't do this. Suddenly scared, she desperately searched her brain for an excuse, *any* excuse that would . . .

She had it.

Grabbing a hank of his thick hair, she pulled his head up. Glazed silvery eyes tried to focus on her. "We can't do this, Hunter."

He stared at her, frozen to the spot. Then he nodded, as if he understood what she was saying. "It's okay—I'll deal with the fact that you're a writer."

May's eyes darkened. "No, you numbskull! I'm not talking about that. I mean we can't do this because we don't have . . . protection." There. That seemed an excellent reason. The best reason. She was very proud of herself.

Dazed, Hunter paused, his kiss-swollen lips parting a little.

The poor thing.

Then a slow, calculating smile creased his passion-etched face. She did not like that look. "What are you smiling for? Didn't you hear me? We have to stop and I—"

"May."

She stopped speaking to stare up at him.

"Don't you want to feel the driving thrust of my steely manhood between the petals of your tender femininity as I masterfully take you to a place where only the angels dwell?"

This he rasped in that perfected husky murmur of his.

"That is, until we float back down from the stars to the safe cushion of our entwined bodies."

Her face flamed. In some strange way she couldn't define, his words were having the oddest effect on her. It was as if . . . No.

In any case—despite the rather enticing image his

words provoked—they could not go on.

Hunter didn't seem to share her opinion. Taking her silence (and flushed face) as interest, he winked rakishly at her.

Furthermore, the silk shorts were quickly dispensed with.

"Hunter!"

A whoosh of cold air crossed her body as he jumped off the bed. May got a brief flash of something rather . . . robust, before she was presented with his backside as he headed toward the bathroom.

Her sweat pants hadn't lied—Hunter's bulge was nothing less than impressive. His buns weren't bad, either, she clinically noted as he strutted through the door. Not bad a-tall . . .

Realizing she was lying on the bed buck naked, she dived under the covers. Then began to wring her hands. Was that it? Was he just . . . leaving?

Or was he coming back?

May didn't know whether to exhale or take a deep breath.

She soon found that Hunter was coming back.

And in his hands were *dozens* of foil packages. She decided to take a deep breath. Her brilliant excuse had just gone out the window. "Where did you get those?" she gasped.

He grinned at her. "Good ole Billy—your neighbor."

"Billy?" This was more bizarre than she thought. She cocked her head sideways, trying to come to terms with the idea. "He's in his sixties! *At least.*"

Hunter snorted. "So what?"

May plucked at the quilt. "Well, I just thought . . . men that old didn't . . . I mean. . . ."

"You thought wrong. My uncle is seventy-three and he's still pounding his—" He stopped, realizing what he was saying. C. Hunter Douglas turned bright red. "Ah. . . . sorry."

Her lips twitched. He really was adorable. The perfect combination of boyish charm and predatory "hunkiness." She sighed demurely.

Unfortunately, her *nice* thoughts of him shifted to apprehension when he tossed the mound of packets onto the bedside table.

She swallowed. There were hundreds of the little buggers. "You—you're being overly optimistic, don't you think?"

"Nope." He lifted the quilt and climbed into bed.

Before she had time to think of something to say, he scooped her in his arms and rolled on top of her, his lips taking hers in swift possession.

Caught in her own sensuality, May succumbed to his passion—until he began gently to probe between her thighs with his erection, trying to get her to unlock her legs.

"Open for me, honey," He whispered the sweet words against her mouth, and if anything was ever more perfectly done in her life, she hadn't known about it. Still . . .

The wispy words rushed out. "Oh, Hunter, it's been . . . such a long time and—"

"Don't worry, sweetheart, I'll be careful."

May unlocked her legs—a little—and squeezed her eyes shut.

What was this all about? Hunter wondered. Since she had only spread her legs the smallest space, he had to wedge himself in there bit by bit until she finally opened her thighs all the way for him.

Hunter pressed forward slightly.

She was very tight. A little bit more . . .

He felt the barrier.

Astonished, he looked down at the woman beneath him. Her face was drawn up anxiously and she was biting her bottom lip.

Despite the seriousness of the situation, his lips twitched. *Does she think I can't tell?* "May." His voice held a hint of laughter and a hint of reproach.

She did not change her expression or open her eyes. "Yes, Hunter?" she whispered haltingly.

He decided that what he was going to say could wait until later.

"Aren't you going to kiss me?" His mouth brushed her closed lids in a loving caress.

Her green eyes fluttered open. "Oh, yes, of course, I was just—"

His mouth covered hers and he sunk into her, rapidly piercing the thin membrane.

She flinched, then lay perfectly still.

"I'm sorry," he spoke quietly in her ear but May didn't even hear him. She was too wrapped up in the feel of Hunter. He was inside her and it was . . . it was . . . precisely as she had imagined.

Giving her time to adjust to him, he brushed his lips across her slightly parted mouth, back and forth, laving the seam with his tongue, gently suckling on her lower lip.

"*Hunter,*" she uttered tremulously.

"I know, honey. I know." He kissed her deeply.

When he began to gently move in her, May cried into his mouth, small sounds of feminine pleasure that made it very difficult for him to maintain his control. She was driving him crazy. His body was telling him hard and fast, but his mind was cautioning him to slow and easy.

A sweat broke out across his brow but he held to his guarded tempo.

It was May who finally changed the pace.

Wrapping her arms tightly around his neck and her legs securely around his waist, she hugged him to her, her uneven voice shyly beseeching him, "More?"

It was the sexiest thing he had ever heard in his life. Hunter groaned out loud. And gave her more. Much more.

He drove into her with strength and power, releasing the passion he previously held in check for her sake. May went right along with him, encouraging him, begging him, commending him, in the unintelligible words of lovers which always spoke volumes.

A pounding, building tempest overtook her, lifting her higher and higher. It was extraordinary . . . she was pulsing everywhere and she wanted to—had to—

"Let go, sweetheart, let it go," Hunter rasped, guiding her even as he took her.

May cried out and let go and everything simply exploded around her. He thrust into her *deep* and clutching her to him, he covered her mouth with his own, joining her in a powerful release. May was intensely aware of the moment, of Hunter, of their joining.

It was a special gift that she would treasure forever; he had given her what every woman dreams of, hopes for. He had made the reality of her first time a true fantasy. And she would love him forever for it.

Hunter smiled tenderly down at her. He kissed the edge of her temple, feathering her jawline with tiny nibbles. "It looks like my May Bea didn't." He teased her softly. "How did you write all those love scenes?"

May kissed his chin. "Writers don't do *everything* they write about, Hunter."

He thought about that. "True. If Rex Stevens did half the stuff he wrote about, he'd have gotten the electric chair twenty times over."

She nodded. "We only wish we could."

He laughed against her throat. Then nuzzled her collarbone.

May sighed contentedly. Lovemaking *was* all that it was cracked up to be. And it was exactly the way she had written it countless times.

Incongruously, a large grin broke across her face. "Mmm, Hunter?"

Expecting to see a sexy, satisfied look on her face, Hunter was amazed to see a ridiculously huge smile. Confounded, he gave her a questioning look.

"I *am* a terrific writer!" She beamed up at him.

Oh-oh. It was another of those "writer" references that had a tendency to be non sequiturs. He had always marveled when he had seen two writers talking together; they always seemed to understand each other. It was the damnedest thing.

Well, Hunter had no idea what her being a good writer had to do with *this*, but he nodded as if he understood just the same.

He snuggled back into her neck.

And reached for another foil packet.

"Champ?" she whispered teasingly a few minutes later.

"Uh-uh." Smiling, he nipped the curve of her neck.

Chapter Eighteen

Benny woke them up Christmas morning.

The little dog was barking and dancing around the bed, trying desperately to get Hunter to pay attention to him.

They both groaned.

Hunter had made love to May the entire night and they were both exhausted.

"What's the matter with him?" May mumbled sleepily. "Does he have to go out?"

"I don't think so—I just let him out a few hours ago." Hunter yawned, then leaned over May so he could see Benny over the edge of the bed. "Wuzza matter, fellah?"

Benny wagged his tail and barked twice. Then he trotted to the front door, looking over his shoulder to see if Hunter was following him.

"I guess he does have to go out." Hunter rolled over May to get out of bed.

"Hunter!" she complained.

The corner of his mouth lifted crookedly in a smile and he bent over to kiss her nose. "Sorry." Naked, he padded after Benny.

May got a very nice view. She crossed her arms over her chest to watch the show. "Anytime," she murmured to herself.

"C'mon, Benny, we gotta go out the back door—too much snow out there." Hunter started for the door off the kitchen but the wiener dog wouldn't budge from the front door. He stuck his long nose near the bottom crack and sniffed all along the edge, his tail wagging excitedly.

"What is it do you suppose?" May asked.

Hunter scratched his chin. "I don't know. But he thinks there's something out there." Hunter walked over to where the dachshund was standing and carefully opened the front door.

As he suspected, snow was piled three feet deep on the porch and there was no place to go.

"See, boy? Nothing there—"

Benny dived head first into the snowbank.

"Hey!" Hunter lunged after him, trying to retrieve him before he lost sight of the thumping tail.

He pulled Benny back out; the dog had a piece of cloth clamped in his jaws and was tugging furiously.

Curious, May squinted to get a better look. "What does he have in his mouth?"

"It's the sack!"

"What sack?"

301

Dara Joy

"The sack of gifts I was carrying when I came up here. I forgot all about it. I must have dropped it on the porch." Hunter released Benny, putting him behind him; then he yanked the material, trying to loosen the large bag from under the snowdrift.

It came free suddenly, and both Hunter and the sack came hurtling into the room. May giggled.

Hunter regained his balance and gave her a look.

"Well, it is funny, Hunter; I mean, you are naked."

Shivering, he closed the door. "Not for long—it's c-o-o-l-d." He snatched up his shorts and T-shirt, putting them on.

Benny started circling the bag excitedly, yapping his head off.

"Now what?"

May found her nightgown scrunched down at the foot of the bed. She was still buttoning it when she came beside him. "What's in there?"

"Just gifts I was supposed to deliver." He reached into the bag and pulled out a red package with a big white bow. A small tag dangled from the top.

Benny barked louder.

"To Joanna," Hunter read the tag, "Merry Christmas from Santa Claus."

Benny sat up, waving his front paws madly.

"I think he wants you to open it."

Hunter shrugged. "Why not?" He unwrapped the gift. A huge grin filled his face.

"What is it?" May looked at him inquiringly.

Hunter reached in the box and held up a plate of candied sweet potatoes.

May's eyes glazed over. "*Hunter.*"

"*Woof!*" Benny concurred.

"That's why he was barking, he could smell the food."

"Do you think it's still okay?"

Hunter dipped his finger in the sauce and licked it off. "Mmmm-hmmm. Natural Maine refrigeration. It's perfect."

May rushed over. "Open up the others, quick!"

Hunter grabbed the next package. "To Alicia, Happy Holidays courtesy of Ingles Delicatessen, where Katya and Rolph say every bite of our food tastes like a little bit of magic." This one held a scrumptious-looking pecan pie.

May and Hunter's eyes met above the plate.

In the next instant they were both diving for the boxes, tearing the wrappings open.

"To Jennifer . . ." May opened a tray of assorted hors d'oeuvres.

"To Chris . . ." Hunter held up a tureen of creamed pearl onions.

"This one is to Ted . . ." May pulled out a pair of bayberry candles and holders.

"For Richard, Happy Chanukah . . ." A dish of giant potato pancakes. They both licked their lips.

Next came a box of dog biscuits with "Benny's favorite" taped to the box. Hunter tossed him one, then reached in the bag to get the biggest gift out.

"To Johnny . . ." They both held their breath as he unwrapped it. It was a big Christmas ham.

May ran into the kitchen to get some plates and silverware. Hunter took the quilt off the bed and spread it before the fire. They were going to have Christmas dinner.

Soon they were seated before the fire feasting on the riches they had found.

May looked at the wonderful food before her, the sweet puppy lying contentedly by the fire, chewing on his hambone, and the man next to her, who against all expectations had turned into a real-life hero.

Her eyes filled with moisture. "This is the best Christmas I've ever had, Hunter."

He put his fork down to cover her hand with his. "Me, too, May."

They came together to kiss.

"Casper?" She planted a soft kiss next to his dimple.

"No, honey."

May sat back on her haunches. "Then what *is* it?"

Hunter grinned at her. "Christopher," he said nonchalantly.

"*Christopher?* But that's a nice name!" She was indignant.

He laughed. "I never said it wasn't, Ms. Bea. That was your idea."

"No wonder you had on a Santa suit," she grumbled. "With that name you were a shoo-in. How come you don't use it?"

"My grandfather's name is also Christopher. It got too confusing at family get-togethers."

As simple as that. No wonder he wasn't a writer. A writer would have a much better story than that.

However, flights of fancy notwithstanding, she was absolutely crazy about the publisher.

Hunter reached over, his hand clasping her about the neck. "You know what?" Their noses were almost touching.

"What?" she purred.

"I think I'm in love with you."

May blinked, stunned.

"Know what else?" he went on unperturbed.

"N-no."

"I think you love me, too."

A writer and a publisher? How existential . . . May's thoughts were interrupted by his next question.

"Know what else?"

May shook her head.

"I predict that you and I will be here next Christmas and we'll be old married folks." He stopped to stare at her poignantly. "What do you think of that, May?"

She did not have to think. "Mmmm, I just love sequels . . ." May closed the small distance between them.

After they ate, May went to store the leftovers in the refrigerator and Hunter was picking up in the room. He had already replaced the quilt on the bed and was in the process of folding the large cloth sack when a small card floated out of the bag to fall at his feet.

Thinking it was a tag that had fallen off a gift, he bent down to retrieve it and was about to throw it away when he spotted *his* name on the front of it.

Gingerly he opened it and read:

To Hunter,

  It seems Benny and you are a perfect match. The other half of your gift is a lifelong one—something you've been needing for a long time. Remember, it only comes from following the "directions" exactly. Merry Christmas.

Your Friend, the Old Coot

P.S. It's a good thing I have an extra suit.

A cold sweat broke across Hunter's brow. He suddenly remembered the names of some of those nurses in the hospital. Nurse B. Litzen? Nurse Donner? And that little red-haired one . . . Rudy.

No way.

What about that deli that supplied all those gifts for the children? Katya and Rolph Ingles . . . K. & R. Ingles . . . Kringles?

It couldn't be.

At that moment May came back to the room. Seeing his ashen expression, she asked, "Is something wrong, Hunter?"

He rubbed his hand across his face. Who would believe it? "No, everything is fine, sweetheart. C'mere, Benny." He patted his leg so the dog would come to him.

Benny obediently left his mangled hambone and trotted Hunter's way.

When the dog was sitting by his feet, Hunter reached down and untied the blue ribbon around the dog's neck. "Welcome home, boy." He ruffled the fur on Benny's head.

Tongue hanging out, Benny gave his new master a look of pure adoration.

The burst of static from the radio surprised both of them. "Hey, Douglas, you there?" It was the sheriff's office.

Hunter went over to the radio, flicking the switch. "Yeah, go ahead."

"I have an urgent message from your editorial director."

Hunter took a deep breath. "Go ahead."

"She says, 'Rex's manuscript arrived last night from

Sri Lanka. It's a knockout. Relax and enjoy the holiday.' "

Hunter was nonplused. Rex had come through. Big time. He actually felt his eyes get damp.

"We should be able to dig you out day after tomorrow," the sheriff continued.

"That's okay, Sheriff." He met May's eyes. "Take your time." He switched the radio off.

May beamed at him. "You got your manuscript!"

Hunter hugged her to him. "That and a whole lot more."

"*How romantic!*" May gazed up at him, love shining in her eyes. "Oh, Hunter, I absolutely adore you!"

He looked down at May and sighed. *Writers.* They were the best.

A GIFT FOR SANTA

NELLE MCFATHER

Lovingly dedicated to my Aunt Guinelle, who is an adventurous romantic just like my heroine.

Chapter One

Christmas was in the air. Cornelia Armstrong Carswell sniffed the fragrance of the basket of pinecones on the front stoop of Catshead Peak. From her lofty hill overlooking the tiny town of Darien, Georgia, she could see the early signs of preparation for the coming holiday. Miss Dovey, the mistress of the nursery/kindergarten, already had her enclosed play yard full of festive figures. Angels mingled with Bambi-sized plastic deer, and a chubby Santa was lord of the sandbox.

Even the Trash brothers, making their Monday morning collection in their worn-out old Ford pickup, were wearing red caps with pompoms. The two men waved up to the young woman at the top of the hill. "Howdy, Neely. It's a fine morning, ain't it?"

"It sure is," Cornelia called back, smiling at the way everybody in town had quickly reverted to using her childhood nickname. The "Trash brothers," actually

Easter and Head West, had grown up and gone to school with her. Coming back to Darien after ten years away as a Navy wife, she was grateful that most things about her hometown had not changed. The garbage collectors were still as cheerful as their late father, Wilde, whose penchant for giving his children whimsical names had perpetuated the humorous streak in Darien's poorest family.

The fact that the West family could maintain a sense of humor was remarkable, Neely thought, her smile fading as she reflected on the poverty they lived with. Although they worked tirelessly, the Wests had never been able to overcome hardship after hardship. Sunshine, Easter's wife, who cleaned and cooked for Neely, had explained why the family stayed so poor. "It's like they say—hard luck hits those with no luck at all. Poor Easter and his brother built up that garbage business on a pin and a shoestring. But ever' time we look like we gone get ahead, have a little dab of money, something happens and we're back to hard-scrabble lane."

The pride in the family would not let them take "money for nothing," so Neely contented herself with sending food and clothing home with Sunshine every time she could come up with a plausible excuse.

Thoughts of the Wests and their lamentable state gave way to other reflections when she saw Miss Dovey down the street. The years had not been kind to Miss Dovey, who had grown more and more into the bitter, dried-up stereotypical old maid that she hated herself for being. She doted on her charges, but even the children lamented that their teacher never smiled or seemed happy. She was as "balled up as that stringy bun of hair," one of the mothers had once commented.

Neely chided herself and waved enthusiastically.

The headmistress, coming into the schoolyard with a bevy of children clinging to her, waved back. "Emma's walking home for lunch," she called out. "I'll watch her from here."

Neely's reply was drowned out by the roar of a motorcycle. She winced as she watched Cash Bidwell's Harley barely miss the huge oak tree around which Main Street curved. "I wouldn't miss you, Cash, but I'd hate to see our Christmas oak banged up." She watched as her daughter crossed the street, making sure that the town scalawag didn't swerve toward the kindergarten.

Neely had gone to school with Cash, too, and couldn't believe he was still just the same ne'er-do-well now that he'd been back in Darien Elementary. What was it her mother was always saying? "That sorry Bidwell boy! He'll never amount to a hill of beans."

Cash was a career redneck, poaching deer and running around town on the motorcycle that he'd bought with his welfare checks. Neely had once commented to one of her friends, "The only thing he's missing is a dog named Booger."

Cash, unaware of Neely's unflattering thoughts, gave a wolf whistle and then hollered at Neely. "Hey, stuck-up, you're shore looking fine. How's about me and you going to Little Knights for some dancing tonight?"

Neely didn't deign to answer and Cash roared off. As her mother had said when Cash asked Neely to go with him to the junior prom, there was no insulting the man.

Thinking about her mother made her sad. It had been almost seven years now since Neely had gotten the telegram about the plane crash that had taken her parents' lives. How they would have loved her being back home, and how they would have adored their darling granddaughter! But Neely had vowed when she was widowed by the accidental death of her husband, Dane, that she would not dwell on her losses. Emma needed a happy environment, not a gloomy mother who dwelt in the past.

Coming home to rear her little girl was one of the smartest things she had ever done, Neely decided, watching her child walking up the hill. Everybody on Main Street called out to Emma, even the rocking-chair contingent sitting on the porch of the Darien Hotel. She was a child to charm anyone's heart, Neely thought with a lump in her throat. How cruel fate had been to rob such a loving, sweet little being of her father. Neely had vowed fiercely after her husband's death that she would never let Emma be hurt again.

They both loved Darien, its people and especially Catshead Peak, the old homestead. Neely could almost feel the ghosts of her kin and often sensed the distant echoes of gaiety and laughter. Never once had she passed the picture of Susannah, her great-great-grandfather Ward's sister, without feeling a jolt of familiarity. It was as though the woman she resembled so closely was her guardian angel. She often heard tinkles of laughter in the windchimes, saw shadowy figures happily dancing in the moonlight . . .

"Mama, you're dreaming again."

When Emma came running up to her, Neely hugged her more tightly than usual. Then she smiled down at her daughter, noticing that the child's chestnut curls were almost as dark as her own now. Certainly the retroussé nose and heart-shaped face marked her as "one of the Armstrong women." Their Scottish ancestry had created a long line of dark-haired, creamy-skinned, blue-eyed females. Emma was a carbon copy of the original, Dorothea, whose portrait hung in the living room of the house.

"Mama, can I bring Nick home for supper one day this week? Can I please, pretty please, Mama?"

Neely tucked her daughter's hand inside her jeans pocket where a Christmas cookie was nestled. As Emma nibbled on the treat, Neely answered, "Honey, I haven't heard anything about what you're doing in school. All I hear about is Nick, Nick, Nick. Who is this guy, anyway?"

She listened to her daughter's enthusiastic description of the homeless man that Miss Dovey had taken in some weeks ago. Even the kindergarten mistress, the soul of discretion when it came to bringing a stranger in amongst her "children," was reluctantly singing the man's praises to everybody. Nobody could quite believe that the prim schoolmarm had taken in a virtual hobo.

"Honey, I'd be happy to have you bring your friend for supper. How about tomorrow?"

"Oh, Mama, thank you, thank you, thank you." Emma hugged her mother even tighter. "You're going to love Nick, you really are. Why, even Miss Dovey almost smiled when he teased her this morning about how she looked like a Christmas angel."

It sounded like this Nick was a real slick operator, Neely thought. But she trusted her daughter's instincts about people. "Well, I wouldn't quite go along with that comparison, darling, but it is sweet of him to be nice to Miss Dovey. I'm glad she took him in to do odd jobs for food and board." People in Darien were still reeling from Miss Dovey's uncharacteristic generosity. "This friend of yours certainly has a way with old women and children. I'm eager to see if he has a similar effect on your mother."

"Oh, I can't wait for you to meet 'im. And maybe he can meet Freckles and Nub Nose, too. I told 'im about our little pet deer and he actually lit up, 'stead of looking sad like usual."

"Well, I know you and how you feel about those animals. Sounds like we've got another animal-lover on our hands." For Emma and Neely both, a direct gauge of a person's worth was how he responded to animals. "I'll have Sunshine make something special for dinner tomorrow. Speaking of dinner, it's at five tonight since I want an early bed for my little girl. After all, you stayed up late last night watching *Miracle on 34th Street*."

"Oh, Mama, wasn't it wonderful how Santa helped that little girl get a new daddy?" For a moment, Neely was afraid Emma would start crying again as she had during the movie.

"That was a four-hankie movie, all right."

"I saw you crying, too, Mama, when the little girl saw the house she'd been dreaming about."

Mother and daughter were by now tucking into the chicken and dumpling casserole Sunshine had left for their lunch.

"You've got me there, sweetheart. I'm a sucker for happy endings. I just hope that you and this Nick friend of yours are not scheming to find us a new daddy."

"Well, I need a daddy, unless you want me to grow up to be one of those wild teenagers with rings in my nose and tattoos and orange hair . . ." Emma started giggling along with her mother at the unlikely image of prim and nearly prissy Emma Carswell as a juvenile delinquent. "Or maybe you could marry Mr. Cash. He's always chasing after you. And isn't he the one who tormented you in grade school? Hey, that's a great idea, you and Mr. Cash, I mean. Then you could be a biker mom and I'd be real cool riding behind on your Harley."

They dissolved into laughter at that unlikely image. After Emma went down for her nap, Neely dawdled for a long time over her coffee. The movie the night before had stirred some old feelings inside her—the feelings a woman had when her family was complete, the feelings a mother had when her child had a happy life with both parents . . .

"Oh, stop it. You promised yourself when you came home there'd be no self-pity, no whining about the past."

But as she cleared the dishes and looked out the window at the beautiful sweep of lawn and trees, she almost imagined she saw her ancestor Susannah strolling with her husband and child. The funny thing was that Neely, like the little girl in *Miracle*, believed that dreams could come true.

"Oh, yes. And there's really a Santa Claus, Cornelia Armstrong Carswell."

On that self-mocking note she went up to nap with Emma and their cat Marmalade.

Neely had one of her dreams that night. It always happened when she was on the verge of some big, exciting change in her life. In her ancestor Susannah's journal, there had been several entries about the black heron that her ancestor had seen before important events.

Neely had searched the cliffs for that black heron, but she'd never seen it. In a way she was glad. One should have one's own omens, and she had the dreams.

In them, she felt as if she were Susannah, waiting for her brother to come home from the Citadel. (Neely knew from the family history that this was where Susannah's brother Ward had gone during the years just preceding the War Between the States.) Neely's dreams featured exact pictures of Ward and his sister, since she had seen their portraits.

But the arrival that really excited her was that of a handsome young man whom she knew in her waking hours to be Morgan Dancey, Ward's Yankee roommate who would someday be Susannah's husband. In the dream, Neely rode horseback, spent hours walking on the cliff, enjoyed the great Yule fire and other Christmas festivities. When she and Morgan were alone together, they made plans for the future—between passionate kisses.

Then the blackness and the fires and the horrors of war came and Susannah would weep on the cliffs for her sweetheart, who was now the South's enemy and therefore hers. She prayed for the safety of her brother, who was fighting Morgan's troops in the desperate battle of Savannah.

Usually, the dream ended as the lovers were reunited, but this time it was different. Neely became herself again, and Susannah drew her into the shadows and took her by the hand to the big oak tree. "Under this oak tree you will meet the man you will love and marry," Susannah murmured. "He will come for you very, very soon."

Then Neely was alone under the oak, her heart beating fast as she saw a figure coming toward her.

"It's you," the man whispered. "It won't be long. It won't be long, my darling, before I can hold you in my arms."

She held out her hand as he stretched his toward her but they couldn't touch, and she knew it was only a dream. "Don't go. Please don't leave me."

When she awoke from the dream, she could hear herself repeating the entreaty. She felt warm and blushing as though she'd really been with a lover. "Darn it, Susannah! Where is this dream lover you're promising me? Carswell, you are going off the deep end just because of that damn movie. There are no eligible men in Darien and you bloody well know it."

She pounded her pillow and put her still-warm cheek on the cool satin. It was just terrible being a hopeless romantic, she thought. And she'd given birth to another one just as guilty.

Still, there was a smile on her face when she drifted off to sleep.

The next morning she was awakened by Emma bringing her a cup of coffee. "Sunshine says I can start bringing your coffee before I go to school."

"Just be careful not to burn yourself," Neely warned, feeling a lump in her throat at how grown-up her little girl was trying to be. If she had a full-time father, she could go back to living out a real childhood, instead of helping her mother cope with being a single parent. "I dreamed about Great-aunt Susannah again last night."

Emma's eyes shone and she climbed up on the bed with Neely. She loved hearing stories about their beautiful ancestor. "Tell me, Mummy. Tell me all about it."

"Honey, if I do, you'll be late for school. Now give me a kiss and be on your way."

Chapter Two

When Emma came home from school that afternoon, she found her mother pensively looking out over the river. "Hey, are you still thinking about that dream you had? Must've been some dream!"

Neely had the grace to blush, realizing she *had* been thinking about the man she'd met in her dream. "Well, that and other things. I was thinking about your friend Nick and how much it must mean for poor, lonely Miss Dovey to have someone to help her out. For some reason, I've had Miss Dovey in my thoughts lately. I guess because it's Christmas, the loneliest time of the year for people who are alone. I think it's great that she's overcome some of her sticky old ways and has taken in this Nick of yours."

"Well, actually, I think it's 'cause they're both so sad. Miss Dovey told me she never met anybody as sad as herself till Nick came along. I wonder, Mama"—

Emma looked sad herself—"did Miss Dovey ever have a boyfriend?"

"Not that I know of. You say this new friend of yours is sad, too? I wonder why. He's a bit mysterious, isn't he, just showing up in our little town and not appearing to have any ties elsewhere."

"Miss Dovey thinks something happened to make Nick wary of people. He wouldn't talk much at all, except to us kids."

"Is that what she said? Emma, is this new friend of yours really all that unhappy?"

"You'll see. It's like, well, he's sad, and all, but that's not how he was meant to be. Maybe you can figure out Nick."

Neely was beginning to see more behind her daughter's entreaty to have the handyman over than a casual invitation to supper. Emma was convinced that her mother was the wise woman of the universe who could solve any and every problem.

Somehow this looked like a more complex problem than the ones Emma usually brought home for her mother to solve.

"So I finally get to meet my daughter's wonderful new friend Nick. I am so excited." Neely held out her hand to the man Emma had so proudly presented to her at the front door. "Please, Nick, come in by the fire and see our tree. Emma and I finally finished decorating it last night."

Neely was chattier than usual, mainly because there was something about her guest that made her feel a little strange. Neely had never seen a man whose eyes held such deep sorrow. Now she understood why her daughter had taken this man under her angel's wing. She was a natural caretaker who always took in wounded strays, animal or human. Neely loved that quality in her daughter but wondered if, this time, she had not taken on a man too steeped in sorrow ever to respond—even to Emma.

"What a beautiful tree." Nick wandered around it, examining it solemnly. "Not many people use the old-fashioned decorations anymore," he said wistfully, "like popcorn and cranberries and . . . what's this? Oh, my, what a special angel."

"It is special." Neely went over to touch the smooth applewood of the ornament in question. "My great-aunt put this on the tree the night her brother and sweetheart were trying to get home to her from the war in Savannah. In the stories I've heard she always swore that the angel brought them home safe."

"Umm. I need something like that," Nick said. He looked around the room. "This is an interesting house. I notice there are windows on the front but none on the back. There's a reason for that, I reckon?"

"You reckon right. It's sort of an early version of the solar heating system. Works, too, doesn't it, pussy-cat?" Neely tweaked Emma's curls. "Speaking of working, shouldn't you be in there helping Sunshine get dinner on the table?"

Emma was reluctant to leave but did so, apparently content to leave her beloved friend with Neely, who seemed to like Nick as much as she did.

"That's one special little girl," Nick said. "I hope you know that."

"Oh, I do," Neely responded. "I do, indeed. I'm so glad she has you as a friend."

"And I'm so glad she has you as a mother. But I'll be honest with you, that little girl needs more. She needs a daddy, a good one, like the one she had . . ."

"There'll never be another one like Dane," Neely said sadly.

"You don't replace someone you love, you add one."

The sound of a sharp rifle report startled them both. "Oh, my God," Neely exclaimed, "hunting season's on us and the poachers are on my land again."

When Emma appeared, her eyes wide with fear, Nick bounded into action, hardly waiting to hear her frightened words. "Someone's trying to shoot Freckles and Nub Nose!"

"The shots are coming from over there, near the cliff." Neely tugged at Nick's arm, hoping he wasn't too old to be running around in the cold like this. But she couldn't allow Emma's beloved pet deer to be killed. Her little girl had too little to love, she thought fiercely. "Oh, no they're shooting again! Emma, you get back in the house. Now! Get back inside."

A voice rang out in the cold night air, one that resonated with authority. "You out there, you with the guns, show yourselves."

"Out of the way, old man, and git the woman and the young'un outa the way. We're out to get us a coupla deer."

Nick walked toward the voice in the woods. When Neely looked at his face, she clutched Emma close to her. Nick's eyes were as steely cold and hard as ice. "You'll not be shooting anything tonight. Put your guns down and walk into the clearing, or else."

A sudden wind blew up and an owl hooted clearly in the woods. Behind that sound came a low growl that Neely couldn't identify. She'd heard there were panthers in these woods. Other sounds of the forest joined in; a cloud covered the moon and dark wings flapped nearby. Then Neely heard a very different sound, kind of a human moan.

Cash Bidwell and his hunting crony walked into the clearing and put their guns down. "My Gawd, that was creepy. I coulda sworn I heard a panther growling. Can't see a thing in this dark."

Nick picked up the discarded gun of the leader. "Nice rifle. I don't hunt myself, don't like killing living things, but I respect the idea of hunting, when it's fair." He whistled between his teeth and the two spotted deer came running up, nuzzling at the old man's knees. "But I don't call slaughtering babies in the woods fair." Blue eyes held like steel grips on the man being chastised as gnarled hands gently stroked the deer's downy heads.

"Hey, okay, I gotcha. Now go easy on the gun. Oh, man!" Cash's and his companion's eyes grew wide as saucers when Nick slowly put down the gun and reached for the tire iron Neely had grabbed on her way out from the porch. "What you gone do with that? Them things can hurt a body."

"This is what will happen to your beloved firearm if you ever show up here again, bent on shooting innocent wildlife."

As they all watched in amazement, Nick slowly bent the tire iron into a Q-shaped piece of worthless metal.

"Gawd," Cash's cohort breathed before making a run for it.

"Brave fellow," Nick said with a slight smile. "Care to follow him, or would you rather hear the lesson that goes along with the demonstration you've just seen?"

"Neely, you got yourself one crazy hobo here, but notice I ain't moving till I hear whatever he's got to say."

Neely squeezed Emma's hand to keep her from giggling. "Smart move, Cash. Maybe you'll learn something tonight.

"The lesson is, my friend, that you never do anything without a good reason for doing it. If you're gonna kill something, make sure it's for a good reason. If you don't, you might wind up with that rifle of yours bent around your neck." Nick bent and picked up the gun and handed it to Cash. "Here. Think about what you can do to turn your love for hunting and killing into good. Think about it hard, Cash, and don't come poaching on Miss Cornelia's land ever again."

"I don't think God wants me to," Cash said. Then he looked at Neely and shook his head hard as if trying to digest all he'd seen. "You always did have weird friends, Miss Neely." His eyes lit up. "Hey, you never took that ride on the Harley with me."

"I'll go," Emma put in cheerfully. Her mother stifled her with one hand. "Mmmm . . ."

"That means good night, and not *arrivederci*. Nick, would you be so good as to escort Mr. Bidwell to the curb and join my daughter and me in the kitchen for hot chocolate and popcorn?"

"I ain't invited?"

Cash escaped the boot aiding his departure by a very narrow margin.

* * *

"He's not a bad fellow—just misguided. Umm. The popcorn was excellent, but this is the best candy I've ever had in my mouth, and I've had a lot of candy in my day." Nick and Emma and Neely were seated around the fire after a delicious dinner.

"That's Great-grandmother's special praline candy recipe, but wait'll you taste the Lane Cake and pecan pie . . . if you're going to be around here for Christmas, I mean." Emma looked up anxiously into her friend's face. "Are you?"

Neely was gazing at Nick's face, too, but for a different reason than her daughter. His blue eyes sparkled and his big face glowed with color. She looked at Emma to see if she had noticed the transformation in Nick since the episode in the wood.

Her daughter was gazing admiringly at her friend and hanging on his every word.

Nick changed the subject, smiling and pointing at the window to the front porch. "I think our little friends out there are looking for a Christmas treat." They all laughed at the sight of Freckles and Nub Nose with their noses pressed against the glass. While Emma was outside giving the little deer a dish of dog morsels, Nick said more seriously, "We were interrupted earlier, Cornelia. Emma desperately wants a father. Why do you think she attached herself to me so quickly? That child has so much to give. She needs a better father figure than an old fogey like me can be."

"You're not an old fogey. And after what you just did, you're our hero. As for being attached to you, that is something I can completely understand." Neely got up to give the old man a hug. "You're absolutely lovable. I'm already as attached as Emma. Nick, how did you bend that tire iron? I mean, I haven't seen you lifting weights down at Pogo's Gym."

Nick's eyes twinkled as he sipped his coffee. "Umm. Luziannne, good old chicory. Haven't had coffee like this in maybe a hundred years." He corrected hastily, "Well, maybe fifty. I'm not *that* old. But to answer your question, any of us can do anything we want to if the motivation's there. Haven't you heard about those folks that lift an automobile off a loved one single-handedly? I happen to have a real soft spot for deer. Wouldn't want to see those two harmed in any way. And I'd do just about anything for little Emma," he added, a tender note in his voice.

"Well, we're very grateful. Oh, my, look at the time! I still have to help decorate the Christmas oak this evening. And have you heard about the upcoming town meeting about the new road? I hope you'll be there. We'll need all the help we can get to keep those Department of Transportation people from running all over us. There's talk that they plan to cut down our three-hundred-year-old tree just to keep from having to run the highway around it!" Neely's indignation was fierce.

"That oak means a lot to you people, doesn't it?"

"Oh, my, yes. I can't imagine Darien without the Christmas Oak. Why, General Oglethorpe camped under that tree with all his troops. And then during the War Between the States, it was almost destroyed when the freemen burned down the town. But there it was, after all was done, standing tall and proud and invincible. I think it's a symbol of hope for all of us, just like it was then. We've had weddings and dances and even christenings under that old tree." Neely got up to clear the dishes. "It's been a tradition, Lord, I don't know how many years, for everybody to hang an ornament on the oak to bring us prosperity the following year."

Nick's eyes lost some of their brightness. "Tradition's a wonderful thing, but sometimes people aren't good enough to live up to it. Don't you have thieving? Ornaments stolen or vandalized? That tree's right out there in the street, ready to be pilfered."

Neely laughed as she picked up a box and carefully chose an ornament from her own tree to put inside it. She knew just which one she wanted to hang on the Christmas Oak this year. "Do you think for one moment that I would put my precious angel on that tree if I were worried about vandals? Lighten up, Nick! The world's not full of bad people. I mean, you said yourself that not even Cash is really a bad guy. Hey, why don't you come with me? You'll see everybody in town there if you stick around long enough."

Nick got up and put on his jacket and an old wool cap that Neely was pretty sure had come from Miss Dovey's late daddy's closet. "Thanks, I'd like to see this tree you hold in such high regard. Then I've got to gather some wood for Miss Dovey. That lady may be prickly as a cactus, but she insists on doing everything for herself. I have to convince her that she needs a little help around that place."

Neely looked at him, her hands on her hips, and shook her head. "I haven't known you very long, but I feel like I have. You sure are a puzzle to me, doing kind things for Emma and me and Miss Dovey and then the next minute acting like there's no good in the world."

"When you've seen what I've seen and lived even a tenth as long, you'll feel differently about the world, I'm sorry to say."

"Well, I lost my parents and my husband within a period of seven years and I could've been the most bitter person in the universe. But you know what? I thought about what Mother used to tell me every time we lost a relative or a pet or had disappointments and reverses. 'It's not what you've lost, but what you have left that counts.'" Her eyes soft and misty, Neely looked out the window where Emma was playing with Freckles and Nub Nose. "And I have so much left that counts." She caught herself up with a sheepish laugh. "Oh, my Lord, I sound like Pollyanna or something. Well, I may be an old marshmallow, but I certainly hope life doesn't turn me into a cynic like you."

They waited for Emma to join them on the front stoop. As Neely watched Emma slip her little hand into Nick's big red one, her heart constricted with tenderness. If only Dane could have lived to be a father to this darling little girl. She heard Emma giggling and Nick laughing. Laughing? Nick laughing? Neely scurried to catch up with the pair, not sure she was believing her ears. "What are you two whispering about?"

Emma giggled again and looked at Nick, who laughed again, this time so heartily that people walking toward the Oak turned to stare, especially Miss Dovey. "Secrets. We're talking about what Santa will bring me this Christmas. Nick thinks he'll bring you something, too. Like a handsome husband to be my daddy."

Thoughts of her dream popped into Neely's head. "Well, that would certainly be a big surprise . . . and a miracle, if you ask me."

"Miracles sometimes happen around Christmas, like my meeting this precious little girl and her mother and having the chance to save something they love." Nick hugged Emma to him. "You've done my heart a lot of good, sweetheart. Now, I see that Cash fellow over there. I think I've got some ideas to run past him. I was talking to Sunshine after dinner. She's Easter's wife, right? And those folks have been having a rough time putting meat on the table. Right?"

Neely nodded, thinking how rare it was for Sunshine to talk about her problems even to her—and here she was opening up to a virtual stranger. Nick could make a rock open up and talk, she decided. "Well, they're proud people, too proud to accept food stamps or welfare, but, yes, they are very poor and sometimes the food I make Sunshine take home is all they have."

"Well, we'll just see if we can do something about that. Come on, Emma, you can smile at ol' Cash, butter 'im up while I make 'im a proposition."

Neely walked over to a group who were struggling with some ornaments that just wouldn't hang straight and offered to help. She never got over the town spirit that was always engendered by the traditional decorating of the big tree. Someone had brought a portable CD, and carols filled the air, with most people singing along. There was eggnog and wassail and every kind of cookie and cake set out for the decorators.

When it was done, everyone joined in a circle and sang softly "O, Christmas Tree." Neely thought back to when she had done this with her mother and father and felt like crying. Yet she was incredibly happy at the same time.

As the song was coming to an end, she heard a ripple of surprise start in the people around her. The crowd shifted and somehow Neely was left standing a little apart from the others as she turned slowly to see what had caused the commotion.

And then her heart stopped as a tall, dark-haired man in casual work clothes moved into the clearing under the tree where Neely stood, an ornament frozen in her hand as she watched the man in her dream approach, his eyes as startled as her own when they met.

"It's you," she said, not believing it. "It's you."

He tried to say something, but his astonishment apparently left him speechless and he just stood staring at her.

Nick and Emma, their business with Cash Bidwell complete, moved over quietly to witness the scenario that was unfolding under the oak tree. "You did this, didn't you?" Emma asked him.

"Do you like his looks?" Nick whispered to his co-conspirator. "I was beginning to wonder if he'd make it down here in time."

"I like the looks of him just fine. And look at how they're staring at each other, like they can't believe what they're seeing." Emma looked at Nick sternly. "You checked him out, of course. He won't hurt my mother or anything like that?"

"Do you really think I'd do anything to hurt that lovely lady?" Nick smiled as he saw Neely and Hunter McGrew moving closer together under the oak tree, totally oblivious to the activity around them or the fact that they were being spied on. "To hear you talk, you'd think I have a lot to do with what's happening over there."

Emma nodded. "I'm beginning to think that you have a lot to do with a lot of things happening around here. And around the world."

"Shh. Don't tell anybody. Let's go and meet Cornelia's new fella. What do you say?"

Emma thought that was a great idea.

Neely was delighted to see her daughter and Nick approach and introduced Hunter McGrew as "a visitor to Darien who's heard about our tree."

Hunter shook hands with Nick and melted over Emma, a fact that Neely did not miss. Her inner excitement was so intense that she exclaimed with enthusiasm, "Isn't this beautiful? Aren't we lucky to have the most magnificent Christmas tree in the whole world?"

A shadow passed over the man's face as he looked at Neely and then up at the tree. "Luckier than most people in the world, who don't think tradition's worth as much as an extra buck or two."

"Why, Mr. McGrew, we already have Nick as our resident cynic. Surely you aren't going to join his club."

The two men looked at each other. "You're a cynic, after spending time with these two, in this town, under this tree?" Hunter shook his head. "I don't believe that."

"Well, believe that if you're in town for Christmas, you're in for a treat," Neely said, tapping her new friend on the arm as the Darien Kilt Dancers came into view, then swung into a lively Scottish dance. The bagpipes drowned out his reply as the descendants of the Highlander settlers of Darien got into the spirit of their ancestral music and dance.

"It's not Christmas in Darien without the traditional skirling under the oak and then up Main Street," Neely told Hunter as she clapped along with the rhythm.

"I'm beginning to think that this is where Christmas originated," he answered. "Are you sure Santa doesn't live in Darien?"

He and Neely were too deeply engrossed in each other to notice the looks exchanged between Emma and Nick.

Chapter Three

Emma had lunch with Nick the next day, sharing her sandwich and fruit and also the news that she'd been bursting to tell him. "Mama's going out with him today. They're going over to Jekyll Island to have lunch."

Nick's blue eyes gleamed with satisfaction. "Now, didn't I tell you nice things happen to nice people? Well, usually. I like that young man; he's got what it takes. There's only one problem. He works for the wrong people, and when your mother finds out . . . well, I just hope it doesn't blow up the chances for a fine romance."

Emma stopped eating, her eyes wide. "What do you mean, 'he works for the wrong people'?"

Nick, who had done his research, told her.

Meanwhile, the subject of this earnest conversation had arrived after much anticipation at the front door of Catshead Peak. His heart hadn't stopped pounding since he'd lifted the door knocker and he knew he was in serious trouble when the door opened to reveal a picture of sheer delectability.

"Am I early?" Hunter caught his breath at the sight of Neely dressed in a midnight blue suit that captured the depths of her dark-fringed eyes.

"No," Neely said, smiling and feeling less nervous now that she could see that her date was nervous enough for both of them. "Welcome to Catshead Peak."

"What a wonderful house! I love it. Looks like it just grew right out of the marshes and sands."

"Well, it sort of did." Neely got her bag and pulled the door shut behind her as she stepped out to join Hunter. "It's made of something called tabby, which is peculiar to the coastal region. It's a mixture of shell and sand and seawater and, like those elements, lasts forever." Neely looked back fondly at the house as she walked down to Hunter's truck. "Emma and I love living in the midst of all this history."

"Speaking of Emma—who's totally charming, by the way—I bet she wouldn't be impressed by her elegant mother going out with a man who drives a pickup. She's probably used to you going with men who drive BMW's."

"My daughter, like her mother, does not make judgments on the basis of what sort of vehicle a man drives. As for me being wooed by BMW types, you don't know Darien very well yet." Neely smiled at her companion, almost making him forget what gear to use. "Now, are you going to go on trying to make me out to be some sort of snobbish Southern belle, or are you going to put on that Travis Tritt tape I saw you hide behind the visor?"

Hunter laughed with sheer happiness. "A woman who likes country music! Neely Carswell, I don't know where you've been hiding, but now that I've found you, you're stuck with me . . ."

He didn't say "for the rest of your life," but the addendum hung in the air between them as they listened to the heartfelt lyrics of a country boy's pain.

"My granddaddy said he used to come over here when he was a little kid, after the millionaires had abandoned their 'cottages.' " They were having lunch in the sprawling hotel that had once been the clubhouse for the rich people who had bought the island to use as a private resort. "This place was planned by the same man who designed the hotel that Jack Nicholson ran amuck in the movie *The Shining.* Don't you love the music from that piano bar?"

"I love everything. I wish this day would last forever. I don't want to go back north, ever again."

Neely laughed. "North! Why, you only came down from Atlanta."

"Well, it's cram full of Yankees now and rampant crime. You're lucky, having a place like Darien to raise your child in."

"I still haven't heard you say exactly what you're doing here." Neely looked down at her plate, missing the shadow that came over Hunter's face.

"I . . . I'm looking over the terrain, doing a feasibility study, sort of, for the company where I work." How Hunter dreaded telling Neely the truth about what he was doing in Darien. *You can't put it off forever,*

McGrew. She'll find out soon enough, he argued with his conscience. He didn't want to spoil this magical day with the woman of his dreams.

Neely would have pursued the subject of Hunter's job, but a friend from St. Simon's came over to say hello, and after a few words with her, she and Hunter found themselves walking on the beach, holding hands. Hunter had gotten a warm jacket for Neely to wear against the December wind gusts. "I'm glad I called and asked Sunshine to look after Emma till I get home. Sunset is so beautiful on the beach."

"Sunset isn't the only thing that's beautiful." Hunter looked at the woman walking beside him, loving the way her face welcomed the salty spray and the way her lustrous hair caught the dying rays of the sun. "I wish I could have grown up here with you. I bet you were as adorable as Emma is."

Careful! Neely could feel herself succumbing to this beguiling stranger. She felt as if she already knew him. If only he didn't have that crisp, curly hair that made a girl want to run her fingers through it. Why did the man have to be trim and tanned, with brown eyes and lashes to die for? "I was more of a tomboy. The Trash brothers and I used to play cowboys and Indians out in the woods behind the cliffs."

She told him stories about her childhood, and then the reminiscing turned to serious wishing that they didn't have to go home. When the sun sank into the Atlantic Ocean, Neely's resolve to be cautious sank with it. With a sigh she went into Hunter's arms and felt the wind and the sea and the dying sun melt away as her lips met his.

They kissed for a very long time. When the cold air

became colder and the tide threatening, they went back to the truck and kissed some more. When they pulled up in front of Catshead Peak, they necked like teenagers. "Omigod," Neely said when she came to her senses. "Everybody in town is probably watching. They all know that we had a date, probably even know what we ordered for lunch. Hunter, this is downright dangerous."

"You're right about that." He drew her close again. His mouth closing on hers was as sweet as strawberries with cream; his hands tangling in her hair brought life back to forgotten parts of her. She was remembering what it was like to be adored, to be cherished, to be loved in the way that a woman needs to be loved.

"Hunter, I have to go in," Neely said breathlessly. "My reputation will be ruined." As if on cue, two lights went on just down Main Street. "See what I mean? The Widow Carswell has been Out With a Man. Everybody in town will be talking about this tomorrow."

"They could do worse than have such a delicious subject to talk about." Hunter looked at her wistfully. "Just one more kiss? And then I'm outa here—I promise."

Neely granted the mutually desired kiss, then watched from the steps as the pickup took off with a youthful squealing of tires. She could hear Hunter singing along with Travis Tritt all the way down Main Street. Lights started dotting his path and Neely went into her house, shaking her head.

Oh, those Armstrong women.

Chapter Four

It was the night of the big meeting. The town hall was packed when Neely got there. She squeezed onto a bench next to Miss Dovey and whispered, "Am I late? Have they started already?"

"No, it's just that everybody wanted a front seat to hear what that big muckety-muck Yankee has to say here tonight. I wonder if those rumors about cutting down the Christmas Oak are true. I've heard that the D.O.T. can be real bossy when it comes to other people's property.."

"Shh. There's Mr. Langdon, the man from Washington." Neely strained to see all the figures on the stage. When she came to the figure on the end, she half rose out of her chair in shock. "My Lord, what's Hunter doing up there?"

"I thought you knew. He's the chief engineer of the road project."

Neely made a little whimpering sound and covered her mouth. "Oh, no." She thought about Susannah at that moment. "Like you, I'm consorting with the enemy," she whispered.

"What did you say, Cornelia?" Getting no answer, Miss Dovey pointed a skinny finger at the stage. "Look at 'em, all those foreigners coming in here to plan our town's future. They've messed up every big city in the country, and now they're starting in on the small towns."

One of the Trash brothers leaned over from the other side of the schoolteacher. "Why you think we all come to this meeting? I've been hearing rumors all day that the engineering plan's already been accepted and they're planning to start work on it Monday morning. And nobody knows nothing, 'cept that there's going to be a bigger road right through the middle of town."

"Hush now, Easter. The mayor's introducing the Washington man. Hmm, I taught Bill Riley in the first grade. You'd think his grammar would be better. No wonder those federal and Atlanta people are up there smirking like we're a bunch of backwoods crackers."

"Ladies and gentlemen, I thank you for coming out tonight." Mr. Langdon was smooth as a newly skinned snake and just about as slippery, Neely decided as she listened to the man lead into the issue at hand so subtly that she almost missed it when he said with an earnest voice, "And that's why we came down here tonight, to explain to you personally why we feel the new road must be completely clear of any dangerous impediment . . ."

Someone up front jumped to her feet amid the jumble of surprised comments from the floor. "Are you talking about cutting down the Christmas Oak?" At the swell of protest, Mayor Riley stepped to the podium, banging on it with his gavel and saying sternly into the microphone, "Now, folks, we're a reasonable bunch and we can at least hear what Mr. Langdon's got to say about this. Y'all will get your chance to speak after these folks is done."

"Thank you, Mr. Mayor." Langdon turned back to the crowd. "Please understand that we at the D.O.T. are all aware of your attachment to this landmark and your desire for its preservation. But progress in Georgia cannot be stopped because of one oak tree, no matter what its sentimental value to the community. Think about it—don't you want more people coming to your businesses, to your hotel, to your real estate offices and residential areas? Don't you want to grow?"

About half the people in the room provided a chorus of "No!"

As though he hadn't heard it, Langdon went on smoothly, "I'm sorry you don't recognize the economic advantages of providing safe, unimpeded access to the interstates and major arteries that will bring in unparalleled new trade and growth. Perhaps, then, I can remind you that your fine little city has had at least three fatal accidents, all involving the awkward placement of your beloved oak in the middle of a main road."

Someone shouted, "Those were three drunks that tried to go through the middle of the tree!"

"Mr. Baretta, I now turn the program over to you to explain to these good people how our program will be implemented." His smoothness somewhat ruffled by the hostility of the townsfolk and their murmurs and mutters, the big-government representative escaped by a back door.

Mr. Baretta spent the next hour trying to soothe the residents of Darien, but finally stated that the contracts were signed and in order, the engineering plans were in place, and work on the road would begin right away. Then he too made a hurried exit. Before he did so, though, he stopped Hunter McGrew from making a stammering apology to the audience, saying in barely audible tones, "Hunter, I'll remind you that you're not only under contract to my agency, you are also in the position of being sued by the state for all you've got."

His jaws tightly muscled, Hunter cast one despairing, pleading look around the room, dwelling on Neely when he saw her standing at her chair, her fists clenched, her face tight with fury. *I'll talk to you later*, he mouthed silently.

"Like hell you will," Neely muttered. Oh, the humiliation of it all, falling for a liar and exploiter. She should have listened to her mother, who'd always said Georgia girls should never fall in love with any man who'd been brought up further north than Macon.

They gathered in knots under the oak, downcast by the realization that their tree would soon be destroyed. "We won't let it happen," Neely shouted. "We'll get a lawyer, we'll picket, we'll sue, we'll do what we have to do." Someone had lifted her up to the back of a pickup truck and she stood there shaking her fist, eyes blazing, as she railed against the cold-blooded usurpation of a small town's autonomy. "They can't cut our oak down, we won't let them." When the crowd had dwindled, leaving a hard-core group of protestors, Neely quickly made plans to meet again, to form vigils, to devise strategies to save their tree.

When she walked home, weary and depressed, she was not surprised to find Hunter waiting for her in the shadows of her porch. "Leave me alone, you traitor. The least you could have done was to tell me who you worked for. But you never even said a word about this meeting."

"I couldn't, Neely, not after seeing you under the oak, realizing what that tree means to you people . . ."

"You can actually keep on working for someone like that? Do what they tell you to do without your conscience telling you how wrong it is?"

Hunter's gesture was one of hopelessness. "You heard what he said. My contract gives me no out unless I want to lose my job, maybe everything I own. Neely, I swear I would never have signed on this job if I'd had any idea . . . look, you may not believe this, but I'm the reason they even came for this meeting. They were going to have our team sneak in here on Christmas morning, chop the tree down, and be gone before anybody in Darien had finished their Christmas brunch. I yelled and cussed, saying I'd leak it to the papers and there'd be hell to pay if they didn't even have the decency to tell the townspeople what was going to happen. They didn't like it, but they called in the big gun and came down here to talk."

"Big deal, talking to us. Why didn't they ask us if we

even wanted the damn road before they started making all these plans?"

"You know the answer to that. Bureaucracy. You're just lucky they didn't get their lawyers in here and have everything on the street condemned and demolished. I've seen that happen."

Neely stomped her foot. "Hunter McGrew, I'm not talking about bureaucrats. Dammit, I'm talking about you, about human decency, about trusting a man that I thought was someone I could . . . I could . . ." Neely slapped his hand away when he reached out to her. "Don't you dare touch me, you . . . you government-controlled weasel. I hate it that I let you take me in, I despise what you stand for—and what you don't stand for!" Her eyes spat fire, her body trembled as she tried to keep from bursting into tears.

"Neely, please. I didn't know about the tree. I didn't realize when I took this job that it was anything more than coming down here and planning a highway project. I swear it!"

She ran up the porch stairs and turned at the top to fling one last barb. "Did your beloved bureaucrats tell you about how to worm your way into our good graces? They know how we are down here, how we take strangers in, how we're hospitable to people—even when they turn out to be snakes." Over Hunter's agonized protests, Neely ground out, "Don't—you—ever—come—near—me—again. You hear? Don't ever set foot on this property, do you understand?" She opened the front door with a jerk and slammed it behind her as she went inside, then ran to Susannah's favorite window seat and cried her eyes out.

* * *

Emma knew there was something not quite right with her mother the next morning when she brought her a cup of coffee. "Couldn't you sleep last night? I heard you go downstairs a couple of times."

Neely smiled wanly, "Oh, I was just upset about the meeting, darling. I thought a little hot chocolate might help me sleep."

"You should have called me." Emma wiggled under the covers with her mother and kissed her. "Didn't we promise to talk to each other about problems?"

Neely hugged her. "We sure did. But this is a problem I'm not ready to talk about just yet."

"It's something to do with Mr. McGrew, isn't it? Not the meeting at all."

"You're too smart, pussycat. Yes, it is, but I don't want to get into it just yet. Say, I haven't really had a chance to talk to you since you went out to make some visits with Nick."

Emma jumped out of the covers, almost spilling Neely's coffee in her enthusiasm. "Sorry. Oh, Mama, if you could have seen the look on Easter West's face when Nick told him what Cash Bidwell is planning to do. He's going to keep the family in deer meat and fish in return for having dinner with them once in a while."

"Cash is feeding the Trash brothers and their families? Are you making this up, Emma Carswell?" Neely said suspiciously.

"No, no, I'm not. I heard him myself. He said that he had more game and fish than he could ever use himself and that his cooking was so bad that eating Sunshine's home cooking once in a while would be a gift from heaven itself."

"Well, I never."

"That's not all. We went out to Miss Dovey's little house and Cash went with us. Do you know that Cash can't read? Miss Dovey said she'll teach him in return for doing some work at the school."

"Well, I knew that Cash got by on social promotion up through the tenth grade, but I didn't know he was illiterate. How in the world did Miss Dovey find that out?"

Emma was smug. She liked being in on the epiphanies that seemed to happen around Nick. "He told Nick about how ashamed he was and how that was one of the reasons he went around bullying people so much. And Nick talked to Miss Dovey about teaching him and . . . Mama, you're not gonna believe this . . ."

"I'm getting to the point that I'll believe anything that Nick has a hand in."

"Miss Dovey acted like she's starting to like Mr. Cash. She's always just hated him, told people how sorry he was, but when we left she was reading a story to him and he was sitting at her knees for all the world like a little boy."

Neely shook her head in amazement at the picture. Would wonders never cease? Long after Emma had left for school, she sat with her cold coffee, pondering the unusual events that had occurred in the past few weeks.

"And it all started with you, Nick the saint."

The ringing of the doorbell stopped her musing. Her heart beat fast as she grabbed a robe and went down to see who was paying such an early call. She didn't know whether it was relief or disappointment that flooded her when she caught sight of her visitor.

"Nick! My goodness, you're out early. Come on in and have some coffee." When they were seated in the kitchen, she said cheerfully, "You're looking mighty fit these days. I like the beard, by the way."

"And how about this gut?" Nick rubbed his thickening belly, his eyes twinkling. "Miss Dovey's vittles have sure filled me out."

"I heard about what you pulled off with Cash Bidwell."

"And I heard from my young friend Hunter what he pulled with you. Anything I can do to cheer you up?"

"Yes. You can tell me what the dickens I can tell Emma to make her understand a world that can't slow down enough to go around a centuries-old tree instead of over it." Neely slammed her cup down so hard it splashed coffee on the table.

"Careful. You're wasting the coffee I love." Nick hadn't missed the dark circles under Neely's eyes. "Tell me about Hunter and how he stands in this and how you feel about it."

She did, ending up crying over her Luiziane. "I'm just so disappointed, I can't tell you, Nick. I was starting to think Hunter might be the one for me. But a man who won't stand up for what's right, I can't bear that."

"Well, you need to look at it from his point of view, girl. He didn't grow up with that tree, didn't hold it in regard like you and your folks did. He's an engineer. A tree's something to cut down if it's in the way. What if he tried to save every tree everybody wanted to leave? There'd be no suburbs, little girl. There'd be no shopping malls. There'd be no stadium for the Braves, for heaven's sake!"

Neely sniffed. "Here I thought you were on my side in this."

"I am. I just think you're looking at things from a narrow point of view. I've learned a lot since I've been in your little town of Darien, a lot more than I ever dreamed I'd learn."

"But you're still cynical," Neely accused.

"With good reason. If you had known me the way I used to be, you'd understand. I was famous, beloved, people built their hopes and dreams around me—especially the children. Why, my name was better known than the Easter bunny, and my visits were probably the most anticipated of any in the world."

"Were you some sort of world-famous philanthropist or something like that?"

Nick smiled. "Something like that. How about one more cup of coffee? I know I'm wasting your morning, but I had a feeling you could use a friend along about now."

"You were right as usual. As for wasting my morning, I can't think of any way I'd rather spend it than talking with you."

"Then let's stop talking about me and talk about what's really important. Little girl, I don't think you know how much I've begun to care for you and that precious daughter you're raising. I know the modern thing is being strong and independent and not needing a man when you're a woman on your own, but that child of yours needs a daddy."

"Oh, Nick, don't be so old-fashioned."

"Old-fashioned? Is it old-fashioned to think that a lovely mother and her child need a good man to protect them and love them?"

"What about your family?" At the look of bewilderment and sorrow on the old man's face, Neely was full of chagrin at her insensitivity. "Oh, I'm sorry. I didn't mean . . . it's just that you're so kind, so beloved by the children, I . . ." Neely swallowed and decided to tackle the issue head on. After all, he knew everything about her family situation, while she knew nothing about his! "What about your children? Grandchildren?"

"Great-grandchildren, great-great-grandchildren? I probably have a million of 'em."

"Don't joke." Neely sensed that Nick's withdrawal meant she'd hit close on a touchy truth. "Did you abandon your family, Nick? I sense such a longing in you sometimes, especially when you're around the children. Is that it?" She put her arm around him and peered closely into the blue eyes that she felt held so many secrets. "You can trust me."

Nick cleared his throat. "I need to be getting back to my room. Miss Dovey worries when I'm not around." He shook his head, laughing. "That woman! She's about as good as they come, trying to fatten me up, pay me for working. I tell her the same thing I'll tell you. Finding a good person in this old world is payment enough."

"You do so many things for people and won't let them do for you. That's not fair, Nick. Giving is the best part of living."

The old man looked startled, stopping to stare at Neely in the midst of donning his worn-out jacket. "Say that again. I've gotten more hard of hearing than ever just lately."

She repeated what she'd said.

"That's it, all right. You've hit the nail on the head. All my life, all I ever did was give, give, and give some more." An edge of bitterness crept into his words. "I used to think that was the way it should be, that I was the one meant to give and not receive. Well, I had the shock of my life when I discovered the meanness people can have in 'em, even when you've given all you have to 'em. And that's when I started noticing that all my giving hadn't saved me from finding out the hard way that people don't care anymore and won't give back. I tell you, till I came to this town, I had no hope for the human race. But meeting you and Emma, folks like Easter and Miss Dovey, even Cash, I can feel myself starting to trust the world again. Thanks to you and all of them, I've rediscovered the joy of giving—and the benefits of receiving that joy."

The phone rang. "That'll be Hunter," Nick said with a little smile.

"And how can you be so sure of that?" Neely made no move to answer the phone.

"Because I had a little talk with him and told him if he gave up on the woman that he was meant to meet and marry, he was a fool who didn't deserve anybody better than that little Charmaine chick who waits tables at Junior's and has already started running after him."

He could not have said anything more effective. Charmaine Haley had been after anything in pants since junior high. Neely made a face at Nick, who was sneaking out the door, then spoke tentatively into the phone. "Hello?"

"Neely? Please let me come by for a minute. I can't

stand the way things are between us. Let me come by to talk, won't you?"

Neely could almost see Nick watching her and giving her the high sign. She could even hear his voice in her head. *Give the man a chance, little girl. He's coming from a different place from you, that's all. Give 'im a chance.* "All right, but you can't stay very long. I have to meet with the committee at Hofyl plantation to plan the decorations for the Christmas Eve party."

"If I had a hat, I'd have it in my hand. Will a dish of humble pie do as well?" Hunter's pleasure at being allowed to come was audible. Neely could feel herself weakening in her resolve to be stern with him.

"Neither, thank you."

Neely barely had time to get dressed and build a welcoming fire in the living room before he was standing at her door with a huge planter of poinsettia in one hand and a bottle of wine in the other. "Pick a hand?"

Neely laughed and waved him inside. "I'll take both." She placed the plant on the foyer table and took the wine, peering at the label with mock seriousness. "Hmm. Mad Dog, no year. Excellent selection, Mr. McGrew, I'm sure I'll be amused by its impertinence."

"There you go," Hunter said, shrugging off his jacket, obviously relieved that he had not entered a war zone—at least not yet. On impulse, he grabbed her and held her close. "God, how I've missed you. Neely, Neely, I've been miserable."

She drew back, fighting her own desire to stay in those safe, strong arms. "I'm sure Charmaine helped you along with those blues."

He looked startled. "Nick told me. I suppose you

351

were drowning your sorrow last night at Junior's since it's the only place open after ten o'clock."

"Dear God, is there anything a bachelor can do in Darien and not get caught at it? I didn't floss last night either. Is that on the Internet?"

His lighthearted banter got them over the awkwardness and they were seated in front of the fire with cups of hot coffee very soon. "I hated being on the other side from you and your people," Hunter said, looking broodingly at the fire and then at the woman by his side. "I talked to Nick about it. He's the only one who seems to understand. I couldn't be disloyal to the ones I work for, yet at the same time I feel like a traitor to you and your town. What is it about this tree, anyway? Think about the traffic you'll bring in with the new road. Think about the benefits to your merchants. Lord knows they could all use some new business."

Neely sighed. "If I have to explain to you what that old tree means to us, there's no use in us sitting here."

"There's some use in it, according to what I feel." Hunter put his arm around Neely and drew her close. "Let's forget about the tree and concentrate on that fire there. Look at those flames, licking around the logs like dragon tongues . . ."

"My grandmother used to read me a story, kind of a scary one, about snapdragons. The flames were snapdragons."

"I'd like to have grandchildren with you," Hunter said huskily, his lips nuzzling the soft flesh beneath Neely's ear.

"There's a big step in between," Neely said, laughing and pushing Hunter gently away. "Grandchildren come much later. And before you and I can even talk about such a commitment to the future, we have to work out the present."

"That's what I'm trying to do right now—work out the present. Neely, honey, can't you understand where I'm coming from, even a little bit? I'm not your enemy. Can't you see that I want what's best for you and your town?"

He was a convincing kind of man, she could tell, but they had a long way to go to be on the same side. "Hunter, let's go outside for a stroll. I want to give you a little bit of history I think you've missed out on."

Hunter thought that was a great idea.

"Mornin', folks." The old men were wrapped up in their scarves and sweaters on the Darien Hotel porch and Hunter and Neely stopped to chat a moment. "It's a fine, mild day for December, ain't it?"

"Hee-hee. Yep, George here is down to his last three sweaters."

"Well, that's a mighty handsome one you're sporting, Mr. Scranton. Early Christmas present?" Neely knew that not one of the old men had anybody but each other, and certainly no money for gifts.

"Matter of fact, 'tis. You know that Nick feller who works for Miz Dovey? He come over first cold snap, got our sizes, showed up the next day with woolies for everybody. Even brought us longjohns," he whispered to Hunter.

"This here scarf was brand-new, not no Salvation Army hand-me-down."

After all the men had shared their descriptions of the "goodies" Nick had provided, Neely and Hunter continued their stroll. "Hope I don't wind up like those old geezers."

"Well, now, I wouldn't say that," Neely said, bristling. "Those 'ole geezers' worked hard all their lives and saved their money so they could at least live independently in their old age. I don't think you ought to go around criticizing our way of life, Mr. McGrew."

"I'm beginning to think I shouldn't open my mouth about anything that could be taken as criticism of your beloved little town." After the silence that fell between them lingered on the chilly air, he ventured, "That was nice of Nick, wasn't it?"

Neely warmed up again. "I've never seen anybody like him, Hunter. Oh, hello, Mr. Meeks. How's business?"

The barber was opening up his shop. "Well, if I have as busy a day today as I had yesterday, I'll have to stay open on Sundays. That Nick, your little girl's friend, brought in a whole gaggle of little black children from the Baptist Children's Home and had me cut everybody's hair. Said there weren't many barber shops left like mine and every little boy ought to get his hair cut the first time in a real old-fashioned barber shop."

Hunter and Neely looked at each other. "Well, I'll be coming by for a haircut pretty soon, Mr. Meeks."

"Oh, no, you won't," Neely told him as soon as they were out of earshot. "I have something in mind for you, and a haircut would spoil the effect."

"Your wish is my command," Hunter replied with a grin when she refused to elaborate on her enigmatic comment. "Now, can we get moving before one more person stops us to tell us another Nick story? I want to be alone with you. And I want to hear about the Christmas Oak."

"Well, I just wish you had read up on our history before you and your D.O.T. people came down here to run roughshod all over it. Just look at the Christmas Oak. Oglethorpe and his men slept under that tree. The Scotsmen who founded this community skirled and danced beneath it over two hundred years ago. What in the world makes a stupid ole highway more important than the history of a place?"

"Neely Carswell, what you still don't realize is that you and I are on the same side. We're just coming from different places to get there."

"My ancestor Susannah often met her Yankee sweetheart under that very tree." Neely sighed. "It was such a romantic story. Susannah lived in the house where I live. Her brother Ward brought home his roommate Morgan Dancey, who was from the North. That was before the War Between the States broke out. They both became officers—one for the North and one for the South."

"I can almost relate to that," Hunter murmured.

"What?"

"Nothing. Go on. What happened?"

"Well, Susannah was in love with Morgan and he with her. But she couldn't see him after the war started, since he and her brother were on opposite sides. Both men fought in that last big battle, you know, the one in Savannah. That terrible Sherman gave Grant Savannah for a Christmas present."

"Neely, please don't start the war up again. I know how things turned out between the North and South. What I want to hear is how it turned out between

Morgan and Susannah." It was important to know if Morgan got his girl.

"On Christmas Eve she waited up till midnight, praying that her brother would come home safe. She had a carved angel that she put on the tree to watch over those she loved. And do you know what? Morgan found Ward wounded and he brought him home. After the war was over and things had healed some, Morgan and Susannah were married. Oh, that was such a romantic time."

He took her by the shoulders and kissed her, right there in the middle of Main Street. "There. Now you can't accuse me of not being romantic."

"Everybody in this town will be talking about us smooching in front of the Christmas Oak, Hunter McGrew. I am tee-totally mortified."

"Well, I'm not. If you're going to put an old tree between us, keeping two people who belong together apart for the sake of an ancient piece of pulpwood, then I'm going to have to get the town on my side." He kissed her again and some people emerging from the City Cafe applauded.

"Way to go, fella," Maude Gilliard, the owner, called as she looked out the door. "I like Christmas weddings best, Neely. So you just call me when you're ready and I'll put that rehearsal dinner together pronto."

"I am not getting married," Neely called back in a steely voice. "Hunter, I am going to kill you. Right here on Main Street in front of the whole damn town."

"She said thanks very much," Hunter called over to the cafe owner, his arm around Neely's stiff shoulders. "Darling, now I know what it is I love about small towns."

Neely's anger was about to explode, but Cash Bidwell chose that moment to roar up on his bike and add to her frustration. "This dude botherin' you, sugar? You just say the word and I'll . . ."

Neely said something unprintable that applied to all the men in her life at the moment and then she stalked back up the hill.

"Hey, man, she p.o.'ed about something?" Cash fingered his single earring and watched Neely admiringly. "Whoa, she's, like, mad, but you ever see such a nice behind on a high-class lady?"

"Bidwell," Hunter said between his teeth, "if I ever hear you make one more of your redneck comments about that lady, I will put your tire iron up tight where the sun don't shine."

"Whoa. I'm scared to death. What is it folks have about my tire iron, anyway?" But Cash saw the gleam in Hunter's eyes and didn't stick around to see if the city dude was all talk or not.

Chapter Five

The campaign to save the tree was firmly launched, with Neely as its spearhead. Even Cash Bidwell got into the act, chaining his motorcycle to the oak every night in case the D.O.T. got sneaky and tried to cut it down at night.

In fact, there had been a rumor to that effect. Easter West reported to the group meeting at the cafe just two weeks before Christmas that he'd heard that an unscrupulous pulpwood poacher had been hired to do that very thing. "How we gone keep 'em from cutting 'er down, Neely? Most of us is in bed come nightfall, fast asleep."

"Well, we'll just have to start having a night vigil," Neely said fiercely.

"Shoot, I'll just sleep up in the damn thing," the other Trash brother said. "There's a low-lying limb wide enough for me to tie my sleeping bag up there.

They cut that tree down, they'll have to cut me down with it."

Several enthusiastic volunteers offered to take turns sleeping up in the Christmas Oak. Neely just wished Nick was around to observe the way the people of Darien were rallying to save their landmark. "Just be very careful that none of you starts dreaming and falls out. We don't want anybody hurt."

Despite her disappointment about how the campaign seemed to be getting nowhere, Neely plunged headlong into preparations for Christmas. With Emma's help, she heaped aromatic pine boughs on mantels, filled baskets with apples studded with cloves, strung holly garlands on stair railings, and generally re-created Catshead Peak's centuries-old aura of holiday spirit.

When Sunshine started the baking, filling the house with delicious smells, Neely and Emma were right there in the middle of it. Their game of drawing straws to see who got to lick the bowl with the Lane Cake mixture set Sunshine to laughing. Good cheer and holiday spirit overpowered the recent pall from the crisis on Main Street.

"Mama, I don't understand why Mr. Hunter hasn't been around more." Emma had won the draw and was licking cake batter from the wooden spoon that had been her great-great-great grandmother's. "Are you two mad at each other? Darla Carradine says she heard you had a big fight."

"Well, I wouldn't go so far as to say we had a real fight. We just disagreed strongly on something."

"The Christmas Oak?" Emma put on her most serious expression. "Miss Dovey asked all of us to draw a picture of the tree, all lit up and everything. She said that might be all we have left of our tree after Christmas. Is that what Mr. Hunter wants?"

"No-o. He doesn't want that, not really." Neely sensed that her daughter was slyly boxing her into a corner.

"And you don't want that, either, so you two really want the same thing." Emma licked the last of the cake batter with her finger. "Right?"

"Don't use rude manners. Yes, you're right. Hunter and I do basically want the tree to stay. But he's forced to do what he's ordered to do, and I'm on the other side . . ." Neely paused with her cup of coffee at her lips, suddenly realizing how unfair she'd been. Out of the mouths of babes . . . "Honey, you stay here and help Sunshine with the divinity, and try not to sample too much of it. You'll be sick. I've got to go see somebody."

"Mr. Hunter?" Emma's smile was triumphant.

Neely tousled her daughter's hair as she got her jacket from the coatrack. "I'm a grown-up. I don't have to tell you who I'm going to see. It might be Fred the barber's wife. I heard she's been down with the flu, really bad. Miss Dovey said Nick's been sitting up with her several nights so Fred could get some rest."

After the door closed, Emma said knowingly to Sunshine, "She's going to see Mr. Hunter, I'll bet you three pralines and two pieces of fudge."

Sunshine, a good-natured woman who was secretly hoping for a match between Emma's mother and the visiting engineer, laughed. "I've learned not to take no bets off you, Miss Smartypants. Now you rinse out that bowl and get to hulling them pecans. They're cracked and all you got to do is pull off the hulls."

Emma got to her assigned task. In between popping broken pieces (fair game, in her mind) of nutmeat into her mouth, she kept grinning and grinning.

Great-great-aunt Susannah had married a man from the "other side." He was a Yankee, but nobody had ever seemed to hold that against Morgan Dancey, from the stories Emma had heard about that legendary marriage. Cornelia Carswell might just do the same.

Emma's grin widened even more. There was still time for her Christmas wish to come true. Hadn't Nick told her that if you kept on wishing right up till Christmas Eve your wish would come true?

"Neely!" The look on Hunter's face when he opened the door of his cottage on the edge of Hofyl Plantation reminded Neely of a little boy's expression when he discovered that Santa had come after all. "Oh, God, I can't believe it's really you. I was just . . ." He stopped short of *thinking about you* and motioned her inside. "You can't imagine how much I've dreamed lately of things getting back to the way they were. Come on, sit by the fire."

"Am I interrupting? I know you've been busy with the plans for the new road." Neely glanced over at an old oak partners' desk that held an array of drawings and charts.

"No, no, I'm at a perfect stopping place. You came at a good time. I was struggling with a real . . . problem."

She followed him around the sofa and sat down.

361

"Nice fire. We're having a chilly Christmas."

"Yes, we are. I was just perking a pot of coffee. Want some?"

"I'd love it." While he was busy in the little kitchen that opened to the great room, she called out, "Heard you were up in Atlanta."

He came back with steaming mugs and a plate of macaroons. "Miss Dovey brought these over. She's the only one in town who's not mad at me. I'm not sure why."

"Miss Dovey's like that." Neely munched on the macaroon and wondered how they were going to get around all the small talk. "You have two other defenders as well. Nick and Emma. They think I've been too hard on you."

Hunter looked at her with a hopeful expression. "What do you think?"

"I have to agree." Neely looked at the fire and wondered if those were the same snapdragons she'd seen in another fire, at another time. "I've always thought of myself as a fair-minded person, but in your case I rushed to judgment. I'm sorry, Hunter. I know you were between a rock and a hard place." She turned to look at him, feeling a meltdown inside that had a lot to do with his looking so boyishly handsome in his fisherman's sweater and faded jeans. His flustered pleasure at her unexpected apology helped, too.

"Hey, you have a right to be mad at me. I come down here and everybody goes all out to make me feel at home, then I turn out to be part of the outfit that's set out to change everything."

"Emma made me see it a little differently. You

know, for a little girl, she sure can come up with some straight thinking."

Hunter shook his head. "That's some little girl. And she's got some mother, too."

"I can't take full credit. Her daddy was . . . well, let's just say that Dane was the best husband and father a man could be." Neely couldn't believe she was talking to another man about the one she'd been married to and loved so dearly. "He wasn't perfect, by any means, but you would've liked him, too. Dane would have stood up for his principles like you have. We didn't always agree, either. Maybe that's why I'm here right now."

"Whatever brought you here, I'm glad." Hunter took the cup from between Neely's tensely gripped hands and set it on the table. "You're going to break that mug, and it's one of my few matching ones."

Her heart pounding, Neely realized she was about to be kissed. "I'll give you another set for Christmas."

"I'd rather have . . . this." Hunter pulled her to him and put his hand under her chin, turning her face up to his. "You are a most beautiful human being. If I just had the words, I'd spout a poem about how beautiful you are." His lips found hers and the flames inside them both leapt with those behind the hearth. Neely felt a moment of gratitude toward the sweet angel that had led her back home to find a new happiness and a new kind of love.

The phone jangled, breaking into their heated rediscovery of closeness. "Rats, that's a call I've been waiting for all morning." Hunter traced the full lips so recently opened against his own, hardly able to abandon the sweet moment. "Please save my place?"

She heard him make the required transition from lover to professional. "Yes, this is McGrew." Pause. "Look, there are no ifs, ands, and buts about it. The new plans are being drawn up as we speak. The highway will go around the tree, and that's final." Pause. "You're scaring me to death, Baretta. As you say, the big boys at D.O.T. can fire me after my contract is finished. But in the meantime, my contract puts me firmly in charge of what goes and what doesn't on this project. And I say the oak tree stays."

Hunter gently replaced the receiver on the hook and then did an amazing thing, in Neely's eyes. He let out a full-fledged Rebel yell, then grabbed Neely up and swung her around in a dizzying twirl. "Whoo-ee! I knew this was going to be my day. First you, then this. Whoo-ee! The Christmas Oak is no longer endangered."

Neely managed to right herself and regain her balance. "Hunter, that's wonderful. And I'm so proud of you for being firm and forceful and not letting them intimidate you. But I have to ask—if you had the power of yea or nay over the tree all along, why the heck didn't you go ahead and make that decision when you first came?"

"Because, my darling, I'm a professional. I had to see for myself what was involved here and be careful that our tax dollars didn't go into preserving the self-interest of a small segment of our state. I'll admit that it was hard not to give in to my own sentiment right away, but I had to follow the correct procedure instead of making a snap decision based on personal feelings."

"Hunter McGrew, I don't know whether to belt you

364

one or give you a very big hug."

"I'd prefer the latter," he said, opening his arms.

Later (a lot later), Neely raised her face to Hunter. "I can't wait till the town hears about this. You'll be the toast of Darien."

Hunter drew her back into his arms. "No, I won't. *We* will. Look at all you did to convince me how much more important the oak tree was to your people than a shortcut at the expense of tradition and history. We did this together, remember, except for one little period of misunderstanding—and 'we' is the operative word."

Neely liked the sound of that. "I'm so glad you're on the side of the angels. Without you, I felt so very much alone."

"You'll never be alone again," Hunter whispered huskily as he lowered his mouth to hers.

Christmas was coming early, Neely decided. *Thanks, Santa,* she said silently before giving all her attention to the man who'd just revived her intuitive faith in mankind.

Chapter Six

"Mama, Mama, you'll never guess what happened today." Emma, her eyes wide and excited, ran into the kitchen where Neely and Sunshine were making lunch. "Miss Dovey went for a ride on Mr. Cash's Harley."

"She didn't!"

"She did so. She was celebrating, she said. Nick put her name in a big supermarket contest and she won! She won a ten-day cruise to the Virgin Islands this summer."

Neely was still struggling with the unlikely image of the prim schoolmarm on the back of Cash's Harley. Imagining her doing the Bahama shuffle on a "Don't Worry, Be Happy" jaunt stretched her imagination to its limit. "Goodness gracious, there are a lot of good things going on around here, not the least of which was Hunter saving the tree."

"Yes, the news about that is all over town. The other kids treat me like a movie star just because I know him."

Neely sprinkled pepper on the green salad she'd finished making. "What other miracles has Nick wrought lately? I'm having a hard time keeping up with 'em."

Emma pursed her lips and thought. Then she ticked off the list on her fingers. "Let's see, besides Miss Dovey, who's changed so much after all Nick's help, there's Mr. Cash. He's started taking meat to the mission as well as to the Trash brothers. And I heard he was working the soup line on Fridays. Then there's the children's home. Nick has done ever much for them, taking them on little trips—"

"I heard about the haircuts. Emma, you see things through the wise, clear eyes of a little girl. What is it about Nick? How can he help so many people and do so much for everybody? He is a saint, no question about it."

Emma smiled and nodded. "He's a saint, all right. More than anybody knows."

"What? Well, I think it's time the town of Hofyl Darien rewarded our resident saint. You know I've asked him to play Santa at the Hofyl Plantation Christmas Eve party. Well, here's my plan. Tell me what you think." And she confided the secret plan she had conceived. "He told me once that nobody ever gave him anything. Well, it's time we changed that."

Emma's face glowed with approval. "I can't think of anything that Nick would like better. He loves the people of Darien and says they gave him back his life, but I think we need to show how much we love him."

The sound of the doorbell ended their scheming. "Now who in the world would that be, calling right at lunchtime?"

"Oh, that would be Nick. I hope you don't mind that I asked him. He said he'd heard about Sunshine's salmon croquettes and since that's what we were having . . ."

Neely hugged her again while Sunshine looked on, pleased as punch. "I'll get the door, sweetheart, while you set another place."

"No, I want to let him in." Emma ran to the front door and opened it. There stood the object of the recent conversation, and Emma couldn't resist a little teasing. "So Saint Nick is here for lunch. Shall I invite Freckles and Nub Nose so you won't miss Rudolph so much?"

Nick looked startled, then broke into a rumbling laugh that made his stoutening girth shake like Jell-O. "Oh, now we're being a bad little girl right before Christmas. Tsk tsk. Need I tell you that Santa knows what every little boy and every little girl is thinking?"

"Don't worry, Nick. Your secret is safe with me," Emma said with a conspiratorial smile. She took the chubby hand and squeezed it, then led him into the living room. "Mama wanted to talk to you for a moment before lunch." At Nick's quizzical look, she shook her head. "Not about you-know-what. It's something else."

Neely jumped right into the subject of the Christmas Oak. "I know it's something you did," she said. "I told Hunter that before you came to Darien, none of these wonderful things ever happened."

Nick's face was a picture of innocence. "Who, me?"

"Yes, you. We're going into the dining room for lunch, Nick, and then you and I are going out for a nice long walk on the bluff."

"This is your future, Cornelia. Your future, your present, your past. It's all here."

They were standing on the bluff looking over the river. Neely saw the herons rising from their quest for food and felt a chill at Nick's words. "I'm not afraid of the past, and the present doesn't bother me because it's what it is, but the future . . ." Neely shivered. "Nick, I just wish I could know what that future holds."

"You will, my dear, you will. Take it from ole Nick, you will."

"Who are you, Nick? Why are you here?"

Neely didn't mean to ask those questions, in fact she couldn't believe the temerity of her own words when she heard them fall upon the still air.

Nick wasn't insulted. "You'll know, little girl, in good time. You'll know and understand. Now, are you ready to get started on that future you keep wondering about?"

"Well . . . yes."

"Then let's go back to your house so you can try on that Scarlett O'Hara getup you were talking about wearing to the Christmas Eve party."

"We've got to work out your outfit, too."

Nick groaned. "Oh, no. I can't believe I let myself be conned into taking the Santa role. Cornelia, if you have a shred of compassion for this old man, you'll get me out of that."

"No way," Neely told him cheerfully. "If I've got to play Scarlett, you're stuck with Santa. That's the way it is."

Neely and Emma had a ball getting ready for Christmas Eve now that they didn't have to worry about the big oak. Emma was thrilled that her mother was back on good terms with Hunter, so thrilled, in fact, that she used all her saved-up allowance on a present for the man she insisted on calling her new daddy.

She wouldn't even tell her mother what she'd gotten, teasing, "You can't shake it or break it and no matter how much you ask, I won't tell you what's in it."

Hunter had fun with the mystery gift as well. He was coming over for dinner nightly these days, to Emma's delight. "Won't you give me just a hint?" he prodded on one occasion. "I can't stand the suspense."

"Nope." Emma was just as stubborn as her closest relative. "And we don't open presents on Christmas Eve, neither. So you have to wait till Christmas Day."

Hunter groaned dramatically. "You learned how to torture men from your mother, I can tell."

"I heard that!" Neely was taking a break from her preparations for the big party. There were so many last-minute details to attend to. But the most important ones, those having to do with the big surprise for Nick, were all taken care of.

They were all so happy that the house seemed to be filled with their joy at being together. Even Emma, who was usually a practical-minded little person, mentioned the phenomenon while Neely was tucking her into bed. "Mama, all ghosts aren't bad, are they?"

A Gift for Santa

Neely had a quick answer for that one. "Not the ones I know. Honey, the people who lived here a long time ago have nothing but good wishes for you and me."

"Like Susannah?" Emma snuggled up under the sheets and comforter. "I know she likes us. She told me so."

Neely smiled, wondering if she'd overdone her efforts to teach her daughter about the history of Catshead Peak and the heritage of its family. "She told you so? In person?"

"Yes," Emma said, closing her eyes. "She loves us. And I love you, Mama."

Neely didn't answer because she felt a strong, sweet presence at her side. Emma smiled in her sleep as if she felt the touch of unseen lips.

Chapter Seven

As Emma had said, everyone in town knew about Hunter's role in saving the Christmas Oak. Word was clearly out that the former engineer was the hero of the day. As Neely and Hunter strolled down Main Street, everyone waved and called out to him. "Atta boy, McGrew! You sure showed them Atlanta ragtails!" "Hey, Hunter. You want a job hauling trash with us?" This from the Trash brothers, hanging off the side of the new truck that Nick had talked the town council into financing. Proudly painted on the side was DARIEN SANITARY DEPT. Sunshine had confided that the garbage collection contract had made a world of difference in their financial situation.

"I might just take you up on that offer, Easter," Hunter called back with a laugh. He whispered to Neely as they sped up their pace to her house, "Maybe I can get the mayor's job." More than a dozen jovial compliments later, he turned and suddenly pulled Neely into his arms and kissed her, ignoring two little boys on bicycles who sniggered and made catcalls. "Everybody's so happy about the tree, it makes me want to share something else, something that'll make me the happiest man alive."

Neely's heart fluttered at the notion of what that something might be. She had always dreamed of having a wedding under the big oak at Christmastime. With Dane, it had had to be a fast trip to Folkston, Georgia, since he was getting his Navy deployment papers and was going to be transferred out of Cecil Field.

"Have I thanked Nick for bringing you to Darien? Somehow I feel that he had a hand in it."

Hunter grinned. He still couldn't believe the miracle of finding a woman like this one. "Only a few hundred times more than I have. You know, that guy is really something. When I first met him, he looked like someone who had lost everything he had. He didn't even act as if he *liked* people much. And now . . ." Hunter shook his head in amazement as he thought about Nick's contributions to the people of Darien.

Neely thought about how her life had changed and expressed her own wonder. "Maybe he's benefiting from what he does for folks just as much as they are. Have you noticed how much happier he looks these days? How his eyes twinkle like stars all the time now? And Emma is crazy about the beard and mustache he grew. He says he did it just to tickle her nose."

"Well, if I don't stop partaking of the Southern hospitality around here"—Hunter rubbed his flat stomach—"I'm going to be as round-bellied as he's gotten to be."

Neely hung their jackets in the foyer and called Emma to come save Hunter from Marmalade, who had wrapped himself around the man's legs and wouldn't let him walk to the kitchen.

They all laughed when the little girl came and retrieved her cat, whose baleful look at Hunter for rejecting his attention was openly accusing. "Marmalade is used to getting what he wants," Neely pointed out after the cat stalked off, his huge tail switching.

"So am I," Hunter murmured with a meaningful look at the woman next to him. Emma, who hadn't missed a thing, danced off to the kitchen to help Sunshine set the table.

At the excited chatter emanating from the kitchen, occasionally punctuated with "Hunter" and "Mama" and Neely was afraid to know what else, Neely said, "Let's take a short stroll before lunch. I think my daughter needs time to calm down."

Hunter seemed very pleased that Emma appeared to be as thrilled as he was that he was no longer persona non grata in her mother's life. "That sounds great. I've got some treats for Freckles and Nub Nose if we see 'em."

Later that afternoon, Hunter, Neely and Emma sat comfortably ensconced before a roaring fire. The threesome had decided their new Christmas tradition would be roasting red and green marshmallows on the fire.

They were in the middle of that activity (which Marmalade found amusing since Hunter would let him bat the stick before loading it with the gummy candy) when Neely thought for the hundredth time about how well her beloved fit in at Catshead Peak. Not only had Emma and Sunshine taken him into their hearts, every animal on the place seemed to have adopted the engineer. "Did I tell you that we're getting Nick to play Santa at the party? Won't he be just perfect?"

"Now that he's gotten, uh, kind of plump," Hunter said.

"Well, it wasn't easy talking him into it. In fact, he acted kind of strange when we asked him if he'd do it." Neely didn't notice her daughter's knowing smile since the child was bent over Marmalade. "Miss Dovey's making a costume for him. He'll look just like jolly ol' Saint Nick. . . . Hmm. What do you think about *my* outfit?" Neely held up the velvet dress she'd been taking in at the waist. Last year's Scarlett O'Hara had been a tad plumper than the new one.

"Well, it beats the living room drapes. Hey, what's in that big box over there? You've been awfully secretive about it ever since it showed up."

Neely tried to look innocent. "Oh, that? Just another costume for someone. Say, have I told you lately how much I love your mustache?"

Hunter rubbed the thin line of hair he'd been cultivating at his sweetheart's request. "Well, at least it's stopped itching. But I sure don't know about these sideburns." Hunter smoothed the sleek black lines nearly reaching his cheek.

"You'll look absolutely adorable as Rhett Butler."

Hunter rose, unceremoniously dumping the cat off his lap. *"What?"*

Neely cocked her head and looked him over, her lips pursed thoughtfully. "Actually . . . if you could do something to make those ears stand out a little more, you'd be a dead ringer for him. At least, for the Clark Gable version."

Hunter stared at her, his mouth open, then at the big box and then back at Neely. "Oh, I get it. You want me to . . . you've got me cast in your little party as . . ." He shook his head and backed away as Neely opened the box and took out the famous barbecue outfit that Clark Gable had worn as Rhett Butler.

"Darling, surely you know enough about Scarlett to know that she always gets her man?"

As dusk fell on Christmas Eve, Rhett Butler led Miss Scarlett O'Hara down the porch steps of Catshead Peak to where the Trash brothers were waiting with the carriage and four that was kept at Hofyl Plantation for just this occasion. "Ah must say, Miz Scarlett," Hunter drawled as he offered his arm to the green velvet-clad vision with the adorable feathered hat, "you look ravishing, my dear."

Scarlett tapped her handsome escort coyly on the arm. "Why, Mistuh Rhett, how you do run on."

"Let's go eat some barbecue before I get sick."

But even Hunter fell into the festive mood of an old-fashioned Southern Christmas as they moved down Main Street in their elegant vehicle. Everywhere on the street, people dressed in Civil War period clothes waved and cheered. "Rhett" and "Scarlett" nodded and smiled and waved back. As they passed under the Christmas Oak, Neely could swear that Susannah was there, waving and smiling and cheering the couple, along with the whole town.

Historic Hofyl Plantation was a picture to behold. From the time they turned in through the gates, Neely was oohing and ahhing and grabbing her escort's arm to point out some new vision of holiday splendor. "Look, look!" she cried when they turned the curve of the lane of decorated trees and glimpsed the house. "Have you ever seen anything so beautiful?"

"Only in the seat next to me," Hunter replied. But he, too, was impressed by the spectacular sight of the Greek Revival mansion with its majesty lit up at every window, every column. A huge wreath with sparkling lights formed the entrance to the veranda. The scene was almost eerie, with the people dressed in their old-fashioned clothes and no trace of the modern world to be seen.

"We should have stopped first under the Kissing Oak," Neely whispered, referring to a tree that was decked with mistletoe for young lovers to take advantage of. "But you know what they say about couples who kiss there on Christmas Eve . . ."

She didn't finish because they were pulling up in front of the house and everyone on the veranda was cheering and clapping. Neely caught sight of Emma standing at the very front of the receiving line and waved. Her daughter looked adorable in her ruffled frock and bonnet.

The Southern "belles" forming the welcoming committee paid more attention to "Rhett" than to his companion. Before Neely knew what had happened, two of the young beauties had Hunter in tow, and she was left behind.

Not for long, though. Two sideburned beaux were quick to offer their arms and Neely was soon inside the huge ballroom. Thanking her escorts and assuring them that she would be able to find the punch bowl on her own, she looked around the room, awed as always by its immensity and luxury. They said that the Marie Antoinette chandeliers may have been the real thing, bought clandestinely from a French antique dealer. The furniture had all been custom-made, except for a few authentic pieces brought over from the original owners' ancestral home.

"May I serve you, ma'am?" The familiar voice at her shoulder made Neely turn away from her admiration of the room.

"Nick! Oh, my Lord, look at you! If you aren't the closest thing to the real Santa, I don't know who is."

She missed the look on his face, being enthralled with his larger-than-life presence.

"Well, I'm glad you approve. I haven't worn a getup like this in quite a while."

"It's quite handsome. So are you. I declare, Nick, you really do look like jolly Saint Nicholas."

"Why couldn't I be Rhett Butler?" Nick asked ruefully, looking over at the fireplace where Hunter was circled by ringleted belles. He laughed, shaking his tummy comically. "Ho, ho, ho—right?"

"To me, you're the most romantic figure in this room. Think about it. Where would this world be without a Santa? What would the children do without Christmas, without their dreams of what that jolly man from the North Pole would bring them on Christmas Eve?"

Again she missed the look on Nick's face, since she was furtively keeping an eye on the action around the fireplace. But her attention was brought back when

Nick responded with deep sadness, "They'd have to face the harsh reality of the world. They would have to realize that without kindness, compassion, and love for one's fellow man, there can be no Santa."

Neely stared at her friend. "Nick, you're the kindest person I've ever known. If you don't believe in Santa Claus, we're all lost."

"Did I say I didn't believe in him? Hey, little girl—"

"I'm not a little girl, but I still believe in Santa."

"Well, hey, big girl then. Did you ever stop to take a look at it from Santa's side? I mean, does anybody think about him and his emotional needs? Sure, there are the milk and cookies and the songs and stuff. But did anybody ever send Santa a thank-you note after Christmas? Noo-o. He gets plenty of mail during the month leading up to the big event, sacks and sacks of it, all listing desires and pleas and even demands. But after Christmas? Ha! His mailbox has cobwebs in it from December 26th to Thanksgiving."

Neely didn't know quite how to respond to such a passionate outburst from an ordinarily mild-mannered fellow. "Why, Nick, I never realized . . . good gracious, you talk about Santa like he's real, like he's somebody you know personally."

"Real? Real!" But Neely was spared the remainder of Nick's reaction when Miss Dovey came bustling up.

"Dears, you need to be up front, on the stage. Oh, Cornelia, darling, don't you look lovely, and that sweet young man of yours . . . umm, umm. Now, Nick, what in the world are you looking so grumpy about? We can't have a grumpy Santa, now, can we?"

"Why not?" Nick muttered. "How many of the little

rascals are lined up to beg for their goodies?"

"Ohh, you." Miss Dovey patted him. Behind his back she winked at Neely. When "Santa" had gone on ahead of them, she whispered to Neely, "I don't know what put him in this mood, do you?"

"He's thinking about how Santa never gets any Christmas cards or gifts, and nobody has any use for him after the big day."

As Miss Dovey left, "Rhett Butler" showed up. Neely pretended to be put out with him.

"Well, I'd hate to be you if the real Scarlett was here tonight. She'd have you spitted over the barbecue pit."

"Can I help it if I'm irresistible?" Neely had to laugh when Hunter made the muscles in his arm ripple. "Forget all this. I'm ready for the Kissing Oak."

"Shh. They're introducing the Highlands dancers, then they'll introduce us, stage the Christmas pageant, and then Nick will do his thing."

The kilted dancers were enthusiastic and soon had the entire crowd clapping as they did their high-kicking dances. The bagpipes sent chills through Neely's veins. "Oh, Lord, I'm going to cry," she said after the plaintive notes faded away.

"Don't cry, Miz Scarlett." Hunter offered her a handkerchief, and after using it, she handed it back. "You need it, too," she sniffed, noticing that his eyes were wet, as well. "You don't fool me, Hunter Rhett Butler McGrew. You're another old softie just like me."

He didn't try to deny it.

As the evening wore on, it became increasingly obvious that Nick was regretting his role as Santa.

Though he certainly looked the part, he seemed hesitant, uncertain whether he really wanted to throw himself into his role. Neely found Miss Dovey and whispered, "We have to get this thing started or Nick's gonna bolt on us."

There was a drum roll and the lights dimmed, leaving only the Christmas-tree lights under which Nick sat. Someone lit the candles around the room. "Ladies and gentleman, we all know who's the most important Christmas figure outside the religious ones we all revere." Miss Dovey made a bow to the group who'd performed in the Christmas pageant and waited for the applause to subside. "You enjoyed the appearance of Mr. Rhett Butler and his lovely Scarlett O'Hara, I'm sure." More applause followed, with a few catcalls for the two participants. "Now, we give you that icon of the Christmas holiday, that bearded wizard of generosity, our very own patron saint of the Yuletide holidays—Santa Claus!"

To a barrage of cheers and clapping, Nick rose from the chair placed under the Christmas tree on stage. "Thank you all, good people of Darien." He was a magnificent figure, Neely thought, catching her breath at how much he looked like the real thing. Again, he seemed larger than life. She was not the only one to respond. All over the room people fell silent and stared at the glowing figure on the stage.

"Santa" looked down into the faces of the audience deep and long, and then he let out a booming, "I wish each and every one of you a merry Christmas. Ho, ho, ho!" He turned in his chair to look at the Christmas tree. "But how can Santa do his job without any presents? Where are the gifts for the children?"

Nelle McFather

That was Neely's cue. With a nod to the drummer of the little band, who sounded a drum roll, she stepped up to the middle of the stage. "Friends and neighbors, tonight we would like to depart from our usual tradition of 'An evening with Santa.' Instead of the children making their requests of the benevolent old saint, we'd like to turn things around." She turned from the mike and smiled at Nick, who was staring at her openmouthed, positively dumbfounded. "We'd like you to know, Nick, that we think you embody the spirit of Christmas, and how much we appreciate you for being our very own Saint Nick."

With that, it began. One by one, person after person filed across the stage, giving his or her testimony about some good deed or small favor that Nick had bestowed. The gifts left at his feet were simple—a jar of honey, a carved duck caller, an old book of church hymns. Each giver spoke quietly of what had prompted his gift, and gradually the ubiquitous compassion of the man known only as Nick was revealed to the people of Darien.

In the dim light, as the procession continued, Nick's joy positively lit up the stage. With each person's testimony, with each gift, his face glowed with more happiness. He embraced each gift-giver with a great bear hug.

Neely couldn't help it. She wept openly. Watching the trash brothers giving Nick a carved wooden set of deer, seeing Miss Dovey drape an afghan she'd knitted around his shoulders, she felt tears streaming down her face. When the children from the Baptist orphanage presented Nick with their present, a handpainted box with all their signatures on it, her tears turned to smiles.

When Emma's turn came and she gave him a copy of Susannah's portrait in a tabby frame, she whispered, "How will you visit all the homes tonight? You don't have a sleigh, no reindeer. There's not going to be any Christmas this year, is there?"

Nick drew the girl to him. "Shh. Not to worry. The night's not over yet and neither are the miracles."

About that time, Cash Bidwell made his way to the stage. He got down on his knees in front of Santa. "Old man, I owe you one. You made me see the light, and that ain't easy, me being a stubborn redneck and all. But I tell you what, you made a gift to me that I won't ever forget. You told me to use the hunting I love for the good of somebody, and you know what? That stuck in my gullet and that's just what I done. I thank you for teaching me the joy of giving. And I thank Miss Dovey for teaching me the joy of reading. I'd like to read something for you just now."

"I'd like nothing better," Nick said with a smile.

"This is from the Bible. I wrote it down out of Miss Dovey's Book. 'It is more blessed to give than to receive.' That's right, ain't it?"

"That's right, my boy." Nick embraced the man and said softly, "Keep on looking after Miss Dovey like you've been doing."

Nick put his hand on the man's shoulder, and the gesture seemed to make Cash look taller, almost statesmanlike. "Those are fine things you've done. I always knew there was a lot of good in you."

"Well, I'd like you to have something from me to show my appreciation. But we can't have it in here.

You reckon we could all go downtown and gather under the Christmas Oak? I'd sure like to make you a special gift."

"Is the party about over?" Nick asked Neely and Miss Dovey. They nodded and soon everyone was on the way to see what more excitement this very special Christmas Eve held for the townspeople of Darien, Georgia.

Neely could swear that there was a new glow in the sky. She could hardly breathe for the sense of anticipation. Hunter held her hand tight on one side and Emma held on to the other as the trio waited with the others beneath the Christmas Oak.

"Mr. Nick, I hereby present to you my most treasured possession." Cash spoke with great solemnity, his voice quavering with emotion. "I can't think of nobody I'd ruther have driving my Harley than a fine gent like yourself." He handed the keys to Nick, and everyone applauded wildly.

Nick looked down at the keys and then back at Cash. "You don't know what you've just done." He looked around over the crowd. "All of you. A year ago, I thought the spirit of Christmas was dead. Now, after being among you, after tonight, I know there is hope for the human race."

He climbed onto the Harley and put the key in the ignition. "I'll be leaving tonight. But I won't be leaving my memories of you good people of Darien. You'll have my good thoughts not just on Christmas but every day of the year."

"Bye, Nick," the people called as they dispersed. It seemed that nobody wanted to watch as Nick left the place that had known so many good things by his hand. When the crowd had thinned to only Emma, Neely, and Hunter, Nick said softly, "Do you mind if Emma stays out here with me a little bit longer? I want our good-bye to be a private and very special one."

"Of course we don't mind. It was Emma who first found you and she should be the last to see you go." Neely embraced Nick warmly, as did Hunter.

And then Emma and Nick were alone under the big tree. "So it's you and me, kid. I'm going to tell you what happened a year ago tonight, because only a child would probably believe it. You see, when I parked my sleigh last year, I was mugged and robbed and left for dead. Dead I might as well have been, for while I wandered, homeless, despondent over what mankind had come to, I had no faith in people. Not until I came here to your little town. Like this tree, this town will live and grow and thrive. You and the people of Darren gave me back my faith. So remember when you set out your stocking and milk and cookies . . ." His voice broke when he looked at Emma. "Think of your very own jolly old Saint Nick.

"Well, it's time for me to be off if I'm not going to disappoint the little children." Nick put two fingers between his teeth and gave a shrill whistle.

In no time, Freckles and Nub Nose bounded up. Nick looked at Emma. "They'll be well taken care of, I promise, so don't you worry."

"I won't, Nick." Emma gave each of the deer a hug and stood back as the motorcycle emitted a mighty roar. Freckles and Nub Nose ran in front, and to her amazement, the entourage took off.

She craned her neck as the amazing vision rounded the oak and she clapped her hands in delight when the Harley turned into a sleigh and the two small deer stretched into antlered reindeer. As the incredible team sailed on into the sky, backed by a silvery moon, the Christmas Oak lit up like a beacon, windchimes tinkling from every limb.

Emma watched in awe and called as loud as she could, "Merry Christmas, Santa!"

The deep rumble of a voice from above replied, "Have a happy Harley Christmas, Emma!"

"Mama, Mama! Hunter!" Emma ran up to the house as fast as her short legs could carry her. When she burst inside, Neely and Hunter rushed to meet her. "You're not going to believe what happened after everybody left!" She was all out of breath, and her mother knelt, putting her arms around Emma to calm her down.

"What in the world? Emma, slow down. What on earth are you talking about?"

The little girl described what had happened, words tumbling over one another as she told them about the magical event. "He's really Santa, Mama. I knew it almost for sure, but when that Harley turned into a real sleigh, with Freckles and Nub Nose pulling it . . . they had antlers, Hunter. Big antlers!" She showed how big with her hands above her head and said excitedly, "They all flew off and . . . Mama, he was mugged last Christmas, that's why he was so sad. People had let him down. And then he came here, and people were good and he could be Santa again and . . ."

"Whoa." Neely looked at Hunter over the top of her daughter's head. "Honey, what you saw was what you wanted to see because you loved him so much. It's a beautiful story, though."

"Mama, it's not just a story, it really happened." Emma saw the looks being exchanged between her mother and Hunter and she sighed. "Well, at least the little children will have their Christmas Eve. Maybe Freckles and Nub Nose will be a part of the team from now on, like Rudolph."

"Maybe so. Those little hams would definitely like that." Neely kissed her daughter gently. "You've had a big, wonderful evening; we all have. Don't you think it's time to get to bed and let those visions of sugar-plums dance in your head? Won't be long before Santa makes his stop here."

Emma's smile was knowing. "Well," she said, yawning as she climbed the stairs to her room. "You two have a happy Harley Christmas!"

That's what Nick was having, she thought happily as she went up to bed.

Epilogue

Christmas Eve, One Year Later

The house was decorated to a faretheewell, the candy and fudge were all made and set out in sinful plenty, the stockings were all hung on the great fireplace of Catshead Peak.

Neely Carswell McGrew inspected the three stockings which Miss Dovey had knitted for her favorite new family, putting the names Hunter, Neely, and Emma in festive red and green letters. She sighed as her husband of six months came into the room. "I just wish Miss Dovey would spend Christmas with us this year. But every time I mention it, she tells me about all the unfortunate people out in the country who don't have Christmas dinner or any gifts for the children and how she feels the need to take care of them. Plus, now that Cash is working for her, she doesn't want him to spend Christmas by himself." Neely shook her head in wonder. "I still can't believe her change since Nick. And Cash! My God, the man works harder than the Trash brothers."

Hunter put his arm around his bride. He wondered how one man could be so lucky as to have such a beautiful wife and child. "I guess when Nick left, she kind of took over for him, helping people and doing for them like he used to do."

"Just think, he's even now getting ready for his big night. Hunter, don't you sometimes wonder if what Emma told us really happened?"

Hunter took a cup of wassail from the steaming, fragrant punch bowl that had come down from Neely's ancestors. He handed it to her and got one for himself. "Well, Emma certainly believes it happened. She and the children at Miss Dovey's have made up their own storybook about the year Santa was homeless and lived in Darien. She showed it to you, didn't she?"

Neely smiled at the thought of how her daughter was blossoming in the happy atmosphere of her new two-parent family. "It was charming. I think she may have the makings of an artist, like her great-great-great grandmother Dorothea. Oh, Hunter, what if things had turned out differently? What if we hadn't had Nick to bring us all together, to help us save our relationship?"

He kissed her gently. "I mention him in my prayers every night, just like your daughter does."

"Emma says she loves having her father come in and say her prayers with her." Neely could not get over how quickly Emma had accepted Hunter as a real "daddy." Neely had explained to her, when the girl asked about it, that calling Hunter "Daddy" in no way diminished the memory of her late father. "Look on it this way, darling. Dane loved you with all his heart and wanted more than anything in the world for you to be happy. I know your having a wonderful new daddy makes him smile up in heaven."

"Well, her prayers are beginning to include your entire menagerie. We even have to include Freckles and Nub Nose. She still misses those little guys, and, you know what? So do I."

"Me, too." Neely cuddled up on the sofa with her spouse and dreamily watched the fire. "Emma still swears that they pulled Santa's sleigh that night. You know, when we never saw them again, I thought Emma would be devastated. But all she said was that Nick needed them more than she did."

Hunter shook his head. "Well, wherever they are, they're part of the legend."

Emma came running into the room, all excited. "Mama! Daddy! Mr. Cash is on the back porch and he says he has a big surprise for me. He wants you to come right now." She tugged at Hunter and her mother. "What do you suppose it could be?"

Hunter got up, pulling Neely with him. "Well, it can't be as wonderful as the present you gave me last year." Hunter stopped at the end table and picked up the little boy angel that had been Emma's surprise gift the previous Christmas. "Nothing could be nicer than my angel—except my two real ones, here."

Emma was pleased, though a little impatient with the grown-up dawdling. Surprises weren't meant to be kept waiting, to her little-girl's way of thinking.

"Well, I thought you needed one to go with the angel Mama inherited from Great-aunt Susannah."

Cash called to them when they all came out on the porch. "I'm out here."

Emma caught her breath when she saw what he had brought. "Oh!" She knelt down beside the two fawns that were licking salt out of Cash Bidwell's hand. "Oh, aren't they the most precious things." Her eyes huge and filled with wonder, she looked up at the man standing over the deer. "Where did you find them? Can I keep them?" She petted the sleek heads and laughed when they both nuzzled her hands. "They're smaller than Freckles and Nub Nose, but just as darling."

"Where did you get them, Cash?" Hunter joined in the petting and looked up at the man who'd changed more than anyone in Darien during the "year of Saint Nick."

"Someone shot the mother—not me!" he added hastily. "But I found the little critters and took 'em home. I been looking after 'em, feeding 'em and all." He cleared his throat and looked a little embarrassed. "Crazy, ain't it, how attached you can get to these little things? They act like I'm their daddy or something."

Neely laughed and hugged the rugged huntsman. "In a way, that's exactly what you are, Cash."

"Well, I'm scared to keep 'em out where I live. You know, some of them scalawags out in the backwoods are just as likely to shoot these little fellers as look at 'em." He didn't see the amused exchange between Hunter and Neely, who were thinking about how that "scalawag" might have been Cash a year ago. "I was thinking, you got such a big place up here, and you've got that nice penned-up yard where they'd be safe . . ."

"Oh, please, can I have them?" Emma's face was all alight. "I'll take care of them, I promise."

"Wel-l. All right." Actually Neely could no more have said no than fly to the moon. There was something symbolic about the fawns being found and brought to Catshead Peak that very night.

"I wonder . . ." She looked after Cash Bidwell, who was helping Emma put the fawns in the fenced-in yard, and mused, "Do you suppose that Nick had something to do with this?"

Hunter laughed. "It's Christmas Eve, and by now you should know that anything can happen—like this." He scooped his wife up in his arms and whirled her around till she was laughing like a child. "I'm glad you're letting Emma keep 'em. We can always use the meat in case my job at Lowry Construction doesn't pan out."

"Oh, you awful man!" Neely made him put her down for saying such a terrible thing and they went back into the house, leaving Emma outside to play with her new friends.

That night as the couple were preparing for bed, Neely said impulsively, "Are you sleepy? I'm so excited about it being Christmas Eve that I honestly don't want to go to bed yet."

"I feel the same way. I keep listening for that big clock to sound midnight and to hear the clatter of hooves on the rooftop."

"Let's put on warm robes and go out on the cliffs. It's such a beautiful night."

First they went down the hall to see if Emma was

sleeping soundly. "Look at that. Look at that little angel." Hunter drew Neely close to him as they gazed down on the child. "Thank you, darling, for marrying me and giving me such a special gift."

"It's our first Christmas as a real family," Neely whispered back. "Thank *you*, Hunter McGrew, for making our home complete with a wonderful husband and father."

"We sound like the Waltons," Hunter said, a little ruefully. "Are we corny, or what?"

"I like being corny." Neely tucked the spread under her daughter's chin and adjusted the large teddy bear that was no doubt tickling its owner's nose.

Out on the cliffs, they looked up at the moon and stars and at the river below. Neely took a deep breath. "Have you ever seen anything more beautiful? I love living here. I hope you didn't mind our staying here instead of buying another place."

"Are you kidding? I love it, too. It thrills me to become a part of your family's past and heritage."

"Well, you have to accept the ghosts as part of that. Sometimes I would come out here before we married and imagine I saw Dorothea and Angus Armstrong taking their stroll along the cliffs. Everyone says that they stayed romantic lovers until the day Angus died."

"I want us to be like that, too." Hunter took Neely into his arms and kissed her deeply. He could never get over how sweet she smelled, how soft her skin was—how totally happy he was to be married to this woman. "Have you seen any of the ghosts since we've been married?"

Neely thought about it. "Come to think of it, I haven't. Now, why is that?" She looked up at her husband. "Unless it's because they know I'm safe now, with you, and don't need them anymore."

"I will always keep you safe, Cornelia McGrew, and Emma, too. Always."

They kissed once more beneath the lovers' moon, and then retired to their bedroom to continue the tryst. Emma might be awake and looking out the window, and for her to witness a passionate love scene would never do, not on Christmas Eve, which rightfully belonged to children.

The house was quiet; the only creature stirring was Marmalade the cat, whose tail switched ominously as he decided whether or not to jump up on the table by the fireplace. He was not a cookie man, but the glass of milk looked tempting. His tail switched as he debated the wisdom of getting into trouble with the mistress of the house over a treat.

"Don't you even think about it, Marmalade." The fierce whisper in his ear made the cat start, then fall to licking his paw as though sampling that glass of milk had been the farthest thing from his mind.

"Shh. Be very still. We're not supposed to be here." Emma crept over to the sofa and lay down, pulling an afghan over her knees. The cat curled up beside her. The ticking of the clock seemed louder and slower as it approached midnight. Emma's eyes fluttered and closed, then opened and closed again. The cat gave a big yawn, growing bored with the vigil, and put his head down for a long winter's nap.

There was a swoosh at the chimney and the cat lifted his head, his big yellow eyes watching the red-suited visitor who put his finger to his lips and rested his bag next to the big tree. He stood looking down at the sleeping child, then went about his business. Marmalade watched, yawning, not catching the scent of catnip toys or anything in the bag for him.

"Here, kitty." Marmalade stretched and jumped down to lap up the milk Santa put in a dish for him. "You be a good cat and I'll see you next year." He reached into his sack and pulled out his last gift for Emma. "This is for you, sweetheart. You be a good girl and it will watch over you always." He placed the present tenderly in the curl of her arm.

Thus was a new legend born at Catshead Peak, on Christmas Eve, 1996—that of Emma's angel, her very own gift from Santa.

High Energy/Whirlwind Courtship
Dara Joy/Jayne Ann Krentz writing as Jayne Taylor

High Energy by Dara Joy. Physics. Zanita Masterson knows
nothing about the subject and cares little to learn. Until a reporting
job leads her to one Tyberious Augustus Evans. The rogue scientist
is six feet of piercing blue eyes, rock-hard muscles, and maverick
ideas, and the idea that he is seriously interested in her seems insane.
But a night of monster movies, cookie-dough ice cream, and wild
love is almost enough to convince Zanita that the passion-minded
professor is determined to woo her—with his own masterful equation
for sizzling ecstasy and high energy.

And in the same heart-stopping volume...

Whirlwind Courtship by Jayne Ann Krentz writing as Jayne Taylor.
When Phoebe Hampton arrives quite by accident at the doorstep
of Harlan Garand's mountain cabin, he is less than pleased.
Convinced that she is another marriage-minded female sent by his
matchmaking aunt, Harlan would gladly throw her out. But Phoebe
is a damsel in distress, and an attractive one at that, so against
Harlan's better judgment he lets her stay—even though she wishes
she were a hundred miles away! Grudging host and grudging guest
will just have to put up with each other for a few days. After that,
they'll never see each other again—or will they?

___3932-X   (two passionate contemporary romances in one volume)

$5.99 US/$7.99 CAN

MELODY MORGAN

Defiant Hearts

By the Bestselling Author of *Abiding Love*

To Katie O'Rourke, a pioneer of the daguerreotype, capturing the lives of everyday people on film while wagonning west is going to be the adventure of her life. But having to share that dream with a bossy, arrogant, and ruggedly handsome man infuriates the young photographer.

Since Spence McCord owes Tim O'Rourke a favor for saving his life, he promises to deposit Katie on her brother's Colorado doorstep. But Spence never imagines that repaying his debt of gratitude will lead to battling harsh prairie fires, fiendish outlaws, and the irresistible beauty of the independent redhead.

From New York to Colorado, Katie and Spence's passion mounts beneath the prairie skies. But it will take more than Spence's warm embrace to convince Katie's defiant heart that his picture of blissful love is worth more than a thousand words.

_4053-0 $4.99 US/$5.99 CAN

Don't miss these passionate time-travel romances, in which modern-day heroines fulfill their hearts' desires with men from different eras.

Traveler by Elaine Fox. A late-night stroll through a Civil War battlefield park leads Shelby Manning to a most intriguing stranger. Bloody, confused, and dressed in Union blue, Carter Lindsey insists he has just come from the Battle of Fredericksburg—more than one hundred years in the past. Before she knows it, Shelby finds herself swept into a passion like none she's ever known and willing to defy time itself to keep Carter at her side.

__52074-5 $4.99 US/$6.99 CAN

Passion's Timeless Hour by Vivian Knight-Jenkins. Propelled by a freak accident from the killing fields of Vietnam to a Civil War battlefield, army nurse Rebecca Ann Warren discovers long-buried desires in the arms of Confederate leader Alexander Ransom. But when Alex begins to suspect she may be a Yankee spy, Rebecca must convince him of the impossible to prove her innocence...that she is from another time, another place.

__52079-6 $4.99 US/$6.99 CAN

Dorchester Publishing Co., Inc.
65 Commerce Road
Stamford, CT 06902

Please add $1.75 for shipping and handling for the first book and $.50 for each book thereafter. NY, NYC, PA and CT residents, please add appropriate sales tax. No cash, stamps, or C.O.D.s. All orders shipped within 6 weeks via postal service book rate. Canadian orders require $2.00 extra postage and must be paid in U.S. dollars through a U.S. banking facility.

Name_____

Address_____

City _____ State_____ Zip_____

I have enclosed $_____in payment for the checked book(s).
Payment <u>must</u> accompany all orders.☐ Please send a free catalog.